OLD-TIMERS

Magnificent stories from mighty Australians

SANDY THORNE

ALLEN&UNWIN
SYDNEY • MELBOURNE • AUCKLAND • LONDON

This edition published in 2013

First published in 2011

Allen & Unwin
Sydney, Melbourne, Auckland, London

83 Alexander Street
Crows Nest NSW 2065
Australia
Phone: (61 2) 8425 0100
Fax: (61 2) 9906 2218
Email: info@allenandunwin.com
Web: www.allenandunwin.com

Cataloguing-in-Publication details are available
from the National Library of Australia
www.trove.nla.gov.au

ISBN 978 1 74331 182 0

Internal design by Darian Causby
Printed in Australia by McPherson's Printing Group

10 9 8 7 6 5 4 3 2 1

CONTENTS

OLD-TIMERS

OLD-TIMERS

This book is dedicated to Banjo and Ava Thorne,
both born in the early part of this century.
Their generation will gain so much from reading these stories.

ABOUT THE AUTHOR

Sandy Thorne is a baby-boomer Queenslander, bush poet, yarn-spinner, and the oldest jillaroo in the west. She shot through from school at age fourteen to go mustering on stations, and educated herself by reading almost everything she could get hold of. She has now written eleven books including *I've Met Some Bloody Wags!* (1980), *Wags in Verse* (1984), *Battler* (1984), *Laugh Yer Guts Out!* (1991), *Beyond the Razor Wire* (2003) and *Working Horses* (2005).

Her books are based on the wags and dags Sandy has met and worked with on the vast outback stations on Cape York Peninsula, the Gulf of Carpentaria, the back of Bourke and the Far North. She was brought up in the Golden Era of the 1950s and 60s and has mustered wild scrub cattle with the toughest, most chauvo men in Australia. She spent a year opal mining in Lightning Ridge in the early 1970s but left the Ridge for a station at Bourke, returning 30 years later in 2002. Her life has been a series of extreme ups and downs, and many great adventures.

Sandy launched her first book on national television by ripping the top off a stubbie with her teeth, which launched her into a new career as a bush humourist, performing bush yarns and her own verse at festivals, conferences and functions. She has appeared on television and radio, all over Australia, for 25 years. She has made people laugh in several countries, and taken 'outback culture' to the likes of David Letterman, Larry King and Michael Parkinson.

A radical mid-life career change saw Sandy have another great adventure as a detentions officer in isolated immigration camps, which she trained for in a maximum security prison. With the help of her diary, she wrote *Beyond the Razor Wire* about her experiences.

She currently lives and works on a station near Lightning Ridge, which she describes in good seasons as 'the hub of the universe' and in summer and drought time as 'Planet Mars'.

For more information, visit the author's website:
www.sandythorne.com.au

CONVERSION TABLE

10 acres	4 hectares
6 fathoms	11 metres
8 inches	20 centimetres
1 foot	30 centimetres
10 miles	16 kilometres
10 shillings*	1 dollar
1 florin	2 shillings
1 crown**	5 shillings
6 pence	5 cents
4 farthings	1 cent
1 pound	2 dollars
4 gallons/44 gallons	18 litres/198 litres
6 stone	38 kilograms

All conversions are approximate or rounded.

* Currency conversions are based on those used in 1966, when decimal currency was introduced in Australia.

** Crowns were British currency and only issued in Australia in 1937 and 1938.

New South Wales

1. Bega
2. Bendick Murrell
3. Bourke
4. Brewarrina
5. Clarence River
6. Cobargo
7. Collarenabri
8. Come-by-Chance
9. Coonabarabran
10. Coonamble
11. Dubbo
12. Euchareena
13. Goodooga
14. Grafton
15. Grawin
16. Helensburgh
17. Iluka
18. Ivanhoe
19. Lightning Ridge
20. Manilla
21. Mogriguy
22. Moree
23. Narooma
24. Narrabri
25. Orange
26. Parkes
27. Qurindi
28. Redfern
29. Tenterfield
30. Tilba Tilba
31. Walcha
32. Walgett
33. Wallaga Lake
34. Warren
35. Warrumbungles
36. Wilcannia
37. Wollongong
38. Woody Head
39. Yamba
40. Yetman

Northern Territory

1. Bagot
2. Daly River
3. Darwin
4. Katherine

Queensland

1. Alexandra Headland
2. Aramac
3. Baffle Creek
4. Brisbane
5. Charleville
6. Dalby
7. Gargett
8. Gaynah
9. Glenmorgan
10. Gold Coast
11. Granville
12. Gulf of Carpentaria
13. Kingaroy
14. Mackay
15. Maleny
16. Mapleton
17. Maryborough
18. Southport
19. Texas
20. Toowoomba
21. Townsville
22. Tully

Western Australia

1. Fitzroy Crossing
2. Kununurra
3. Ord River
4. The Kimberley

INDIAN

OCEAN

Perth

INTRODUCTION

A greeting from the author to the reader

G'day. You've chosen to read this book because, like me, you love Australia and its history, and you love our 'old-timers'.

All my life—since I was a small girl growing up in the greatest era of all—the 1950s—I have loved being in the company of 'oldies' and listening to their stories. They have worked harder than most of us could even imagine, they put their lives on the line defending our country from foreign invasion, their heads are full of knowledge only experience can pass on. They are our living treasures.

I have wanted to write this book for a long time. I wish I could clone myself so I could gather the thousands of other great old-timers' stories out there, particularly from our World War II veterans, to whom we owe so much. I know you'll enjoy reading this collection as much as I enjoyed meeting the wonderful people who kindly spent time with me. I hope you enjoy this poem I wrote in tribute to all of Australia's elders.

THE GREAT OLD-TIMERS

Our original pioneers: the explorers
the men who had no fear
They died of thirst or fever,
or felt the hostile spear.

The settlers following their tracks
who slaved to build their runs,
then left their womenfolk behind
to face the enemy's guns.

They strived to forge our nation,
with efforts, so immense
By 2000 all were resting
within the graveyard fence.

Now our new crop of old-timers,
who've passed three score and ten,
have many wonderful tales
to tell of way back when . . .

They've all had hard and tough times,
They've slaved, and loved, and feared,
Their knowledge and experience
is their wealth that comes with years.

What they tell us, we respect
When past lessons they remind us,
And we love to hear their stories
Yes, we treasure our old-timers.

BILL HAMMOND

Pioneer fisherman

Bill Hammond's phone rings at first light. One of the local professional fishermen needs help, urgently. Hurrying downstairs, he decides that rather than getting his car out of the shed, it will be just as fast to ride to the wharves. Jumps on his pushie—bugger the helmet, no time—his long legs propelling him through the streets of Iluka towards the mighty Clarence River. He arrives on his mission of mercy in three minutes flat, skidding to a halt at the marina. Not bad for a 93-year-old. With 80 years' experience to draw from, he soon sorts out the young (63-year-old) fisherman's problem.

A great bloke who loves helping people, Bill lives in one of Australia's magical little spots, where everybody knows everybody. And if anyone needs help or advice about boats, fishing gear or anything regarding the Clarence, Bill Hammond is the man to ask. He's lived and worked there all his life.

The biggest river in eastern Australia produces many fascinating fellers with big stories, and Bill is one of them. In boats large and small, he caught creatures great and small, making a living out of its magnificent wide waters and offshore over its bar since he was thirteen. Before that, he was helping his father to feed the family, gold-mining, farming and fishing since he was big enough to bait a hook.

Born at home at Wombah, near Iluka, in 1916, Bill was brought up at an idyllic spot called Woody Head, near the northern side of the river's mouth. 'We had the most wonderful place to grow up, with the best of both worlds—the bush and the ocean—to play in. We never worried about sharks, even though Shark Bay, where big numbers of sharks of many varieties go to breed, is just a couple of miles up the beach. No one has ever been attacked at Woody Head, or even in the Clarence for that matter—possibly because there's so many fish for them to eat.' There were plenty of fish and wallabies to eat, as well as homegrown veggies.

Bill's father Henry built the house himself in 1923 from local timber. On his 380 acres, Henry always ran twelve to fifteen cows, which were milked by hand. 'To ensure the cows had plenty of grass on that coastal country, we lit fires to burn off early every spring. There were no bushfires back then. Now that it's all national park, with no cattle and horses grazing and no burning-off taking place, the scrub is so thick you're flat out making your way through it—useless . . . and dangerous.

'Because Dad was away mining so much when I was a boy, he eventually surrendered 200 acres of his lease back to the crown. It had been impossible to keep 100 acres of it fenced, with the big southerlies blowing sand till only a foot of the posts would be out of the ground, or the tides left the posts hanging.'

The Hammond children were taught by correspondence by their mother, but Bill admits: 'We weren't keen scholars—we didn't learn much. But in my opinion you can learn more from reading than you learn in a classroom. I've educated myself, thanks to a love of reading.'

As they grew big enough to work, Bill and his older brothers Charlie and Bert often rode off with their father to help him at his goldmining lease 12 miles north, at McAulay's Lead. Henry had been mining there using a pump and slurry table on Jerusalem Creek, with small success, since 1890.

Now when Bill casually informs you of this, you suddenly realise with a bit of a shock that this bright-eyed, sharp-as-a-tack man, yarning away to you while energetically digging up his big veggie garden, goes a long way back—a bloody long way back. His dad was actually goldmining in the 1890s! Wow! You realise you are looking at a piece of living history.

'When the gold finally petered out at McAulay's Lead, my father had to think of another way to make a living and feed us. He sadly and reluctantly abandoned his mine. I can remember the look on his face when we rode off from his lease for the last time—he'd had to let go of his dream of striking it rich.

'He'd decided to clear part of his block at Woody Head and turn it into a market garden. There was abundant fresh water from a spring, right alongside the beach. We were all expected to help with the hard yakka, of course, and I remember there was a lot of whingeing while we cleared the bracken fern, lantana and patches of prickly pear—a really rotten job, but we understood it just had to be done. The prickly pear grew 3 to 4 metres high. We burnt the heaps and buried what was left a metre down—all difficult work. A neighbour had originally advised my father to spray the prickly pear with arsenic, so he experimented on a clump about as big as a loungeroom. Nothing grew in that spot for ten years.'

Clearing completed, Henry ploughed the ground with his two Clydesdales. Bill says: 'I loved watching them working for Dad, and loved helping him groom and harness them. Our daily lives revolved around caring for, and working with, those horses. They also pulled the cart, which we used for everything—like a ute on a farm is used now. Down on the beach, we'd all gather and load pippie and oyster shells, to be burnt then added as lime to the sandy soil. Once the vegetables were planted—a big variety—we gathered sea kelp to use as fertiliser, and spread it. It was a marvellous experience, all of us working together as a family, achieving something together. Kids in town don't get to experience that sort of thing. My sister Mary and I would drive the cart the 2 miles into Iluka, which consisted of 26 houses in the 1920s, every Friday afternoon to sell the freshly harvested veggies that thrived in the sandy soil. Mary and I would be very proud of ourselves driving the horses back home with some groceries—usually flour, sugar, tea—and what was left of the money we'd taken, to give to Mother.'

Treasured memories from Bill's childhood include the family's trips to Sydney. Their mother would get them up at 4 a.m., and make sure they all had dustcoats over their good clothes, before driving to Iluka in the cart. From there, they'd catch the riverboat for the four-hour trip to Grafton. 'I remember the shilling ticket included a cuppa and bikkies. We really looked forward to that. On the way, we'd see men with horses snigging logs on the banks, then rolling them down over other logs onto barges, to be taken to the sawmills. In my mind, I can also still see the big steam train arriving at Grafton station, and still feel the excitement—such an impressive, thrilling sight! Then we'd choose a seat, with our dustcoats back on as the seats would have soot on them. Oh boy, that soot hurt when it flew into your eyes as you'd lean out the windows to wave to the fettlers. Getting a drink of water from the big bottle that sat in a wire rack in each carriage seemed such a treat!

'Another vivid memory is watching my older brother Charlie riding off from home leading packhorses, on his first paying job. Oh God, I wanted to go with him, but my mother would sternly call me back to do my lessons. She knew what I'd rather be doing! Charlie landed the packhorse mail run up to the Chinese diggers who were still persevering in their search for gold at McAulay's Lead. I loved to listen to the yarns he'd tell when he returned home—we all did. As well as carting their supplies, he'd shoot wallabies for them on the way, sometimes managing to drop a dingo for the scalp, worth a pound in Maclean. Charlie was invited to have some wallaby chop suey by a friendly Chinese miner one day, and swore he saw cat's paws out the back of his hut. That didn't worry Charlie—he still thought it was delicious! Living off the land during those tough years was quite normal—if you'd eat a wallaby, why not a cat? Charlie, who was saving up to buy a boat, would send the salted-down wallaby skins to Winchcombe Carson's in Sydney.

'In those days, you did whatever you could to earn a quid. I caught fish for our household—so did my brothers—but I often thought that if we had a boat, we could make a living from fishing. We fished from the beach, rocks and riverbank. There was just no spare money to buy a boat during those Depression years.'

At thirteen, Bill became a professional fisherman when his uncle gave a 4-metre boat to him and his brothers—a wonderful gift which would allow them to catch many more fish than the family needed. They could sell the surplus! It was miles easier to net mullet using a boat.

'When the sea mullet are full of roe, they travel north to spawn, then when they lose their roe, they sensibly swim back to Iluka. The mullet season starts around Anzac Day and lasts around six weeks. When they were coming out of the river we'd see a telltale ripple. We made our cotton nets ourselves, and worked as a team, rowing the boat out, shooting the nets. Our timing had to be perfect. Then we'd communicate by hand signals from the boat, indicating "Out wide!" or "Coming in!" as the school swam into the nets. Then came the hard part—dragging the catch up onto the beach. Our largest haul was 16 tonnes.'

Working feverishly, the brothers packed the fish in baskets, covered them in kelp or bracken ferns, and loaded them onto their Model T Ford truck—so much more convenient than the horse and cart. The three Hammond lads had saved for three months to get the 25 pounds to buy the second-hand truck. Petrol cost 18 shillings and ninepence (less than 2 dollars) for 8 gallons and the bonus was the wooden case, which could be used for many things, including making furniture.

With the truck loaded they'd race through their bush track into Iluka for ice, at 'crazy' speeds of up to 10 miles per hour. 'We were very lucky that an ice factory was so close! Swinging a big mallet, we took turns to smash up the huge blocks as fast as possible, while the others packed the ice between each layer of fish. We were a good team but, then, we had always worked together as a team, helping Dad. We put our loads on either the steamboats such as the *Ulmarra*, which picked up all sorts of produce along the Clarence daily, taking the stacked baskets upriver to Grafton for the train to Sydney, or onto the occasional cargo boats which went direct to Sydney. At 3 farthings a pound for sea mullet, our average weekly cheque back from the fisherman's cooperative down there gave us around 3 pounds each. We'd give 2 pounds each to our mother for board.'

A teenage lad could buy a lot with a pound, or even ten bob, back then, but Bill was saving a little each week to buy his own boat. When he eventually obtained his professional fisherman's licence, he was extremely proud of it and was to hold it for 54 years. Bill fished on his own for 40 of those years. In their early fishing days, when life was good but pretty hard at times, fishermen didn't pay tax. Then in 1939 two fishermen applied for child endowment, and subsequently the government called all fishermen in, ordering them and their retailers or middlemen to keep tally books for the tax department. The party was over—Big Brother was keeping an eye on them.

'Back in my teens when my brothers and I fished together, we also fished for other species. Jewfish of around 65 pounds, or 30-plus kilos, were common.' (Bill is pictured holding one that weighed 64 pounds, which he caught on a 35-pound nylon line, outside the old ice factory.) 'We'd put out 8-inch mesh nets with 6-inch nets inside them, like a corral. At the strategic point and moment, we'd drop a big chain in the water to create noise, then we'd herd the jewfish in like sheep. Strangely, they will not go over the top of the nets.'

In one day, the Hammond brothers, working with the Paddon brothers, 'yarded up' 90 head of whoppers. From the time they put the nets out at 1 p.m., till the last jewfish was packed in ice, they'd all worked for twelve hours . . . but what a catch!

In winter, there were bream and blackfish heading out of the river to sea, to go north. There was that telltale ripple again, alerting the fish-hunters that the chase was on! Bream and blackfish travel deeper than mullet so the Hammonds decided to build a spotting tower at Woody Head. They cut three trees to make a 20-metre-high tripod, with an observation deck. Three other fishermen helped them with the difficult task of putting it up. Bill says it was a bit scary perched up on top, but the tower was a great success.

'For a long time, there was no market for blackfish—people were put off by their unattractive appearance. Lobsters were also plentiful from August to Christmas time, so we thought we should have a go at trapping and selling them, too. Everybody made most things by hand themselves in those days, and we fashioned lobster pots from cane gathered in the Woody Head scrub, with wire woven through it, and cedar floors. A catch of around twenty dozen a day was normal. For these beauties, which would retail in a shop for 90 dollars today, we received about ninepence each from the Sydney co-op. We'd take trays to the Harwood pub, and get sixpence for the smaller ones, 2 shillings for the largest.'

Other men were starting to row from Yamba and Iluka out of the Clarence's mouth and around to Woody Head to share in the bounty. Instead of being jealous of 'their' beach, or greedy, the Hammonds made an effort to get along with their fellow fishermen. A large family picnic was arranged for Boxing Day, with many families rowing there, enjoying themselves, then, after a few nice lukewarm beers, racing each other home. This Boxing Day picnic grew and became an annual fixture, with horseracing, running races and other sports held along the beach to entertain everyone. There might have been a depression on, and not much money about, but people along the Clarence had plenty to eat and a strong community—a good life.

'We had some strife one mullet season, when thirteen Queensland fishermen with two boats invaded Woody Head. They were bloody rude and bloody unscrupulous—their dirty tactics stirred up real animosity, whereas we'd all always got on together. They had no licences and scrawled New South Wales licence numbers on their boats with charcoal, but what we most objected to was the way they butted in on every potential haul, scaring fish away from the locals' nets—it made us all furious. They were not nice fellers at all, so eventually we called in a fishing inspector to "mediate", as they say these days. Fortunately they shot through then and the peaceful life resumed at Woody Head.'

All Bill's teenage years were spent learning more and more about the profession he had 'fallen into'. Before he reached the age of twenty, he'd saved enough to buy his own boat. *Seaspray* was a beautifully crafted 6-metre plywood sailboat but he put a 30-horsepower diesel motor in it. He had always wanted a plywood boat because, unlike timber boats, they didn't have to be regularly drenched with water when beached, to prevent the timber shrinking. He was starting to think about automation and doing things an easier, faster way. 'I got hold of two aeroplane tail-wheels to make a trailer, which made it much easier to pull her out of the water and over the sand, instead of hauling it over a row of poles. It was still hard yakka, so I went one step further, making a winch powered by a 4-cylinder Dodge motor. Mechanisation! It's such a great feeling when you've worked out a way to make your work easier—you feel you're really progressing, getting ahead.'

It took a while longer, however, before he worked out there was an easier way to haul nets full of fish up onto the beach. Old habits die hard. 'It's a bit of a miracle none of us got hernias before we started to use the winch, then vehicles. We were all young and strong and it was such a feeling of satisfaction, hauling our catch out of the ocean with our brute strength. I guess as you get older you get smarter . . .'

Hauling nets, lobster pots and boats constantly for several years had made the teenage brothers, all big fellers, exceptionally strong. In one of his part-time jobs, young Bill could easily carry bags of metal, extracted from the sand by miners, for several metres to load them, whereas most grown men were flat out even lifting them.

In the nets, there were often prawns as well the fish they were hunting. Some of these were cooked up and eaten on the spot, the bulk thrown back. No one thought about selling any or going after them seriously for a long time—they were fishermen, after fish. One day Bill noticed Evans Paddon—after whom Evans Head (further north) was named—trawling up and down off Ten Mile Beach and discovered he was specifically after prawns, and that there was definitely a market for them in Sydney. He converted *Seaspray* into a prawn trawler and became the first local bloke to trawl for prawns off Woody Head and in the Clarence.

'I'd go as far as the Grafton Bridge and would haul in an average of a thousand pounds per trip. At first I had to stick to a limit of prawns at least 4 inches long, which was later dropped half an inch, then done away with altogether. Until then, I kept the smaller ones for bait, hidden out of sight of the inspectors. I'd tow my net for about 20 metres, then idle and pull it in by hand. After returning to Woody Head, I'd cook them onshore in a 150-gallon tank of saltwater, then race off to the ice factory in the T Model to pack them up in baskets for the riverboat pick-up. I'd go like hell, smashing up the ice as fast as possible, using my trusty old bloodwood mallet—talk about doing things the hard way! Even got a sweat up in winter! Eventually the ice factory acquired a crusher—I was laughing then. My brothers soon realised I wasn't mad, going after just prawns, and they joined me in the venture. We threw in 5 pounds each to get a bigger and better net from Sydney, a Frazio that went down 6 fathoms.'

The Hammond brothers all ended up with their own boats and their success led to a few other Woody Head fishermen joining in the hunt for prawns, then fetching about fourpence a pound. All were in small craft around 6 metres long, which became known as the 'Mosquito Fleet'. As they became gamer and went out to where the much larger trawlers—including a steam trawler from Sydney, the *Moona*—were operating, they heard one skipper on the radio saying, 'Gawd, streuth, look at them little boats dartin' about—they're like a swarm of mozzies!' The name stuck.

When the boats were getting full, and nearly ready to go back in, Bill would fly a corn bag from his mast as a signal to their mate onshore, to light the fire under the tank, sitting on railway lines. The water in the huge tank would take an hour to get boiling on a fine day.

'The corn bag came in handy one day when, about 3 miles out to sea, a swordfish suddenly came up and hit the boat, knocking out a lump of timber as big as a fist near the motor. I can still feel the horror when I saw that terrifying sight of green water gushing into the hole. I rammed the bag into the hole and headed for land, bailing like buggery.'

Not surprisingly, Bill faced many 'tricky' situations during his 54 years as a professional. 'Getting back from the ocean into the river over the bar presents the biggest danger, especially when the sea is rough or when a sea fog has set in. It blocks out everything. I remember heading back once in a 6-metre boat when a thick fog suddenly rolled in—too thick to attempt even finding the bar let alone crossing it, so I tied up to a lobster pot to just sit and wait. My eldest brother wanted to go in and, against my better judgement, we set off, but I could tell he was heading the wrong way and stopped him. He was "slewed" and heading back out to sea. We'd have been in a bit of strife if we'd run out of fuel.

'When you're looking for the safest passage to cross the bar, you mustn't take any notice of the wind—it can change. You take notice of the waves, and count the "racers"—count five or seven big ones, then go in during the lull. It can be very dangerous if you don't know what you're doing, and things can go wrong even when you do. I nearly rolled on the bar once when a big southerly had suddenly come up. I had my son, who was fourteen at the time, with me. I thought I counted the big waves right but a huge wave suddenly broke over us, the motor nearly stopped and the boat was on its side. It gave me a fright—we had no lifejackets. They're compulsory now, of course. We survived that episode but I have seen several wrecks on the bar. One day when the wind was particularly strong, a government tugboat with a load of coal on deck, steaming to the bar, hit the spit and rolled over.

'Blokes in tinnies or small craft who don't respect the danger can come to grief so easily. I was anchored out on the ocean side of the bar once, waiting for the sea to calm down. There were big rollers, and I couldn't believe my eyes when I saw three stupid blokes in a tinnie about to tackle them. They ignored the waving and yelling from me and the other trawlermen, and actually waved back, then continued on. The tinnie was almost immediately trounced. A 20-metre Yamba trawler went to the rescue, but in those treacherous waves its nose hit the northern sand spit, turning it over. The deckie came up and then tried to rescue his skipper, who was trapped, but tragically he drowned. The tinnie and the three silly buggers were eventually all rescued. I'll never forget that.

'Another vivid memory is the sight of a German submarine coming up out of the ocean [probably to recharge its batteries] when I was tending my lobster pots fairly close to the heads, just before World War II. A sub was later torpedoed at Port Stephens. Shortly before, a former World War I German ace pilot had called in to Iluka in his yacht for fuel. When war broke out, the thought naturally occurred to us locals that he could have been plotting harbours during his round-Australia trip. Later on during the war, a Clarence tugmaster told the Grafton newspaper that he'd seen a Japanese midget sub near Maclean.'

Over the years Bill has seen many unforgettable sights on the Clarence. 'One day a clip came undone on the Iluka to Yamba ferry and the schoolbus went into the drink. My son Ken dived in and got all the kids out of the half-submerged bus, assisted by a lady in her pants and bra. Ken also saved a drowning man one day, up near the bluffs. He received no official recognition for either rescue, but finally was awarded a medal, along with his brother Ray, for saving the life of fellow fisherman Noel Everson, who'd been hit on the head by his boom while we were both trawling up at Shark Bay. Noel is, like me, still going strong, and still winning rowing races in his 80s.'

Is there something in the drinking water at Iluka? I have to ask Bill his secret for being so fit and bright at 93. 'Eating plenty of fish and veggies, and having a good lady to look after you. I've been lucky twice. My first lovely wife, whom I sadly lost due to a stroke, looked after me, and now my second lovely wife Jean also looks after me. I keep myself busy and active, and I have many friends of all ages.'

Bill raised three sons, Ken, Ray and Doug, and a daughter, Desma, who all, like him, were brought up in the magical setting of Woody Head, riding their ponies along the beach and to school at Iluka. 'They'd leave them in the ice factory's paddock and sometimes the fishermen would leave the rails down and the ponies'd trot home,' Bill chuckles.

When he bought his first big boat, *Hustler 2*, he moved his family into Iluka where the boat could be safely moored and the children were closer to their secondary schools. Bill recalls he and his wife had gone to Brisbane to inspect a boat, but at 23 000 dollars it was too expensive for them so they returned home. Then Ken rang them from Brisbane and said, 'I've found THE boat. Come up and see it.' When they got there, it was the same boat. They went to the Westpac bank to see if they could mortgage either their Woody Head or Iluka house. 'You'll have to mortgage everything you've got,' was the stern reply. Bill's response, 'Including my missus?' lightened up the situation and they got the loan to buy the boat Bill had always dreamt of owning. As well as being safer crossing the bar and capable of bigger catches, to be able to trawl at night also meant a bigger income. As soon as he could afford it, he bought a new Nissan motor to replace the old 5-cylinder Dormon he'd been nursing along. Bill had come a long way from his first vessel—a 4-metre punt which he towed to the ocean at Woody Head behind a horse.

After more than half a century of hard yakka and paying taxes, Bill retired aged 67, unable to get a pension due to assets. During the Bicentennial Year, he was honoured to be invited by then prime minister Bob Hawke to a prestigious black-tie dinner, hosted by the New South Wales Fish Marketing Authority, where the PM presented Bill with a gold medal featuring a fishing boat inscribed, 'To Our Industry's Pioneers'. But Bill—who has been vice-president of the P&C, a trustee of the Soldiers Memorial Hall and on the board of directors of the Maclean Co-operative—is more than a pioneer of an industry: he's part of a community.

Bill feels he has been blessed to be born in one of Australia's most beautiful and productive regions, and doubly blessed to be able to make a living and raise his family there. But even the loveli-est places hold sad memories. In 1977 tragedy struck the district when, during an exercise, an F-111 crashed near Ten Mile Beach, killing both RAAF airmen. Their controversial aircraft suffered a birdstrike at 860 kilometres per hour. There is a memorial to them at the site. Bill remembers that terrible day too well, a day that brought back memories of a similar tragedy there in World War II, when the RAAF base at Evans Head used Ten Mile Beach for bombing run practice. Two men crashed and died. Before the crash, the local fishermen had asked if the planes' approach path could be changed so the noise wouldn't interfere with their liveli-hood. 'I remember the top brass landing on the beach in a helicopter to explain to us why the bombing run approach couldn't be altered. Sixty years later, that same beach was again crowded with locals to see [electronics entrepreneur] Dick Smith land his balloon after his 55-hour record flight from New Zealand. So a lot of history is attached to this area . . .'

Clydesdales and carts, Model T Fords, F-111's, helicopters, balloons and many, many boats—Bill Hammond has seen them all operating in his magnificent bailiwick. Sadly, his family land was taken over by the national parks department in 1981—the first coastal land to be resumed by them—and is now Bundjalung National Park. The locals' holiday huts and caravans, which the family had allowed to be there for free, for generations of holiday-makers, were removed, along with the Hammonds. The government now invites tourists to stay in the house Henry Hammond built himself, with blood, sweat, an axe, an adze and a Clydesdale—for his family, and their families. Bill's house, nearby, is no longer his, and strangers now enjoy it.

It was a sad ending to the story of the Hammonds' time at Woody Head, but surprisingly 'Big Bill' can overcome his sadness to proudly show off the magic place where he once lived. With a positive, cheerful outlook, he smiles as he tells his stories, thankful for the good life he's had, enjoying your company, and enjoying each day as it comes.

A productive, honest life; a great Australian. Big Bill Hammond, we salute you—enjoy your golden years.

SID MARTIN

From Changi to the wharves

A part from underarm bowling, surely one of the most disgraceful chapters in Australia's history was its neglect of our
returned men from the two world wars. Vietnam vets no doubt have
similar stories to tell, of being returned to Australia from active
duty or capture, then simply left to get on with life as best they
could, with no assistance of any kind, no official gratitude for what
they had given their country and its people.

Sid Martin was one of many men who came home after four years
as a POW in Singapore, Indochina, Burma and Japan, to the attitude
from the army on his discharge, 'That's it, mate, now bugger off,' and
even less assistance to recover and get a job from the government of
the time. What happened to 'Lest we forget' back then?

Born in 1918 on a farm at Cobargo, near Narooma, on the
beautiful south coast of New South Wales, Sid, his two brothers and

two sisters walked to school, as everyone did in those days, unless they were lucky enough to have a pony of their own. In a poor one-horse family, the horse was usually needed to shift the cows before and after milking. Sid actually walked to several schools in the district because he kept playing up, getting into trouble, and when he was sent outside the classroom he'd just clear off. After his escape from the local school, his mother sent him to Tilba Tilba, then finally the Aboriginal mission school at Wallaga Lake. None of these educational establishments appealed to Sid—apart from playing footy with his mates from the mission. He was to continue playing for Wallaga—just a little conspicuous as the only 'whitie'—for years afterwards.

So his formal education was not a success, but that wasn't unusual back then. He wasn't stupid, and like many people from that era educated himself gradually through reading, and always found employment. He enjoyed working on farms, ploughing behind Clydesdales, milking cows by hand, building and repairing post and rail fences, and doing all the usual chores on the land—all done the hard way, but time was no problem. 'People didn't rush about, they just got the job at hand done, and did it properly, with pride.'

Turning 21 used to be a big celebration, receiving 'the key to the door' as a symbol of adulthood, but Sid's present was the thought of taking part in the so-called 'grand adventure' of going off to war. When Australia's men were called to arms in 1939, Sid and his brothers enlisted in the army. His mother, who had lived through World War I, and father, who had survived it, had to bear the pain of seeing all their three sons leave the country, knowing they may not return.

Unfortunately for Sid, and brothers Les (nicknamed 'Tibby') and Bill, they joined the ill-fated 8th Division, which was sent to Singapore and Malaya. After the disgraceful military debacle which resulted in the infamous 'Fall of Singapore' in 1942, the three brothers, along with many thousands of other young men, were captured by the victorious Japanese and incarcerated in the prison at Changi, where the airport is situated.

Of the 23 000 men captured, only 11 000 survived the following four years.

Asked if he could attribute his survival of those nightmare years to anything in particular, for example his robust stamina from his farming background, Sid sagely shakes his head. 'Life's a bag of tricks. It was luck, pure luck. Luck is either with you, or it isn't. If it isn't, you're in trouble. That's the same in any situation in life. It's a different world in a war zone, and different again in a prisoner-of-war camp, but you needed luck to survive. There were some poor buggers whose bodies just couldn't handle the constant starvation and beatings, or recover from dysentery and other tropical diseases—they had bad luck. Others somehow survived all that— they had good luck. Having a bloke like Weary Dunlop to help you survive—now that was even better luck.'

Sid's brother Bill was Weary's offsider. However, Sid didn't see Bill until the war was over, and didn't know if he was dead or alive. 'I did see my brother Les, and we tried to keep tabs on each other during the next four years, which wasn't always easy. There was no mail allowed in or out, so my mother and father didn't know if we were alive.' When Sid was imprisoned in Indochina, he managed to get a message to his parents from the World Communications centre at Saigon, just saying 'I'm okay, Les is with me, and Arthur Meade' (a friend from nearby Bermagui). A woman from Broome picked up the message and made sure it reached his mother. But that was early during his incarceration and his parents didn't get any more news until the war was over.

Shortly after capture, Sid was sent to work camps, firstly near Saigon, then to Cambodia, then back to Singapore to build a dock. Next was the worst nightmare: the Burma line. They started at Victoria Point, which was the most southern point of Burma, where all the famous aviators, including Kingsford Smith and Amy Johnson, left on their epic flights. During work on the line, they slept, through sheer exhaustion, out in the open, or if they were lucky in bamboo huts, while enduring the monsoon season. With just a small serving of rice to eat, with sometimes a tiny bit of fish, meat or vegetables added, Sid tried not to look back and think about the comparatively better food they had in the Saigon camp: stewed dogs or horse and eggs. He actually got sick of eggs there, even though he was starving. After surviving the horrors of the Burma line construction, he was sent to Japan, to a camp near Nagasaki, but fortunately just far enough away from the site of the first atomic bomb.

'Burma was bad, but my time at that work camp in Japan was even worse. We worked in the mines. It was an extreme winter and of course I wasn't used to that, and even though we were issued British winter uniforms—most probably from poor buggers who'd died—they were still inadequate and we were freezing all the time, even when we were working. When going to and from the mines in the snow, our legs were always numb from the knees down. Conditions in the mine were like Burma: brutal. Those of us who lived through it attribute much of our survival to mateship—pure and simple. We supported each other. It was hard, it was a cruel, dreadful experience and I don't want to think about that time in my life. I try not to think about what we experienced, and the poor buggers who didn't make it. I try not to have hatred in my life.'

I reckon it must have been hard not to feel hatred when, after Sid's release, he went to the wharves and saw the thousands of Red Cross parcels which were supposed to have gone to the POWs, and might have saved lives if they had, stockpiled by the Japanese for themselves.

Sid was taken from Nagasaki to the Philippines for six weeks, to get fit enough to return home. He was 6 feet tall, but weighed 40 kilos—a walking skeleton, like all his mates. I asked him if he was ever able to face eating rice again. 'Oh, yes, I love rice!' was his surprising answer. He replies in the negative, however, to the question of whether the army put the released POWs on a special diet to recover, or if they received special care. 'No, we got the usual army food, and no special treatment, but we were grateful to be alive and that there were no more bloody Japs yelling orders at us and flogging us. It was wonderful to just hear Aussie and English voices—no Japanese.

'When we were strong enough, we were put on a ship to Walsh Bay, Sydney where, funnily enough, I was soon to return seeking work on the wharves. We were taken by bus to Ingleburn base, sent away on four weeks leave, then called back to be discharged. There was nothing for us, and nothing done for us.'

It was a case of 'the war's over, now get on with life'. But everything had changed and Sid, and others like him, had to change too. After a happy reunion with his family, including brothers Bill and Tibby whom he hadn't seen since early 42, he went to Sydney seeking work. There was little on offer, even to returned men, and only hard labouring jobs at that. He found work on a building site in Dowling Street, but it was only casual labouring. He'd had to line up at the site with a mob of men like him—desperately seeking work. The foreman arrived, looked them over, then asked them to hold up their hands, palms up. After Sid had been chosen he overheard the boss say to the foreman, 'They look like they'll go alright,' to which the foreman, a tough joker, replied, 'Of course they'll bloody well go alright. I looked at their hands.'

Having been reared during the Depression years, and as an ex-POW, Sid knew very well how to tighten his belt, do without, live on very little. He found a tiny flat at Redfern, where he was to live for the next 30 years. Sid eventually went to the wharves in search of further work to survive. Work on the wharves was all casual then. Men lined up at the pick-up points, eagerly hoping to be selected. The selectors would call out, 'You, you, you and you,' pointing to each man, and the unsuccessful ones would drift away, disappointed, to try their luck elsewhere—such a fine way for men who'd fought for their country to be treated. Most blokes were unable to buy even a pushbike to get around looking for work, so it was a case of wearing out your boot leather.

Pick-up points were at Millers Point and Walsh Bay for deep-sea shipping and Sussex Street for coastal. 'Picked' men were taken to the ships by bus or launch. Sussex Street to Hickson Road had been dubbed The Hungry Mile in the Depression years, with hungry men searching for employment. Sid recalls the desperate men, some highly qualified, trying to get a start on the gangs digging and draining the swampy ground that became Wentworth Park (later famous for greyhound racing), during the so-called Great Depression. His father told him the same scenes of desperation could be observed during the 1890 Depression, when the government hired men to build Centennial Park.

Sid fortunately looked like a bloke who could work hard, and was often picked, but also knew the bitter disappointment of missing out. No work, no tucker. The conditions on the wharves were just as hard and unsafe as they'd been on the building sites. Amenities were nonexistent. Loads were manhandled from ships to trucks and vice-versa. Nearly everything was done the hard way, and any existing equipment was primitive and often dilapidated. Some wharves had treacherous loose timber. The men lugged bags of cement, wheat, lampblack, etc., along planks, up and down ladders. They got absolutely filthy, either covered in dirt and dust, cement, lampblack (the worst) or rust from carrying and stacking iron. Men were frequently hurt but, if possible, would keep working. They had sore hands from cement, splinters from timber, scratches, cuts and bruises, but they had to keep working if they wanted to eat, pay the rent and survive.

By the late 40s, mechanisation was at last making the wharfie's job easier, first with steam-operated winches, then electric winches, and forklifts. The Waterside Workers Union was having success in its fight for better wages and conditions and more certainty of a regular income for its members. The union was at last getting many things for them which are taken for granted by workers now: smoko breaks, first aid kits and a first aid room, plus a room and showers for the men to change their filthy clothes at the end of the day. When a bag of soda ash or cement had burst, the men were able to have a shower and wash it off, instead of having to put up with the burning when it mixed with sweat on their skin. Sid learnt to have a cold shower after loading bags of lampblack, because hot water would make things worse, spreading the black all over. 'You can imagine what we looked like when we'd been lumping bags of coal all day! There were still steamships back when I started in the 40s, before they all changed to oil in the 50s. We lumped bags of coal across planks to the holds for hours, we'd be black and buggered, thus the saying "working like a navvy".

'With the terrible conditions we worked under back then, we felt we had the world against us. The wealthy shippers held control over organisations, which filtered down to control over us. We faced a struggle like the early coalminers did. How did *they* feel back in the 1920s when a big owner of the coalmines, John Brown, on being informed the miners' families were starving, said, "Let 'em eat grass". Back when our union was making a stand for better conditions for us, they were vilified by the shipowners, but men can only be treated badly for so long, then they will get together and stand up for themselves, to be treated and paid decently, exactly like the coalminers and shearers had to. The shipowners had refused to pay to have some wharfies trained in first aid. The union paid for training, so there'd be a first aid man available on each shift. The shipowners' refusal to pay for it meant the rift between employers and employees widened. Around the same time, the miners and ironworkers unions were fighting for the same improvements.'

A step forward in the wage-paying system saved the men a lot of mucking around getting their money. At the end of a job they were able to be paid at the job, instead of having to go to the Pitt Street office (although men who finished before the job was completed still had to go to the office). 'At last we were guaranteed hours, and paid a decent rate, which meant we earned, around the early 50s, about 5 pounds a week. Also, we couldn't be sacked on the spot for no reason, at the whim of some boof-headed gang boss in a bad mood. Some of them were bastards and just enjoyed having that power over men with no power. There was a bloke like that called "Sacking Fred", and another called "Stargazing Wally", nicknamed one nightshift when a bloke said to him, "What do the stars say, Wally?" and he replied, "The stars say you're sacked!" Wally thought that was funny, but the poor bloke had to go home and tell his missus. Those were bad days.'

Sid became a union delegate, and one of his finest moments was winning a court case for compensation for a man who'd been injured on the wharves when hit by a bale of wool. The man was to receive compo for his injury, but not for his prescription spectacles, which were smashed. Sid went in to battle for him on this point. The shipowner's representative put up their argument, then Sid stood up and quoted the relevant Act, which stated that 'compensation was to be granted for the injuries to the person, *and articles upon the person*'. Sid had studied the Act a hundred times and memorised it. It was with great satisfaction he heard Commissioner Kline find 'in favour of the plaintiff'. It was the first case the union won and Sid was the hero of the day, even though he received no word of thanks from the bloke he'd stood up for ('a bit of an oddbod'). 'The union has achieved many good things, like stopping the shipment of pig-iron leaving for Japan in Bob Menzies' time. Our members refused to load it as they were sure it would be used as weapons against Australians.'

The hard days, the many hours spent carrying loads like a human mule up and down gangways in all weathers, eventually began to tell on Sid's health by the time he was in his 50s. His years as a POW would have also taken their toll on his body. In the early 1970s he was starting to spend time in hospital, with joint and back problems. Eventually his doctor said, 'Sid, you can't do this sort of work anymore. Your body needs to rest if you're going to enjoy a long life. You deserve an invalid pension—you've worked hard in terrible conditions both during and after the war, and you've paid a lot of tax. Go to repat and see what they'll do for you.' Around the time Gough Whitlam was elected in 1972, Sid was finally granted an invalid pension and could at last take it easy. But—disgraceful as it may seem—he had a frustrating, protracted battle against a repat doctor first.

He lost his flat at Cooper Street, Redfern, in 1978 when the block was sold, and was able to get a housing commission flat, but had to move to Wollongong for it. He still misses Redfern, where he knew a lot of people, but he has friends and family who care for him and keep an eye on him. Sid has always enjoyed helping people, and at 93 years of age still does. He even does the shopping for a house-bound neighbour, scooting off on his motorised 'gofer machine' to the shopping centre to do his good deed.

'If you want to have a happy life, just rule out "What's in it for me?" and do what you can to help others. Kind deeds are worth more than kind words. That's what life's all about. Stick with that, or as near as you can get, and you'll be proud of yourself and sleep well at night. I've never judged people I've just met or hardly know, because that first impression could be wrong—they could be having a bad day and be a different person tomorrow. In life, I've always found it wise not to do certain things in haste, especially important things—that's a quick way of making mistakes.'

I was taken to meet Sid by his second cousins, Christine Hansard and Glenda Robinson (nee Martin), who obviously think the world of him and keep an eye on his welfare. Having known him and been close to him since they were young girls, they offered this comment on his nature and character: 'It is very fortunate that, if once in a lifetime, you meet a person who is humble to one's self, generous to others, honest to all and impartial in judgement. How lucky we have been to share our lives with such a person—a very gracious man, our second cousin, whom we endearingly call Uncle Sid.'

Every year on 15 February, the anniversary of the fall of Singapore, Sid attends his unit's reunion. Sadly, there are only three of them left now—Sid, Jack Boardman and Allan 'Butch' Gaudrey—but the memories which bind them are as strong as ever, on that day and any day.

Good on you, Sid, and thank you. Lest we forget.

JOHN 'JOCKEY' CHARMAN

Coalminer

For many of us, working underground would be a frightening experience, but to John Charman, it was only natural that he would follow in his father's footsteps. Born in Wigan, England, on 20 August 1919, John immigrated to Australia with his family when he was five years old. His father was lured by the thought of having a much easier working life here, compared with the mines in England, where the small seams of coal meant miners had to crawl in to get at them, then dig in cramped conditions.

The family headed for Helensburgh, the northernmost mining town in a string built above the rich seams along the south coast between Wollongong and Sydney. Coal had been accidentally discovered there by three survivors of a shipwreck in 1797, when they found lumps of coal on a beach to use for a fire. Explorer George Bass was sent to investigate, and all New South Wales coal was handed over, as a monopoly, to the London-based Australian Agricultural Company. One and a quarter centuries later, the tough, hard life and deplorable working conditions John's father had experienced in England were not much better in Australia, where mine owners also treated their workers appallingly, with scant regard for their welfare or concern for safety.

By the time John was following him underground, working conditions still weren't much better or safer, so it must have taken a lot of courage, I put to him, to climb into that cage and descend into a dark hole where the possibility of a rockfall or explosion must enter your mind. He laughs (John laughs a lot). 'No, you don't let yourself think about that. You're just going to work underground, like your father and grandfather did before you, and like your workmates who are with you on that shift, and all their fathers and grandfathers most probably did too. I was brought up in Helensburgh, which is a coalmining town—nearly everyone is a coalminer, except for the people who run the shops. It exists because of the coalmine, it was built by coalminers, and we're proud of our mining history. Col Harper discovered coal here and set up the mine, and was the first man to be killed in it. He left nine kids and I went to school with a couple of them. So, you see, our lives here, until recently, revolved completely around the mine. Helensburgh used to be so close, you'd think we were all related. The Burgh, as we call it, is now changing since "outsiders" have started to move in. The word has spread about our beautiful spot, right in the national park, and people from all walks of life now live here and commute up to Sydney. I'm happy about that because I love a chat and it's nice to talk about things other than coalmining.'

John is well known in the Burgh as either 'Havachat' or 'The Hat'. He is rarely seen without his big Akubra on, and a five-minute walk up the road to get the paper usually turns into a couple of hours by the time he's had a chinwag with everyone. John's third nickname is 'Jockey', so when I saw a jockey-sized chap in a big Akubra chatting away with the postie, I knew I had my man.

John's dad wanted him to be a jockey, not a miner, and took him to a trainer's stables near Rosebery the day he finished primary school. It was during the Great Depression, and the family was struggling to survive like everyone else. A coalminer's pay was not much, and it would be a big help not to have a teenage lad to feed. 'I wasn't keen at all on being a jockey. I loved horses but I wasn't a good rider. However, I remember Dad was so keen to get me there. He didn't have a car, of course—hardly any miners could afford one—we all walked everywhere, or caught the train. Anyway, we hitched a lift on a truck to the Princes Highway, then couldn't get another lift so we walked all the way to Mascot in the rain. It was hard, but life was hard back then and you didn't expect anything to be easy.

'I used to exercise an average of sixteen horses a morning on the track. Hard work. I used to get all the bad "pullers" because for some reason I could hang on to them. So I certainly earned my huge pay as an apprentice—ten shillings a week. Of course, it wasn't just riding—there were stables to be mucked out, horses all had to fed and groomed—you were kept very, very busy. My only outings during my six years as an apprentice—apart from going to the races—was to go to the night markets once a week. It wasn't very exciting but it was an outing. When I turned 21 I was qualified, and received a pound a week and my board. To have a job and three meals a day during the Depression meant you felt very fortunate, no matter how hard your work was.

'I was never a successful jockey. I don't know why, but I just rarely rode a winner, even though I enjoyed competing. To survive, I worked the nightshift at a wool mill at Botany owned by Fred Hughes, who also owned racehorses. In the mornings I earned money riding trackwork. When you're young you can work hard. I rode at different tracks—Ascot, which was where the airport is now; Moorefield, where the Kogarah TAFE now stands; and Victoria Park, which disappeared when the suburb of Zetland was built. We used to take the horses to meetings on the train back then. It was a grand era of racing, and I was privileged to count several famous jockeys amongst my friends: George Moore, George Mulley, George Podmore, Darby Munro, Andy Knotts, Billy Lappin, Stan Davis and Harry Dark, who rode the wonderful mare Tea Rose. George Mulley was a wag and sometimes led me astray. When the Second World War started I went to enlist but the bloke in charge owned race-horses and knocked me back.

'I eventually saved enough to buy a house back in Helens-burgh, a little miner's cottage, so I could marry my girl Dulcie and carry her over the threshold. I met her on a merry-go-round at a circus in Ryde; I stayed on so long talking to her I got dizzy. Living back in the Burgh, it was only natural that I went to work in the mines, and gave away what had been an enjoyable, if not a really successful, career on the racetracks. It wasn't long before I was back in the saddle though. A local chap bought a racehorse and I trained it for him, with quite a bit of success. I rode him myself in the Burragarang Cup and he bolted in—what a thrill! But my old bad luck started up when the saddle slipped at Grafton, then the horse bled at Ascot and couldn't race anymore.'

In the mine, John started as a 'clipper', clipping the cables off the skips so the coal could be tipped out and washed, then became a 'wheeler', wheeling the skips into the coalface. The miners put up the timber shoring themselves, working in pairs. All jobs in the coalmine were hard and dirty. Coaldust is very hard to wash off as it has oil in it. Up top, out the back of their cottage, Dulcie worked hard too, scrubbing John's filthy clothes on the scrubbing board, whirling them around in her copper tub of hot water, then pushing them through the mangle. It was tough work but it was still an improvement on her grandmother's time at the Burgh.

Dulcie vividly remembers how she'd help her grandmother carry her washing through the bush to the dam that supplied water for the mine. 'Grandma washed the clothes there like a native woman, then we'd hang the clothes on a wire she'd string from tree to tree. Even though I had a copper at the back of my house, which made things a lot easier for me than my grandmother had it on washing days, I still couldn't waste any water because we only had rainwater tanks for our supply. The Burgh didn't get water on until 1950.

It was while visiting her grandmother that Dulcie first fell in love with the area. 'I loved coming out here for holidays, playing in the bush that surrounded this village for miles. My children did the same, and their children, and now their grandchildren. They all live here and love it. It's still like a little country town, but only an hour from the city.

'We used to have wonderful old-style dances every Saturday night and people would come from far and wide to enjoy our band, who of course were all miners. There was a room at the back of the band hall—which the miners built; they built nearly everything—where the older ladies would play euchre. The men had beer hidden outside, where there was at least one fist fight every Saturday night, because two particular men, good mates, always had a fight after a few beers.

'We all helped each other out in the hard times, and still do. During the strikes, for instance, when there was no money coming in while our husbands held out for better pay and safer conditions, people would share their veggies and rabbits. Professional fishermen would bring us fish from the beach at Stanwell Park, to help us survive. One strike lasted three months—that was hard. We had five children, but we all tightened our belts and made it through. Every strike was for a good reason: to get a decent wage, or to make their work safer. Yes, I used to worry about John getting hurt. I'd see him walking off to the mine with all his mates, all carrying their cribs [lunchboxes], yarning and joking, and hope they'd all be walking back together that afternoon, all black, but safe and sound. Some of them would be carrying a sugar bag of coal from the slack heap— about the only free perk of their job. It was a hard, steep climb home for them.'

Any miner's wife on the south coast line would know the stories of the terrible disasters at Bulli and Mt Kembla. Ninety men died in an explosion at Mt Kembla in 1902, caused by a combination of leaking gas and the highly dangerous naked lights they had to use. Warnings of the gas leakage by miners to management had been ignored, and every miner knew if they pressed the matter they could be sacked on the spot. The mine owners held all the cards. An interesting but quite spooky anecdote from a survivor of that disaster was his recall of waking up one morning, yelling: 'Run! For God's sake, run! She's fired!' Three months later, working underground, he heard a man yell those very words, before all hell broke loose. He lived to tell the tale. A workmate had another horrifying but equally amazing experience, when he was dumped, unconscious, onto the pile of dead men, but fortunately recovered and was able to attract someone's attention and get help. A miner who had the courage to testify at the subsequent court inquiry that his warning of leaking gas had been ignored by the manager lost his job. Such men were 'blackballed' and couldn't get employment in any mine after they spoke up.

After World War I, George Davis, MLA, fought to get better conditions for miners after visiting Broken Hill and seeing that the mines there had begun providing showers for the men to use after work. Men in mines such as those at Helensburgh had to get clean as best they could in a tin tub in front of the fire at home, and often their home, provided by the mine owners, was a one-roomed hut, so there was no privacy. During strikes for better conditions, miners were thrown out of these huts, their furniture thrown out on the street with them.

They were just hard times—very, very hard,' John says. He recalls when he was a youngster and people would talk about the good old days. 'Not in the mines,' the old miners would say, 'there weren't any good old days.'

By 1938 they *only* had a 40-hour week to battle through. For many years before this breakthrough, most miners were too frightened to push for it, in fear of losing their livelihood, and even after that victory it was still not a job for the faint-hearted.

Conditions were certainly challenging, to say the least, when John began mining. He was deeply saddened when a mate—one of many Welsh miners who came to Australia during the Great Depression—was killed in a rockfall. And he could only hope that he wouldn't suffer from the other dread miners have—of getting 'dusted'. Coaldust on the lungs was a major and common occupational hazard. John's father suffered terribly from it, as did many miners, and that was what finally killed him. Known officially as pneumoconiosis, the condition killed thousands of miners.

But there are some good memories, too. John remembers with pride that during World War II, Australia's miners got right behind the war effort, smashing production records, and honouring the slogans printed everywhere on posters: 'Coal to beat fascism!' 'Coal to beat the Japanese aggressors!'

Being a horseman, John also enjoyed watching the pit ponies working. 'They weren't really ponies—they were big horses. There were about 30 underground at a time. They stayed underground for a year and were stabled down there. Their eyes adjusted and at knock-off time, they would push the doors open themselves, finding their way back to their stables. They were taken up after a year, for six weeks' holiday, and they'd just go crazy when they got into their paddock. They would have suffered for a while from the sudden light.'

The horses were eventually replaced by little locomotives to pull the loaded skips. The miners would fill an average of 23 skips in a morning. They each had a leather identification tag on a rope which they'd put in a skip before sending it to the weighbridge, and they were paid by tonnage. John remembers it was freezing in the drift, the tunnel where the skips were taken back up above ground, and he'd wear two jackets.

An injury to his foot in the mine forced John's retirement at age 60 in 1979, but he kept himself busy coaching the Helensburgh soccer team for the next twenty years. He used to go fishing but, as he puts it, 'the fish didn't like me'. He and Dulcie have always had an enormous veggie garden behind their cottage, and give much of their produce away to neighbours and friends, of whom they have many. Keeping up with thirteen grandchildren and seventeen great grandchildren also takes up their time. Neither of them ever learnt to drive, they've never owned a car or felt they needed one, and catch a train when they need to. They remain perfectly happy with their life in the Burgh . . . don't you envy them?

It's nearly 70 years since John fell for Dulcie on the merry-go-round at Ryde and, 66 years after their wedding, they love each other's company just as much and both still have a spring in their step. Under his trademark big hat, John, at 92, still has that twinkle in his eye that tells you, 'Here's a larrikin who knows how to enjoy himself'. Part of our coalmining history, John Charman is a living treasure. Good on yer, mate!

MARY BARRY MBE

The most popular publican in Queensland

Step inside the old Commercial Hotel in Dalby, western Queensland, and you immediately feel welcome. That is the true essence, the essential factor, of a successful pub. A well-dressed, friendly lady smiles, says hello, and gets you a drink in double-quick time. While getting your order, she asks your name, and if she's not too busy, she'll have a chat. If you travel on then return to the Commercial a year later, that same lady will greet you by your name, making you feel even more welcome than the first time. You are amazed she remembers, but that's just one of her secrets of success. When you meet Mary Barry, you soon realise that she is not only a gracious hostess and super-efficient publican, she is also a complete individual . . . you'll never find another like her.

If it's a Friday or Saturday night, the bar will be full of sportspeople, farmers and ag college students. You can't help but notice how fond of Mary they all are, and that she is like a mother to the students and the younger footballers. Generations of locals think of her as their 'second mum'. She's bailed hundreds of them out when they've got into strife, given them advice when they needed it, lent them money, listened to their troubles and encouraged them to succeed in life. Just about every student who's been to Dalby Ag College or played footy or cricket in the region would have a 'Mary Barry story'.

Like Max Offner from Toowoomba, for example: 'My favourite Mary story is from my rugby playing days, in the 60s. During one of many huge nights when the team were all playing up like second-hand chainsaws at Mary's after a match, she put me to bed upstairs so I wouldn't drive home . . . ah, shall we say . . . less than fully alert. Then she rang my mother and said, "Max is staying here tonight, Dawn, dear. He has a case of mild concussion from football and needs a good rest." Of course there'd be hundreds of blokes she's sent to bed over the years when they get legless. There was never any trouble in her pub while she was on deck. She'd stop it before it got going. I'll never forget seeing her literally jump the bar, pearls, twin-set and all, take this big, aggro feller's arm and lead him firmly out the door, saying, "Darling, you've had enough. Out the back!" People can drink as much as they like, have the time of their life, but everyone knows there is a limit to your partying behaviour at Mary's, a line you don't cross, which is good for young people to experience and understand. For them, it's a bit like partying at your grandma's house. Enjoy yourself, but don't go crazy.'

Respect for Mary was so great that her standards of dress and behaviour still rule the Commercial today. Despite working long hours, she has always been immaculate in her appearance. And she won't tolerate Jackie Howe singlets in her bar; she is unable to comprehend how a man could be too lazy or uncaring about his appearance to put a shirt on. 'There was also no swearing,' Max says. 'If a bloke forgot himself and swore, he'd always apologise to Mary. It's amazing. There's that element of respect that permeates even the thickest fog of alcohol. Unfortunately the words "legend" and "icon" are over-used these days, but she is genuinely both a legend in her own time and an icon of the Western Downs.'

Past president of Mary's beloved rugby union club, Leigh Johnston, says: 'The fact that a punch has never been thrown in the Commercial is entirely due to the enormous respect everyone has for this amazing lady. Everyone heads to Mary's after a game—that's our pub—and as you can imagine, the fellers can get pretty lively, whether we've won or lost. If she tells a bloke to leave, but he goes back later and apologises, they're always welcome back. "Don't worry about that. We all do silly things, darling," she'll say. Those words and her smile make blokes feel more regretful about what they did or said, and more determined to behave in future, than if she'd been furious with them. Two big Russian blokes who were working on the Moonie pipeline years ago—tough as nails they looked—started arguing one night and stood up to start fighting. Mary went over to them, clapped her hands, got their attention, and waggled her finger: "Now, listen here. No blueing in this pub. You're mates, so shake hands and behave like mates, or leave." They looked like two naughty boys caught out. They shook hands, sat down and finished their beers, mates again.

'If a bloke gets full and leaves his change on the bar by mistake, it'll be there in an envelope with his name on it when he goes back. Mary creates a sort of wholesome, civilised atmosphere in that bar, that everyone respects. Even when the place is packed and everyone's having a huge party, moving around, you can safely leave your money on the bar—no one would dream of touching it. One night a bloke found 500 bucks in a roll on the floor of the gents. He handed it over to Mary, so she shouted him a jug for being so honest. Another night, one of "her" rugby boys staggered backwards through the front door, smashing the glass. He was mortified, apologising profusely to Mary, who calmly said, "Don't worry, darling, don't be upset. I've got a piece of masonite pre-cut out the back shed. We'll get the glass fixed next week. I'll get Harold to run you home, pet, you need a good night's sleep." A lot of young people love going there because it's nothing like the trendy bars in bigger towns or cities; there's an old-world atmosphere, a last little living example of "the good old days".'

In testimony to her amazing memory, Leigh relates the story of taking his visiting uncle there for a drink: Scotch and water. *Four years later* he was back visiting Leigh, and as he walked into the bar Mary was already pouring him a Scotch and water.

As well as being kind, brave and hospitable, Mary's also very smart, a whiz with figures. When looking at the books, she has always been able to spot an error immediately, a talent she may have inherited from her father, who was an accountant. Born at Gargett, near Mackay, in 1919, Mary grew up in Tully, attending St Clare's School, then the Herberton Convent and finally All

Hallows School, Brisbane. She worked in Tully as secretary of the Canegrowers Council, then in a solicitor's office in Brisbane, where she also helped her mother run her boarding house. That was an introduction to catering for guests at a professional level. In 1952 she took over the lease of the Commercial, then a brewery pub, after a battle with the licensing commissioner, who bit off more than he could chew when he said to Mary, 'Don't be ridiculous, young lady. A woman could not possibly run a pub!' She stuck up for herself and went on to become one of the state's most successful hoteliers. Her friendly, welcoming, well-run country pub was a fine example of the hospitality industry before the term was even popularised, because Mary thought of her patrons as guests and treated them that way.

When she first took over, learning as she went along, she allowed her naturally generous spirit to guide her, giving her customers what they wanted. From the time she opened as licensee, many people from a wide radius of Dalby enjoyed her meals—big, grand meals. Soon the saying 'Meet you at Mary's' spread like wildfire—and it's stuck, still a part of local lingo after all these years. Likewise her favourite saying when she's shouting a drink, which she frequently does: 'Happy days!' No one can leave her bar after just one drink— she calls you back to shout you one. No wonder her customers return and are loyal to her, even if the décor is a bit out of date now—last renovated in 1963. A non-drinker, non-smoker, if Mary joins you for a drink, she sips lemonade. She has one alcoholic drink a year: a pernod on Christmas Day.

Dalby was a prosperous place in the wool-boom years—a great time to be a publican. In fact, the prosperity lasted right through 'til the Whitlam years. But no matter how tough life became for the region's primary producers, such as during times of drought or severe market downturns, they could always drown their sorrows—and find a friend—at Mary's. A good listener, her genuine concern about her customers' problems, and interest in their families, has always been appreciated.

In 1986, Mary bought the freehold. When gaming machines started to appear in pubs she would not consider having them, declaring, 'My philosophy is that this pub is not a money-making exercise—it's a hub for the community.' Countless family and club celebrations of every kind have been held at the Commercial during her reign, with Mary attending to every detail at every function as if it was for her family. The Commercial has also been the venue for the Wambo Shire Council meetings for 50 years. It was a justified honour for Mary to be inducted into the Queensland Hoteliers Hall of Fame in 1970.

As well as being the proud recipient of an MBE (Member of the British Empire) in 1971, she was voted Dalby's Bicentennial Citizen of the Year in 1988, and is patron of the Dalby rugby union and cricket clubs, the ski, polocrosse and darts clubs, the jockey association, the Dalby Thistle Pipe Band and Dalby Jazz Big Band. Her big donations to local causes, like the showground pavilion for example, mean that future generations of Dalby children will continue to benefit from her generosity. Mary says her parents brought her up to support the community, and it gives her enormous pleasure to do so. Now 91, she's served four generations of locals, and regards all the people of Dalby as her family. She was always 'too busy' to marry.

For several years, her busy schedule also included caring for her mother, who lived at the hotel. Mrs Barry Snr was a great friend of artist Hugh Sawrey's mother. Mrs Sawrey often visited the Commercial and Mary was very fond of her. For all Mary's kindness to his mother in her older years, Hugh created a special painting, that hangs now in what's always referred to as the 'Hugh Sawrey Room'. While he stayed at the hotel to paint it, in that very room, he frequently enjoyed Mary's 'merchandise'. A true bushman, Hugh loved good company and having a blow-out now and then. But if he started getting a bit boisterous, Mary would say, 'Hugh, go home to your mother.'

Around the public bar hang photos of Mary with many celebrities, including sporting heroes Shane Webcke, Gordon Tallis and Merv Hughes. Her generous support of many sporting organisations in Dalby is legendary, but her great love seems to be rugby union. She loved to watch 'her boys' play and even went on tour with them once, to New Guinea, as their good luck charm. The local New Guineans, both children and adults, were intrigued and delighted with her, calling her 'Missy Queensland'.

Denise Brady, who has worked for Mary for 35 years and managed the Commercial for the past 10 years, says: 'Mary took an interest in the rugby union club from day one in 1964, when she was asked for a donation to help build a clubhouse. "How much do you need, luvvies?" she said, and then gave the committee "non-repayable loans" to develop their grounds—now called the Mary Barry Sporting Complex. Whenever they tried to pay her back, she'd say, "No, darlings, you just might need it later." She loves to talk to the players about their games and how their training is going. The current players' fathers, who've moved away, now come back here with their sons for a drink and a yarn with Mary during the footy season. It's lovely to hear her reminiscing with them—there's always huge laughter when they recall what they used to get up to here. One of her favourite recollections is the big grand final celebration she let them hold here, and they called it "No Undies Sunday". They all came in hilarious fancy dress and chucked their undies up in the fans.'

One of the grandest nights in the town's history was the rugby club's gala black tie tribute dinner to Mary in 1997, with The Hon. Jim Killen as guest speaker and Alan Jones, broadcaster, as a surprise guest—both famous men are big fans of Mary's. Both declared it to be one of the most enjoyable functions they had ever attended. Major sporting stars of all ages and codes were also there.

As well as helping the rugby and cricket clubs establish facilities with interest-free loans, Mary was responsible for the Touch Football Association's lights going up, which enabled them to expand from eighteen to more than 40 teams taking part in the comp. Typically, she wiped their debt when the bulk of it was still owing, as she has done for other clubs. She likes to think that Dalby's young people have plenty of choice of good healthy things to do, so they will stay in the town and keep it vibrant.

Mary really loves the young people, and they love her. Denise says: 'When she's watching the rowdy ag college students or rugby boys having "boat races" [drinking contests], she has this lovely smile on her face. When one of our young sporting teams lose a match and come in to drown their sorrows, she shouts them four jugs of beer and several big plates of sandwiches and says, "Here, luvvies, this is for playing the game." She takes a great interest in how the ag college students are progressing, what their plans are for their future—that type of thing—and when they go away and return, as they all do, she's so keen to hear what they've achieved, how their families are and so on.'

Locals say you can go away for years and come back to Dalby, and there is a constant: Mary Barry never changes. Over the years, more than one Dalby Primary School child, when asked to write an essay about a famous person, has written theirs about Mary. Some locals describe her as the 'Mother Teresa of Dalby', or 'the finest example of a true Christian', meaning she helps people no matter what their creed. Denise says: 'People would not know the extent of her generosity. She not only supports sporting organisations, she helps more down and out families than anyone will ever know about.'

A great supporter of her Catholic church, Mary in turn enjoys seeing the priests come through her door, to wet their whistle and have a yarn. At one Sunday Mass a visiting priest, Irish as Paddy's pigs, gave a long sermon about the evils of working on the Sabbath. Afterwards, he went to the Commercial with some other priests. 'Mary, we're here for lunch,' he said. Keeping a straight face, she replied, 'Oh, father, we can't possibly help you—no one works here on the Sabbath.' Denise recalls, 'Mary had a great old laugh at the looks on their faces, then went off to get them a feed.'

For her eightieth birthday, Mary received a most unusual and special gift—a mass celebrated in her honour. It was attended by people from all religions and walks of life, who wanted to be part of it, in tribute to her. Most of the congregation, of course, enjoyed a drink afterwards—where else but at Mary's!

'You know,' Denise says, 'you could travel anywhere in Australia and mention you're from Dalby, and it's highly likely people will say, "Oh, that's the town with Mary's pub—had a great time there!"' Mary loves to see people enjoying themselves and, according to Denise, that's what makes her a tough—but fair—boss: 'Because she's always worked hard, she expects you to do the same and if she walks into the bar and a drinker has an empty glass in front of them, look out! You get that finger waving at you, leaving you in no doubt that she isn't happy with you, that you're letting her down. "No one should ever have to wait for a drink" is the motto she drums into bar staff, and of course she's right—there is nothing more annoying to a thirsty person than having to wait. Her pet hate would be seeing an empty glass in front of someone—another is chewing gum, she won't tolerate that. She tells any new staff, "Keep casting your eye around the bar, no matter how occupied you are with what you're doing, and when it's busy, move faster—the customers like that. They see you're making an extra effort to look after them, and they appreciate it. They won't stay, or come back, if they're not happy with the service. And no matter how busy you are, you always have time to give them a smile."

As well as looking after her customers, Mary also really looks after her staff. Denise believes: 'A good indication of what a person is like to work for is the length of time employees stay. Harold Lynch was the manager before me and worked here for 27 years. No one would have a bad word to say about Mary. I consider myself lucky to have worked with her for nearly 35 years.'

Harold Lynch calls Mary the greatest woman he has ever met in his life. He says: 'Mary never says anything but nice things about people. In the hotel business, you see and hear a lot of things people normally would not want you to see or remember. Mary tells her staff: "See no evil, hear no evil, speak no evil. In other words, don't ever blab!"'

When Harold applied for a job at the Commercial, he'd never worked in a hotel. 'I'd knocked around the bush doing all sorts of jobs, rabbit-trapping, rouseabouting in shearing sheds—you name it. I was green as grass, but I was keen to learn.' With her typical faith and goodwill, Mary gave him a go. 'She taught me everything, including keeping the books, and within two years left me in full control. She even bought a house in town for me to live in so I could get away from the pub.'

They had a 'terrific working relationship' for 27 years, but Harold agrees with Denise—Mary was a tough boss and kept him on his toes. He recalls: 'One day I was very upset because I'd made a mistake with the bookkeeping and had rubbed a hole in the page with the eraser. Mary came along and saw I was in despair and asked me what was wrong. I confessed what I'd done and apologised profusely. She opened a drawer and said, "Look, Harold, look what I keep in there—erasers. We all make mistakes, and at least you've realised you made one." She was magnificent in her kindness. After that, we had a terrific working relationship. Of course, I eventually realised that during my early days when I was learning the ropes she was planting little mistakes in the figures, to see if I picked them up.'

Harold says that even though he was the manager, as Denise is now, Mary still acted as 'mine host' in the bar during busy times, and worked hard supervising the very busy accommodation and kitchen side of the business, plus organising all the functions held there. 'She's always loved doing that, and puts as much thought and effort in as if it was for a member of her family—which, of course, they are. For local groups having fundraisers—balls, barbecues, etc.—she gives them their grog at cost price, even though she has to pay for it herself, a month ahead. Everyone in Dalby loves her—you can feel the atmosphere of the bar just lift to a different level when she walks in. I retired at 65 to take it easy. Not like Mary—she's over 90 now but still doing what she can.'

Mary just can't imagine ever retiring. Her life is the hotel. 'I've been here nearly 60 years now and I've loved every moment. I'll just keep going as long as I can and they'll carry me out of this pub in a box. Happy days!'

Postscript: Mary passed on before this book was printed. Her funeral was attended by many hundreds of people of all ages and walks of life . . . Happy days up there, Mary!

KEVIN HOPKINS OAM

Steamtrain driver, sniper, sports star

As a baby boomer, one of my most magnificent memories is the inspiring vision of the steam trains chugging into our station. A visual feast of might and power, those grand and glorious trains were a splendid example of the astounding feats of engineering man can achieve. How fortunate I was to see them and experience riding in them. Even as a horrible schoolchild, diligently carving my initials or swearwords into the beautiful polished timber of the carriages, or chucking water or banana skins at the hapless fettlers, I still loved the steamtrains. Almost every child back then dreamt of being a train driver.

Kevin Hopkins lived that dream from 1936 to 1981, as 'King of the Rails' around Central Western New South Wales, with an unwelcome interlude fighting for his country in World War II. Kevin was born at Bega on the south coast of New South Wales in

1918, where his father was a Postmaster General (PMG) linesman. Now famous for its cheese, the beautiful dairying district was then very isolated. With no trainline on the south coast, goods were brought to Nowra by the steamers *Eden* and *Bermagui*. Passengers usually endured a 'pitching and tossing' trip from Sydney. Bullock drays then hauled the goods to Bega over the dirt tracks. When they bogged, the bullockies had to unload, then reload after hauling the dray out of the mud—a fascinating procedure for a young boy to watch. Kevin remembers staring wide-eyed at the first truck that arrived in Bega—a big Leyland that could travel at an amazing 20 miles per hour! That was the beginning of the end for the bullock teams.

Bega then had six blacksmith shops. Hanging around them, Kevin learnt many new words: 'Like the bullockies, they were always swearing. It was very entertaining.' In those days children rode ponies or drove sulkies to school. 'I tried to learn to ride well,' Kevin says, 'but I spent a lot of time on the ground.

'In the Depression years, many children did it very hard and were hungry and cold, but my brother, three sisters and I were very lucky, because our father was never out of work. A treat from my grandmother was "soft bread", which was bread soaked in milk and sugar—even nicer than bread and dripping. On Saturdays my grandparents, who lived on a farm near Bermagui, paid me threepence for four hours' work. An ice cream cost a halfpenny and I'd save the rest. I used to clean the fowl run, rake their yard, and carry water from the washing to spread on my grandmother's famous hollyhocks.

'She suffered terribly with rheumatism and I would help her

wash her feet and pull her stockings on. She was a tough old lady—delivered all her children at home and cut the cord herself—no midwife. Grandfather had refused to go to school and was illiterate. He signed his name with an "X", but he was clever, could build or fix anything—even learnt how to pull a Model T Ford apart and do any repairs. That was a major achievement for a horseman of that era. He had a collection of snakes in bottles sealed with wax. I remember him steering his horse and cart home with a load of wood on it, with one hand, while holding a snake in the other. He wanted the snake to coil neatly in the bottle. I still treasure a gift he gave me of a wooden cross in a bottle with a tiny ladder, which he'd made from a piece of timber from the shipwrecked *Lyee Moon*. Because there was no communication system back then, everyone on board drowned or perished later, including, he told me, Mary MacKillop's mother.'

When he was twelve, the family moved to Orange, after his father received a promotion. Kevin was enrolled at De La Salle and was in for a shock. 'The Irish brothers who ran the school should have been taken to the high court for cruelty to dumb animals. They caned us mercilessly. Orange is a freezing place, and the school had no stoves in the classrooms, and the windows didn't fit properly. It was miserable—cruel. We ran around at recess trying to get warm. The only mercy the brothers showed us was to give us a choice of being caned on the hand or backside. Because we were half-frozen, the pain of being caned on the hand was murder, so we always chose to bend over and touch our toes.'

Kevin was given a break from the misery of De La Salle when his father returned to Bega to enjoy his six months' long-service leave.

The local convent didn't have French, which he'd been studying, along with the mandatory and dreaded Latin, so Kevin went to the state school. But after two terms, with no cane, it was back to the black-frocked floggers, until he finally escaped them for good after gaining his intermediate certificate.

It was still the Depression years, and jobs were very hard to find, but he managed to get casual work as a messenger boy for the PMG. Soon after, he beat a long line of hopeful boys for a permanent job at the Western Stores as a 'tiger'. The Western Stores sold everything and the tiger was the busy toiler who did all the worst jobs 'out the back', loading and unloading, stacking everything including sheets of iron, timber, bags of cement—hard yakka for a fifteen-year-old. In between, he chopped the firewood, and filled bottles of linseed oil, kero and metho from drums. Naturally the older workers had great sport with him, sending him up the street to get a tin of striped paint, bottles of sparks etc., but he bore all their pranks stoically and hoped to work his way up to being behind the counter. 'When I was actually inside the store I was always fascinated to watch the customers' money being attached to the wire at the counter with a docket, then sent flying up to the cashier's window on the next level. Seconds later, the change and receipt would come whizzing back down the wire to the salesperson. I couldn't wait to do that.'

Kevin enjoys a good laugh recalling an incident that happened when he was the brand-new tiger, naive to the ways of the world. In his realm out the back amongst all the hardware and tools, he was allowed to sell smaller, inexpensive items, which people came to the back door to purchase, if they had the right money—tuppence, threepence or similar. The store manager, on a visit during Kevin's first week, asked how he was enjoying his new job. Kevin very proudly informed him he'd been doing a roaring trade that day selling bottles of metho. He'd had to keep filling them up, they were selling so briskly, he told the manager, waiting for some praise. To his disappointment, the manager just left abruptly. Kevin's supervisor appeared soon after, to inform him that he wasn't to sell any more bottles of metho without calling him first to check out the customer. All the down-and-outers in Orange—and there were plenty during the Depression years—had spread the word that there was a new boy out the back of Western Stores who'd sell you as much metho as your heart and indiscriminate thirsty palate desired.

When an opportunity arose to sit for the railways exam, the thoughts of a career with the Western Stores were easily overtaken, in a sixteen-year-old boy's mind, by the chance to become a train driver. 'After passing the exam with flying colours and being offered a start, I naturally had to begin on the bottom rung, as a call boy, riding around Orange on a pushbike knocking on the doors of men who were being called in for a shift. There was no regular work back then—men took what they could get. I chose to use my own bike because the railways "pushie" took a lot of pushing, having thorn-proof tyres that slowed it down. All roads were dirt back then, and full of cathead burrs.'

He had to find board in town when his father was promoted to line inspector, based at Dubbo. But when Kevin was promoted to an engineman, he was also based in Dubbo and back with his family. 'I never worked the same shift twice all year, and was on call from midnight to 6 a.m. Crews were alerted by the call boy as cargoes became available. We all dreaded getting the "horror trip"—the midnight run to Nyngan. We enginemen serviced the steam engines after every trip. Everything had to be greased, the stokebox cleaned of trapped cinders and ash. The fuelman would get underneath, poke a hose into the stokebox, then take out about a foot or more of ash with a steel rake, which would land in a pit. This old ash would be dug out later by a steam-operated "grab"—the predecessor of an excavator—and taken away in trucks to dump in the washaways on the "mud lines" out west. This was naturally unsuccessful and replaced by stone ballast. "Coaling up" the engine was another task where a steam grab was used, situated on the line opposite, dumping loads of coal from a truck into the tender. Later on, the tender went under a container and coal was dropped in.' It was hard and dirty work, but Kevin was grateful to have it.

Amongst Kevin's worst memories of his time with the railways are the many animals that were killed. Most of the lines he travelled were unfenced, and filling out a sheet stating the number of stock killed was part of the engineman's job. 'After being promoted to a driver, I endured the horrible experience of being powerless to avoid killing animals, several times. I once hit 50 sheep camped in a cutting near Binnaway. It was impossible to stop in time. Then there was the nasty sensation of being derailed—an unwelcome adrenalin rush I experienced twice, when driving light, "42 footers", or rail motors. Both accidents were caused by cattle camped on the line.

'In the first, I was driving from Cootamundra to Parkes, "flat-out" at 50 miles per hour. I had the breeze up, I don't mind admitting.

I can still see, in the glare of the headlights, a big red bull standing across the line a hundred metres ahead, his head turned and staring at me with red-rimmed eyes. The emergency brake couldn't pull up in time and we collided. As the cowcatcher was rolling him along, stones were flipping up onto the line. Finally, he rolled under us, and his bulk lifted the whole rear end of the rail motor up and off its rear wheels. Only the actual weight of the rail motor kept it sitting on the wheels, so they were very unstable. You can imagine how frightened the passengers were, they didn't know what had happened. Luckily no one was hurt, which was a miracle. We were 20 miles from anywhere but I had an emergency railway telegraphic system, and a breakdown crew were sent to jack it up. They were able to fix it overnight. Meanwhile the passengers were taken by taxi back to "Coota".

'Then exactly the same thing occurred after leaving Molong one night. Another big bull stood on the line, glaring at me. I hit the emergency brakes, but he also ended up rolling under and upended us. Again, God was with us—no one was hurt.

'I knew a couple of drivers who'd had the absolutely horrible experience of hitting a person. They could never forget it, of course. Thank goodness that never happened to me but I went very, very close once and I can still see those fellers like it was yesterday. They were driving towards a level crossing and I was pulling the whistle like mad, unable to believe that the driver wasn't even slowing down. By the time the car and I were both reaching the actual crossing at the same time, I had almost pulled the whistle cord out. I could see the blokes by then, talking to each other, not even looking at me. Imagine how I felt when they kept going—it was horrifying knowing that the collision was about to happen and not being able to do a thing to prevent it. But that day just was not their day to die. The bulk of their car had passed over our tracks but the train clipped the end of it, sending it spinning like a top up the road for about 50 yards, round and round and round, till it slowly spun to a halt. By then the emergency brakes had pulled us up and I rushed back to them. They were sitting there completely dumbfounded. They had been talking to each other above the radio, and never at any stage saw the train, so they literally didn't know what hit them.'

While working with the railways was inherently dangerous and stressful, Kevin also has great memories of the railways camaraderie amongst the staff and many larrikin types. 'We had a fireman who was well-known for his love of practical jokes. Before a driver could leave a station he had to have an authority to occupy the track to the next station. This usually consisted of a metal staff with the name of the section of track the driver could traverse safely. At the next station a similar authority was required for the next section of track. If the station was manned, the officer-in-charge would often effect the transfer of staffs without the train stopping. In darkness and with no platform lights at minor stations, the change was carried out by the feeble light of a signal lamp held under the officer's arm.

'One night this wag substituted a dead goanna for the staff. As the station officer grabbed the dead goanna, he screamed with fright and his signal lamp went flying up in the air then smashed on the platform. "What in the hell was that?" said the driver, who, being on the opposite side of the engine and with limited visibility in the darkness, had seen nothing. The fireman was so convulsed with laughter, he couldn't tell him until they were well beyond the station limits. The station officer threatened to bring serious charges, saying he'd almost had a heart attack, but eventually it was all smoothed over.

'Another great joke involved a new driver from Dubbo who boasted he had the ability to hypnotise people, and he liked to skite that he couldn't wait to hypnotise certain individuals and get them to reveal the murky secrets from their past. One of these prospective subjects was a driver from Mudgee—a big bloke who feared no one on earth except the hypnotist. Everyone noticed he went to great lengths to avoid crossing his path—he must have had a lot to hide. One day he was sitting in the Binnaway barracks about to demolish a heaped plate of steak, eggs, bacon, mashed spud and gravy, before going to bed for a rest until he was called to take a train back to Mudgee. Just then the call boy came in to call a Dubbo crew, and seeing the Mudgee driver about to hoe into his tucker, he somehow kept a straight face and casually said, "The Dubbo hypnotist just brought a train in." Well, the Mudgee driver froze for an instant, with a great hunk of steak halfway to his mouth, then, with one sweep of his arm, emptied the contents of his stacked plate into his open tuckerbox on the seat beside him, slammed it shut and disappeared into his room. He didn't appear again till he was due to take his train out. If he'd ever found out the call boy was joking, the lad would've needed to keep a lot of distance between them. We all got many a good old belly laugh from recalling the look on that driver's face, and the way he swept that big meal straight into his tuckerbox, on top of his tobacco, matches and form guide.

'A funny but also true yarn that did the rounds was about the two goods train drivers who were having a chinwag while filling their tenders with water at Narromine. The Dubbo-bound driver said to the driver heading west, "Make sure you stop at the Mungeribar siding before Trangie and fill up your waterbag. The rainwater there is a heavenly drop." Now, the other bloke was not noted for drinking water except in an emergency, but it was hot, and curiosity made him pull up at the siding. He filled his billycan, took a gulp, and called out to his fireman, "Holy Moses! Bring your billy, quick!" They thought the good Lord had turned the water into rum. But on investigating they found someone had hidden a pilfered consignment of rum in the roof gutter that filled the tank. Pilfering on the railways was pretty rife then. Apparently the weather had been so hot the corks had worked loose, and as there was only a couple of rungs of water in the tank, it had mixed up into quite a potent drop. Needless to say the tank was soon drained.'

Kevin thoroughly enjoyed working with the railways, but he also loved his 'leisure time' in the militia with 54th Battalion, before World War II. Camping, shooting and being out on exercises appealed to him tremendously. He'd always been athletic and was also an excellent shot—a talent put to good use later in the jungles of New Guinea where he served as a sniper and saved many allied lives. When he enlisted in 1940, he hoped to join the 8th Battalion with many other young Dubbo men but, fortunately for him, a health problem sent him back to Dubbo till he recovered. The ill-fated 8th Battalion went to Singapore, where most were almost immediately captured and many died.

When he was well enough, he joined the 7th Division, but asked for a week's honeymoon leave so he could marry his fiancée Agnes. Her mother made her a wedding dress in a hurry, friends chipped in coupons for food for the reception and after spending their first week together in Kiama and Newcastle, Agnes returned to Dubbo, while Kevin went to the Army HQ at Sydney Showground. Agnes had been a 'hello girl'—a telephonist with the PMG—but after her marriage she helped her sister run her shop in Carrington Avenue, near the Catholic convent. By sheer luck, Kevin was posted initially to Dubbo's military base, where the zoo now stands. Being able to ride a bike home every night to his bride and home-cooked meals made him the envy of his mates.

Kevin was based at Dubbo for eight months and during that time, as a sergeant major of the 33rd Infantry, he attended various weapons courses and an officer training course at Duntroon. Being a sergeant major was a tough job requiring a man capable of controlling, training and disciplining tough men.

In 1942 they were sent to New Guinea. They went by train to Brisbane, where a thousand men were loaded onto a cargo boat with accommodation for ten. 'We were supposed to sleep in the hull but fumes from thousands of tonnes of stored high-octane fuel made us sick, so we slept out on the steel deck with our boots for pillows. When fresh food ran out we ate bully beef stew for a fortnight before reaching New Guinea. It was rough but we were tough in those days—people walked a lot and most had done a lot of hard physical work.'

Was he scared when travelling to New Guinea to be shot at? 'Not scared, but apprehensive about leaving my wife and brand-new baby son, Robert, behind. There was real fear that Australia could be invaded. The Japanese had shown they were a cruel enemy.'

Kevin is still haunted by his experiences in the Owen Stanley Ranges. He buried many enemy soldiers and always felt sorry for them, believing they were someone's sons or brothers who had been brainwashed to do terrible things for their country. His worst memory of the war was a horrifying accident when a US bomber crashed just 50 metres from a huge allied convoy. 'We were in trucks heading towards the aerodrome, where US and Australian bombers were taking off in large numbers. They were heavily loaded and flying so close above us you felt you could touch them. Wreckage from the bomber smashed into ground bombs and fuel exploded, sending sheets of flames into the trucks, including the one I was in. Men were incinerated. Some men's ammunition belts were set off, some were running, trying to escape, to the other side of a ravine. A bomb skidded over the top of the convoy and landed in the ravine, blowing them up. In the end 60 men were killed and 85 seriously wounded. I lost a lot of wonderful mates and often think about them now, but there was no time to mourn back then. Of course, the concept of counselling didn't exist. We just had to clean up the mess, get the bodies out and the wounded to hospital, before getting back into what trucks were left and heading to the aerodrome.

'Our task was to relieve US paratroopers fighting at Nadzab. First we had to survive a terrifying landing on a roughly levelled-out patch of ground. After hard fighting we got the Japanese out of Lae and proceeded up the Markham Valley, marching through shoulder-high grass in tremendous heat and humidity, carrying a lot of equipment and ammunition. When our sweat dried our shirts looked like they'd been whitewashed. After wading through swamps and creeks, we reached the Finisterre Ranges and chased the Japs to Shaggy Ridge, now famous as the place where more shells were fired than at any other spot during the Pacific war. We then held the valley for a couple of weeks before being taken to Port Moresby, where I was wounded by a booby trap. Then we returned to Australia to prepare for the Borneo "show". I kissed the ground when I got back to Australia.'

The army had wanted to promote Kevin to lieutenant, but the war was winding down by then and the railways wanted him back. An RSL committee member since 1960, Kevin has been parade commander and sergeant major for all Anzac and Remembrance ceremonies in Dubbo since 1962. Although firmly against our involvement in modern 'faraway' wars such as Iraq and Afghanistan, Kevin is proud he served in World War II: 'We needed to take a stand against Hitler, Stalin and Tojo. The Japanese came close to taking Australia and had to be stopped.'

After the war, Kevin began helping many of the less fortunate in his community, through the St Vincent de Paul Society. He visited prisoners in the Dubbo Gaol (now a tourist attraction), writing letters for them, and helping discharged and paroled men, as president of the Rehabilitation Committee. A quiet achiever on many committees over the years, his proudest achievement is his triumphant effort to establish the Ozanam Villa Home for the Aged.

He was honoured with a Commonwealth Recognition Award in 1999, for 'significant contribution to the community', and was described in a letter from Federal Member for Parkes, Tony Lawler, as 'one of the Central West's most Outstanding Senior Australians'.

As well as being an outstanding citizen, defender of his country, and loving father of nine, Kevin Hopkins has also made his mark in the world of athletics. Taking up running at 55 to keep fit, this man, who has always 'eaten sensibly', started competing in veterans' events, and gradually joined the starters in javelin, discus, long and triple jump, steeplechase, marathons and pentathlons, breaking records all over the state. True to his style, Kevin hasn't been content with major success locally, then statewide, then nationally. He entered the world Veterans Masters arenas and, over 33 years, amassed no fewer than *four hundred* gold medals, brought proudly home from many countries overseas. He has twice been awarded the prestigious Marcus Tooley Trophy, in 1984 and 1989, for outstanding achievement by an athlete aged 30–39, from the New South Wales Veterans Athletics Association; the Sports Australia Award for Outstanding Performance in 1990; featured in an impressive book of Dubbo sporting greats; and competed in the City to Surf in Sydney no fewer than 22 times, and was in the winning over-60s team three times. Amongst his treasure trove of medals and trophies stands the beautiful, eyecatching reminder of his most splendid moment of all: his replica of the Olympic torch, which he proudly carried in the 2000 relay around Australia.

Kevin competed and won against the world's finest until he was 88—sadly, his competitive career was brought to a sudden and tragic halt when a large dog jumped on him from behind, knocking him to the ground and breaking his pelvis.

At 93, Kevin Hopkins still looks like he could give Rob de Castella a bloody good run for his money, but these days this immaculate and impressive man contents himself with gardening, emailing his children and grandchildren and helping out fellow RSL members and anyone else who needs his help and guidance.

His parents lived long lives and his sisters, who are well into their 80s, constantly travel the world, so the boy from Bega who remembers the era of bullockies and steamships is bound to get his centenary telegram from the Queen in 2018. I hope I can be there to shake this good man's hand.

DES MORRISON

Lethal weapon—a lifetime of discipline,
dedication and duty

At 85, Desmond Richard Morrison is fit, strong, and more than capable of 'ripping your bloody arms off'. If you are a law-breaker, and cross his path, you should be afraid. If you take him on as an *intended* law-breaker, you have absolutely picked the wrong man. With a lifetime's experience in defence and attack, the last 30 years as a trainer of police and corrections officers who train staff in use of force, use of lethal force, riot squad tactics, control of extraordinary violence, firearms training, knife-attack defence tactics and other useful skills, Des is a man you don't want to upset.

His toughness might stem from being sent off from Africa, aged six, to fend for himself at a spartan Scottish boarding school, but it's most probably inherited from his Scottish warrior father, a veteran officer of the Royal Marines and Rifle Corps Ceylon, a bayonet instructor and rough rider for the service, who was awarded the Military Medal for Bravery in World War I.

Born in 1926 on his family's estate, 'Mini Mini M'Lange', near Blantyre, Nyasaland Protectorate, Central East Africa, Des was willingly indoctrinated from birth with traditional loyalty to the ethics of God, King and country. There followed a lifetime of adherence to 'discipline, dedication and duty', supported by the King James Bible. As Des is fond of saying: 'This minimised doubt and indecision—both negative, time-wasting factors in many people's lives. The fear of God is the beginning of wisdom, as the scripture rightly says. The fear of God ensures people do the right thing.

'I was brought up in the era when the sun never set on the British Empire, it covered so much of the globe. After World War I, my father saw service in the Colonial Police and Prisons in India, Ceylon [Sri Lanka] and Africa. His family and my mother's family clans developed and ran a patriarchal system growing tea, rubber, coffee, coconuts and cardamoms in those countries. My father was sent to Nyasaland to develop land for tea and coffee. He took with him a staff of ex–Indian Army Muslims and their wives for domestic security for my mother, who would be left alone for weeks on end. He also took over elephants from Ceylon to clear the land as African elephants cannot be worked.

'Diseases of all kinds made life a misery for white mothers and their children, hence I was packed off to school overseas at such a young age. My mother was not happy about this, but it was realistic. She was a wonderful character and, being the product of a very different colonial era, used to frequently say things in her very posh voice, like: "Desmond, your father was a good man, kind and just. He only ever shot the blacks when they deserved it."

'The school I attended ran a rigorous regime to "establish moral fibre" through physical training and drill. From dawn we were training under a stern former Royal Marine infantry sergeant, in drill, exercises, gymnastics, cross country runs, boxing and football. All this was designed to prepare a lad to serve his country. The virtues of loyalty, dedication, discipline and a willingness to die for one's country if necessary in war was the unquestioned rock of belief for all in those times. Our education included the history of battles which we had to learn thoroughly, where they occurred and so on, in case we might be sent there one day ourselves, to fight.

'In that completely politically incorrect era of the genuine belief in British superiority as a race, we were also instructed in the characteristics of other nations, the inference being that although they were inferior, they could be useful to work for British subjects. We were continually warned of the papacy's wicked past and the Inquisition. Charlemagne's "Convert or Die" policy implanted in us Protestants (of minor doctrinal differences, which made the Roman Catholic's treachery and blood-thirstiness seem all the more evil) a staunch suspicion of all European Catholic countries. This apprehension, which extended to Islam, Buddhism, Sikhs, Hindus, etc., was to be a policy of keeping men in their place and subordinate, to ensure the advance of the British Empire, and a policy of converting them to Protestant Christianity in order to become civilised.

'So my life was orderly and focused. I saw active service from the age of thirteen, first in the Royal Australian Navy, but even at that seemingly young age, I had been for years set examples of boys going to war for Britain throughout history. Before being confronted with the actual horrors of war, I had been prepared by seasoned petty officers, gunner's mates, bosun's mates and masters-at-arms in what to expect. Before I joined the navy I had, while still at school, decided I could help the newly declared war against the might of the German forces. So I ran away to London, purchasing my ticket courtesy of a loan from the housemaid—I had always carried the coal buckets for her and we were in love. On the way to Waterloo Station, I was seated next to an old man with medals on his chest. I was greatly impressed and he asked me where I was going. I replied that I was joining the Scots Guards. He told me he had joined them aged ten, as a drummer boy, and went to the Crimean War with them. An alert bobby at the station bailed me up and I was soon packed off back to school to receive six of the best.

'Undeterred, I ran away again soon after, heading for Edinburgh to become a boy piper for the Black Watch [a Scottish line infantry regiment]. The housemaid was going to join me there when she could leave. Unfortunately, during my escape, the Luftwaffe dropped bombs near the railway line. Herded off the train into a shelter, I was sprung again by another alert bobby, received another six cuts—trousers down. Hardly suitable treatment for a determined war hero-to-be.

'My parents had been told to take me out of the school, and they decided to send me to a school in Australia. On the same ship was a girl whom I'd known in Ceylon, where both our families had owned plantations. When the Luftwaffe came over strafing the top deck and dropping bombs, I gallantly pushed her into a lifeboat, where we found that fear does not exclude other human emotions. Blimey, I was in love again! So was she, and to this day I feel remorse I did not even keep in touch with her. A man can be a heartless bastard without even trying . . . such is the nature of man.

'Scots College was full so I had to attend an Anglican school, to my father's consternation. I was determined to do a runner when the time was right, as the local Highland Regiment in WA and the 10th Light Horse still had a remount depot nearby. I joined the equitation course at school, run by a World War I veteran light-horse instructor, to pick up skills I knew would be useful when I enlisted, such as troop drill. The sports master, a World War I company sergeant major with the King's Own Scottish Borderers, took an interest in me and taught me to fight. "But ye'll fight like a Scot, laddie—not this pansy English-style boxing nonsense they do here." I was so fortunate to have him as my private tutor. He taught me how to fight to survive, not just box to win a boxing contest. He was the only person who understood my yearning to enlist.

'After two more unsuccessful escapes, I finally made it from school uniform to the uniform of the Royal Australian Navy. I saw action at sea and in landing parties in the Indian Ocean, Burma and the Pacific, including the Ryukyus Islands campaign. Okinawa was part of the Ryukyus Group. This campaign was to seal the fate of Japan. They had begun the war with three million servicemen and by the end had more than five million men fighting us. At that stage of the war, Japan was desperate and sending suicidal forces against us—a truly formidable foe. The presence of kamikaze pilots could strike fear into the hearts of the most courageous men.

'I saw terrible things—men literally splattered all over the deck. Our officers, sending us to clean up the carnage after a battle, would bellow, "Don't feel sorry for them—their worries are over. Get this job done, then get yourselves right for the next encounter."'

At war's end, Des wanted to leave the navy to join the Grenadier Guards, but was put off by the prospect of being posted with them to Norway. The other choice was the Far East, and Des couldn't see the point in serving there and trying to sort their problems out, as he held the opinion, from prior experience there, that 'It'll always be a bloody mess'. He joined the Scots Guards where, because of his underwater clearance experience, he would start as assistant inspector. The Scots Guards were not famous for tolerance of a man's behaviour that was less than braver than the brave, less tougher than the tough (they drilled with swords honed to razor-sharpness). On one of Des's first parades with them, it started raining, and the regimental sergeant major (RSM) bellowed: 'Look at this! Those are not raindrops falling, they are the tears from former guardsmen looking down at you sacks of shit!' The height regulation was a minimum 5 feet 8 inches, but most were 6 feet tall or more. The RSM berated anyone under 6 feet 2 inches: 'You horrible little man! You will hide amongst the tall men in battle, which is why the tall men have the highest casualties. Well, let me tell you this, you horrible little runt, if you do not hide or run away, if you can act like a Scots Guard is expected to, a VC can look just as good on a runt like you as a man who's six-feet-three—UNDERSTOOD?'

The RSM advised them, when going into action, to put paper in their garters, and steel in their gauntlets, for extra protection, warning, 'We live in violent times.' And they were. Des was able to refine his knowledge of the art of cutting a man's throat without any noise occurring. In the war, he'd learnt that because of their helmets, Germans only had a small area to cut; that is, along the mandibular line. Other skills learnt with the guards were the Fairburn timetable of death, depending on which artery was cut, and, when being attacked, to overload an opponent's 'computer' so they couldn't think, by gouging their eyes, kicking them in the shins, then bringing their head down to your knee, and by then it was much easier to break their neck. All this knowledge was to serve him well later in life in law courts as an expert witness on the 'use of force'.

Des also learnt parachuting with them, a skill that would become invaluable. His instructor would say: 'Now, laddies, remember you're in the Scots Guards. Some people go to work in a car, bus or tram, you jump out of a perfectly good aeroplane to go to work, and ye can expect the worst if ye fail.' The Scots Guards, naturally, thought it was 'sissy' to use a reserve chute, and took their chances.

After the war Des met an attractive girl, Valerie, who had been an aircraft plotter during the war—an extremely taxing and important job, plotting British aircraft to and from missions. She had lived at Biggins Hill, which was the most bombed place in England by the Luftwaffe as it was the first town they saw. Valerie had struck up a friendship with Des's brother, a Royal Air Force (RAF) pilot, after plotting him during several missions. He was one of the 'miracle boys' of the RAF who survived the war. Des met her when they were both at the dockside saying goodbye to his brother, who was heading back to their home in Ceylon. Valerie and Des hit it off, and began courting.

Because he wanted to get married, and married men weren't allowed in his unit, Des bought his release for 50 pounds and emigrated to Canada to join the Royal Canadian Police Force, serving as a chief constable based in Victoria, British Columbia. Des was then invited to join an elite military unit that was being formed in Canada, to become known as the Princess Patricias, after their royal patroness from the UK, a granddaughter of Queen Victoria. It was a parachuting unit, a mobile strike force created to parachute into the Yukon to prevent the Russians from claiming it. The Russians were there in enormous numbers, intent on taking over the entire Arctic North, and were reputedly ruthless. The Patricias were warned: 'Don't get taken prisoner by the Russians. It's a death sentence.' As far as Des was concerned, the Yukon should've been *given* to them as a punishment.

The Canadians taught him how to break a man's neck quietly—a handy skill when the situation called for a silent death. Another bare-handed skill he acquired around this time was how to literally rip a man's throat out with his fingers—not easy, Des says, but when a man is fighting for his life, he can do things he normally couldn't do. In return he showed them the fighting techniques he'd learnt from his old sports master at his Western Australian boarding school—not, as he'd told Des, the 'pansy English-style boxing', but the actual skills needed when fighting to survive, using knees, elbows, boots, forehead, teeth, pronged fingers and so on.

Des was also sent into Germany with the Patricias, again to stop the Russians advancing towards Channel ports. He explains: 'The Siberians and Mongolians were sent into Germany by Stalin to indulge in mass murder and rape. They committed appalling atrocities on the German people, especially women.' But they were no match for the Patricias, who not only had advanced battle skills but superior artillery. Des was put in charge of a 50-tonne Centurion tank, which he was very fond of.

Des gratefully recalls the ladies from the Women's Royal Air Force who handed them their parachutes—appropriately known as 'shrouds'—in Canada, before leaving for action: 'They would look us in the eye and say, "I'm Beryl and I packed your parachute myself. It is all perfect. I just wanted you to know that." It gave us confidence knowing that these honest, decent-looking women had carefully packed our parachutes, rather than some careless galoot who might have been on the grog the night before. Women are honourable about things like that, whereas a man is just a man.'

When faced with extreme danger, even this elite parachuting regiment needed every positive on their side, including, Des says, a sense of humour. 'The worst were the night jumps when you couldn't judge the distance. If you hit the drink, for example, you can get tangled up and drown. When someone died that way, or on impact from some disaster, we would joke after headcount: "There's still one up in the air."' Typical of the Patricias' grim humour was a song they often sang in the mess or when heading out to the aircraft they were going to leap out of, with the words: 'They wiped him off the tarmac, like a pound of strawberry jam!'

A highlight of Des's military life was taking part in a 'trooping of the colour' parade to Lady Patricia Ramsay, their patron. To his, and the entire unit's horror, one of their gallant number passed out. The unit had to step over his prone body, not missing a beat. He received a scathing dressing down, a detention and a drop of a month's pay for being 'idle and inattentive on parade', but his wounded pride would have caused him far more suffering. Another happy memory was taking part in the Edinburgh Military Tattoo in front of dignitaries from all over the world. As they were all assembling at the drawbridge for the grand entrance, a rider from the Lifeguard Regiment, resplendent in their red tunic and plumes, was having trouble with his horse rearing up. He didn't realise a microphone was nearby, installed to give the crowd waiting inside the castle the sound of many horses' hooves clattering over the drawbridge on entry. Before the promised clattering of the hooves, the crowd was treated to the lifeguard's exasperated words: 'Get down, you coffin-headed bastard, or I'll break your fucking neck!' The poor bugger was put into a dungeon and sent off to a wretched post in Egypt.

Des's assignments in Germany and the Yukon with the Patricias were complete by 1956, and although he was tempted by an invitation to join the Royal Canadian Mounted Police, he yearned to head to Australia, where the warm and friendly climate matched the people who lived there. His next adventure was as a patrol officer in the Northern Territory, based at Baggit towards Northcliffe, near Darwin, but his duties took him far afield into the bush. His patrols were carried out in vehicles (Landrovers), boats and canoes, on horses and, when necessary, on foot. Des had been hand-picked for his experience to bring law and order to Baggit.

In those days Aboriginal people were 'wards of the state' and it was Des's duty to stop them wasting their lives drinking metho, establish order and discipline in their community, ensure their food rations were distributed fairly and used properly, sort out the problem of excessive dogs, and settle tribal disputes. He also ensured they were paid and treated properly by cattle stations and drovers, and that teachers in settlements respected tribal customs.

Another job as patrol officer was to check the brands of the big mobs of cattle passing through from the Kimberley, looking for stolen cattle and horses. Des trained Aborginal trackers to be his assistants in chasing cattle thieves. Des always employed 'tribal killers' as his trackers: they had killed men in their tribe or from other tribes, but being employed as a tracker gave them immunity to tribal law and punishment. That was a good incentive for them to be loyal to him, watch his back and work properly so they'd keep their job. The Territory was still a dangerous place for white men to move around in.

Back then land in the primitive, neglected and difficult-to-manage Territory was almost there for the taking, and Des bought a block on the Adelaide River, to run a successful sideline with his son Jim, catching wild donkeys, breaking them in and selling them. Val was an asset in the settlements, being a qualified nurse, and their son and three daughters certainly had an interesting and unusual upbringing. Des had gradually built up a cattle herd on the block and the children loved working with the stock and learning from the stockmen who helped from time to time. Their favourite was a wise and highly experienced bushman called Malaui who was of Aboriginal, Afghan and Scottish descent.

Des's patrol beat covered a large portion of the Territory. Later he was assigned a patrol assistant, none other than Ted Egan, later to become a famous entertainer, champion of Aboriginal welfare causes, and top-level public servant in the Territory. Des became the patrol officer in charge, then acting superintendent of Hooker Creek, outside Wave Hill towards the Tanami Desert. Des's lifelong aim has been to always leave a place better than he found it and, for that alone, his time patrolling the Territory was a success. Another wise saying that Des lives by is: 'If you don't do the best job you can do, you are doing yourself a disservice.'

After six years' service, controlling law and order in a wild, untamed and vastly isolated part of Australia, Des resigned to become the ranger at Katherine Gorge, taking tourists on boat trips and collecting firewood for campers. His income was supplemented by a cemetery contract, burying people at Katherine. Many Indigenous people died of leprosy in the 1950s. He also won the government tender to rebury police troopers whose graves were being eroded. It took two hours to dig down to them with a post-hole shovel. They had been buried in corrugated iron as there were no coffins. Des reburied the troopers with an official respectful ceremony. He then won a contract to clean up Larrimah, at the end of the rail line. This meant mustering 1200 head of cattle to put there to graze down the long grass, then hiring a truck to load all the scrap metal lying around. He had—as always—boundless energy, and great physical strength.

When Val became a Jehovah's Witness, he sold his block and took her and the family to the US, where she did a business course and Des and his son established themselves as farriers in Denver. He found the Americans were far ahead of Australians in their corrective shoeing methods for horses and honed his skills accordingly. As his wife and children became completely immersed in the Jehovah's Witness lifestyle, Des found he was considered by them to be spiritually unacceptable. He returned to Australia, to contract muster in the Ord region of the Kimberley, where he also managed a station.

After learning of Des's skills and background, the police commissioner asked him to join the Northern Territory Corrections Service, specifically to train both police and corrections officers in getting and staying fit, plus control and restraint techniques. When he first started knocking the officers into shape, Des's opinion of most of them was that they were 'not worth feeding greasy hobble-straps to'. He soon weeded out the 'crap' and trained those who were prepared to become fit and do their job in a professional, humane and energetic fashion. He trained the police in Darwin up to marathon standard of fitness and led them in a marathon race, backed up by male and female corrections staff. Having instilled in all of them that an ordeal such as a marathon is 'mind over matter', Des kept running even though the heat of the roads had caused his toenails to come out. Naturally, he is utterly appalled when he sees obviously unfit police, military and corrective service men and women today: 'If you are not prepared to be fit, why should you be entrusted to protect people?'

Having trained the best exponents of the techniques required for control and restraint of offenders—such as control of extraordinary violence, and riot prevention and control—to become trainers themselves and pass on those skills, Des was then free to accept invitations that started coming in from correction centres overseas, as his reputation spread. He trained corrections staff in Northern Ireland, Hong Kong, Canada, the US and Mexico. Teaching his methods saved a lot of prisoners a lot of pain, as he trained officers to subdue and restrain them when necessary, with the minimum of struggle, instead of having to rely on brute force and batons as would have happened previously. He believes control and restraint is all about knowing the human body, the nervous system especially, to subdue a violent person quickly, with the absolute minimum of violence.

While in those countries, Des was also able to develop other skills, such as the use of force against extraordinary violence, through liaison with law enforcement agencies including the FBI, the US Secret Service, and various US city and state police agencies. He acquired extra techniques that had not been taught in World War II, such as defence against knife attacks. He learnt that the best knife people and knives (particularly the butterfly knife) were to be found in the Philippines, and that you were out of luck against them unless you had a gun. If you were able to wrestle the knife off an opponent, the best plan, he found, was to then slash an artery in their arm, then their groin, then their throat. That pretty much enabled you to walk away from the villain and have a cup of tea.

In Northern Ireland, where he was head instructor of both the Royal Ulster Constabulary and the prison service, he was pleased to be working with highly disciplined and operationally experienced men. Working with the Mexican prison staff provided a contrast. There, the wardens' solution to every disturbance or indiscretion was to beat the crap out of the prisoners and use gas and other harsh methods of control as a first resort rather than a last resort. So Des sent them on an extremely steep learning curve. The head of prisons said to him, 'Senor, I have never before seen a gringo treat my countrymen with such respect.' He was asked by the top-ranking police to form a riot squad that wasn't in the payment of the drug lords. During this mission, Des, to his amusement, was 'adopted' by a minder, a wild woman with a scarred face, a knife in her boots and a large tattoo saying 'Jesus Saves'. During a riot in a Mexican prison, where she had worked as a guard, she had cut the throats of three men, earning her the respect of the inmates. She and Des were an unlikely but effective team.

Hong Kong's style of 'corrections management' was also politically incorrect. Des was sent with the Royal Hong Kong Police up into the New Territories where a gang was smuggling people over the border into 'Honkers'. Their solution was not quite softly-softly: the gang of six was shot and their bodies chucked across their side of the border. 'I think that will get the message across, don't you?' commented one of his colleagues.

As well as the thousands of prison and police officers Des has instructed to become trainers in skills that can save their lives, save the lives of others and restore peace—and the numerous training manuals he has written to ensure his knowledge continues to be passed on—Des has also trained many females to protect themselves. The majority of these women live in fear of being raped, then possibly killed, because of their work as corrections officers, or because of the dangerous areas they live in. He teaches them self-defence, and advises them to obtain a weapon. 'You can always say you need it to shoot a horse that might need putting down humanely. In my experience, rape doesn't often end with just rape. Isn't it better to be grilled before a jury of twelve, than put in the ground by six of your family and friends at your funeral?' From experience, he tells them: 'When frightened, control your fear by controlling your breathing. The first things that happen when you are frightened are your pulse increases and your sight is impaired. You have tunnel vision. To control yourself, take deep breaths, and keep that up till your heart is under control. Survival can be achieved by mindset.' He doesn't hesitate to set things straight with women who think they are as strong as men when it comes to a close physical struggle— they simply aren't. The best defence, he says, is usually to take out an attacker's eyes and air rapidly—with pronged fingers jabbed into the eyeballs, then the soft area at the base of the throat—then run like hell. He does show them paralysing moves that can be carried out to follow up the initial 'eyes and air' attack, but recommends that if it is at all possible to run and get to safety, do so.

Not surprisingly Des is horrified at the sight of small people, especially women, being allowed into the police force in these politically correct times. 'They are not only a visual joke to crims and thugs, but they—and the ones carrying a lot of pudding—put their partners in danger.'

He feels he is entitled, at his age and with his achievements, to say exactly what he thinks of Australia's current law and order situation: 'Political correctness is horseshit. It denigrates our sense of right and wrong. Australians are now subjected to the antisocial depredations of vicious extraordinary violence from the undisciplined progeny of dysfunctional parentage. Police and prison officers are forced now to suffer riotous behaviour, bashings and kickings etc. in their line of duty from these out-of-control louts and crims. When you control and restrain offenders, you are not incurring brutality, you are submitting them to environmental inoculation. That is, teaching them that they have to behave and obey our laws to deserve living in a lawful, peaceful environment. Political correctness is designed to emasculate everyone who is in authority, trying to do their job. That includes the poor bloody schoolteachers as well, who now reap what was sown by the ratbags in the Whitlam government: No discipline.

'Law-abiding citizens have a right to defend themselves, with whatever force is necessary. This right has been eroded by the unrealistic, ridiculous PC mob. Unrealistic multiculturalism has also eroded and bastardised what our pioneers fought and battled for. The public service and government is full of idiots and wankers bending over backwards to kowtow to the demands of people who won't assimilate. Sometimes I despair for the police and corrections officers of modern times, but I hope they will heed the counsel from my old RSM: "It's not how many times you get knocked down that counts. It's how many times you get up and what you do when you get up."

'The life I have led has been made easier by an early acceptance of discipline. My definition of discipline is "Doing what you *have* to do when you don't feel like doing it, and not doing what you *want* to do when you know you shouldn't do it"—an attitude or credo obviously sadly lacking today.'

Des's awards and medals are too numerous to list, but he is proudest of his campaign medals from World War II, the Canadian Special Service Medal, and the Australian National Medal for both services as a Northern Territory patrol officer and instructor at the police college.

At 85, Des now lives in a peaceful bush setting in the Sunshine Coast hinterland, keeping busy with a permaculture garden, feeding and caring for friends' horses, as well as doing his exercises daily. He is a voracious reader and sharp as a tack, up with everything that's going on in the world. He still conducts occasional courses and has just been engaged to 'sharpen up' the skills of a major Queensland jail's riot squad. He is fond of saying, 'My next career move is death.'

Whether he's gardening or inside working at his desk writing a manual or a letter to an editor, or sleeping surrounded by photos of his regiments and the royal family, pity any villains who have a go at Desmond Richard Morrison. It's highly likely they'll leave his premises in an ambulance.

PAT MUMFORD

Wool classer and the 'baby'
of his bomber squadron

The week I was to meet Pat Mumford to hear his story, I received a message that he'd been called out west to Brewarrina on a job, wool classing. I have to admit to having a bit of a chuckle at this, because Pat is 85. A wool classer is on their feet all day, moving rapidly around the wool table, sometimes grabbing a broom, sometimes picking up fleeces to throw when the pace is full-on. When I finally got to meet him, I could see the man is really, in body and mind, at least twenty years younger than his age.

One of his secrets of eternal youth is swimming. He swims laps every morning with the Diggers Swimming Club at his local RSL, competes in carnivals hell, west and crooked, and has a bloody great time with good friends, male and female, who also worship the 'powers of the pool'. Pat equally attributes his wonderful vitality and robust health to all the walking he did as a youngster, and good tucker—young mutton, fresh milk, fruit and veggies, and plenty of it, all his life. He has never eaten 'smokos'; instead, if he was hungry, he would have a gutful of water. 'I'm sure that used to rinse my guts out—has to be good for you.'

Born at Mogriguy, between Gilgandra and Dubbo, on Australia Day, 1925, Pat quips, 'It was the hottest day Dad could remember, and my mother will never forget it!' Home was a wheat, sheep and cattle farm, called Mogriguy, giving Pat the unforgettable address: Mogriguy, Mogriguy Road, Mogriguy. He walked 2 miles to the little local school, and 2 miles back, every weekday. Then, at Dubbo high school, he walked a mile to and from school, a mile home for lunch and back again. Pat believes that walking 4 miles a day, five days a week, for eleven years, along with the hard physical work carried out on a farm daily, set him up for lifelong good health and strength.

As soon as Pat was old enough to enlist in World War II, he joined the Royal Australian Air Force (RAAF). 'Like every young bloke, I wanted to be a pilot, but my eyes didn't pass the stringent test, so I became a wireless operator, trained in morse code.' His squadron, the 576th, was sent to England to fly Lancaster bombers with the Royal Air Force (RAF). Even though they only received two months training in the Lancasters, Pat says the RAF trainers were 'extremely impressive men'. 'I responded far better to them than to the RAAF instructors I'd had in Australia. They could brilliantly condense a huge amount of information, and put it into your brain, accurately. My favourite instructor was a Scottish pilot, a

DFC [Distinguished Flying Cross] winner with burnt hands and an injured face. He never repeated himself.

'The Lancaster is a beautiful plane to fly empty, but a different beast with a full load of bombs and fuel. They use a lot of fuel climbing with a load on, so the further away you flew, the lighter they got. Then, after we got our bombs away, she would respond and do her best to get us home. At our base, the searchlights were on all the time, a wonderful sight when you were in a plane running out of fuel, or with a pilot struggling to keep a damaged machine in the air. There was a saying: "The only thing better than a Lancaster is a Lancaster with a better pilot."

'Based in Yorkshire, and later in Lincolnshire, our crew naturally became close friends, even though we were a bit of a mixture. The pilot was Welsh, trained in Canada; the bomb-aimer was English and also trained in Canada; the navigator another Pom but trained in South Africa; there were two Canadian gunners; and me, the Aussie wireless operator. At eighteen when I arrived, I was the "baby" of the crew.

'I was a warrant officer by then, and air force personnel in England were considered to be "the elite", but we still had trouble winning women away from the Yanks when we were on leave. They always had more money and smarter uniforms. There was also something put in our food to keep us from being "toey" around women. I don't know what it was, but it stopped us from thinking constantly about getting women into bed—as all young blokes do—and it stopped us from being scared about the job we had to do, the dangers we faced, our prospects of survival.

'One day I did meet a Canadian pilot who had done 29 operations and he was no scaredy-cat, but he just absolutely did not want to go on a 30th mission as he felt sure he would not return. He was all dressed up, sharp as a tack, and told me he had an appointment for an interview with his wing commander. He said he intended to tell the commander that if he was forced to go, he was sure that would mean the RAF would lose the aircraft. If that didn't work, he was going to admit that he was an impostor, that he was really 40 years old—eight years too old to be flying ops. I also heard of pilots who, in a similar predicament where they just knew somehow that their time was up if they went over to Germany again, could not force their body to take the plane up.

'I made it through the last three years of the war over there, flying 22 operations over German territory. The statistics of every operation were roughly like this: 90 per cent of the squadron would return home, 7 to 8 per cent of planes would be lost, the rest came back damaged. Crews had to be constantly trained as replacements for the men who didn't make it back or were injured.'

During one flight over Germany, Pat was sitting with his head out of the astrodome and saw an allied Lancaster in trouble. Its starboard prop was shot off and the engine was catching fire. Two men jumped out, one in the light blue uniform of the British, the other in the dark blue of the Australians. 'I wondered if the poor buggers survived the jump and if they were captured. Shortly after the war ended I spotted an Aussie in a loo, with a brand-new uniform on. Naturally, we had a yarn and he said he'd been shot down and captured, and just released. "Where were you shot down, mate?"

I asked, and when he told me, I couldn't believe it. I said, "I saw you jump, I was right behind you." He said that when he landed, he was immediately surrounded by a mob of blue-eyed, blond, aggressive kids with vicious guard dogs. He reckoned they looked like the selected stud progeny Hitler was supposed to be breeding. The kids were really keen to let the dogs go, but fortunately they were all kept under strict control by a soldier in charge of them. He and his mate weren't treated too badly. I heard many men say they would rather be captured by the Luftwaffe in Germany than captured in occupied France, where there were many different factions and fear and treachery were rife.'

During training, both in Australia and in England, the airmen never received any instruction in parachuting: they were just told to wear the harness at all times and shown how to attach the chute to it. Then the day came when young Pat had to rely on one to save his life. 'We were flying back from bombing a place called Berchtsgarten, our target being the SS barracks where Hitler was reputed to be. One old engine wore out and packed it in so our pilot was nursing the plane back to England, when suddenly the other engine packed it in, too, and the wing was on fire. The pilot somehow nursed the plane all the way from the North Sea to the other side of the Channel. At 1500 feet, he said, "Jump for it, lads." I was the second last to jump, and he ruffled my hair while I waited my turn, as if to say, "You'll be right, son." I'll never forget that. I jumped, pulled the cord, looking up at him. I wasn't frightened, but worried for him. He got out too and survived, thank God, but we lost our navigator and bomb-aimer. I can still hear the plane crashing. One bloke landed in a tree, fell out and broke his leg. I didn't know what to expect but when my chute opened, there was no feeling of falling, just a sensation of floating down like a leaf. I was lucky enough to land in a 2-acre barley field, which was surrounded by concrete ditches, railway lines—any number of things that would've done a lot of damage. I walked to a house and knocked on a door. We were in Norfolk. Those of us who survived were taken to a hospital belonging to a US Liberator Squadron at Hethel Base nearby. We were there for a week and the Yanks really looked after us.'

As testimony to the fact that a parachute saved his life, Pat wears his 'Caterpillar' badge. The badge honours the insect that starts the cycle which produces the silk the parachutes were made of.

War is a terrible thing, ruining so many people's lives, and one person Pat always remembers is a young lady who trained female recruits for the RAF. She had class and, in her quiet but authoritative manner, was doing a fine job of knocking some real rough nuts into shape. She told him her husband had disappeared not long after enlisting and going off to fight, and she had no idea if he was still alive. 'I don't know if I'm a widow or if he'll come back,' she said. Fleeting moments such as that sorrowful statement from a courageous woman can never be forgotten by men like Pat, who faced death themselves at such a young age.

Every Anzac Day since 1950, when he proudly wears his campaign medals, Pat has attended his squadron's reunion in Sydney. 'They were all top-class men. Very fine, very gallant gentlemen. There's only twelve of us left now. But they know I'll be there every year, because I was the "baby".'

After the war, Pat stayed in the UK until November, then had a wonderful 'world cruise' in a Liberty ship, full of RAAF and repatriated US aircrews, via Capetown, across the Pacific to America. Travelling across the States by train, he saw frozen waterfalls and rivers. Then he boarded a French liner for Australia. Pat and his brother, who had been in the Pacific with the RAAF, had inherited the family farm from their father, but the brothers had a less-than-happy working relationship. 'He was lazy and overbearing; I was a toiler. I was always fit, and proud of my fitness and strength. When we were on that farm together, the only time I was happy was when I couldn't hear his voice. He was on my back all day. Thank goodness I was finally able to buy him out.'

In 1947 Pat became engaged to Glenys Joan, whom he'd known at high school, and they married in 1951. Her brother was a Lancaster pilot so they had a lot in common and he eventually married Pat's sister. Pat and Glenys had two boys and a girl, and now have four grandchildren and three great grandchildren. But the mid 60s and early 70s were very hard years on the land.

'Wool and wheat were in the doldrums, and there was a roaring drought. I remember a few drops of rain came down in December 64 and the old-timers were all saying, "This is the start of the 65 drought." They were right and it was a bad one, really bad. On top of that, I was whacked with a big probate bill from my father's death—an iniquitous burden. There was no stability in the rural sector. The Arabs were teaching us a lesson by not buying our wethers. Everyone was chasing their tails, trying to change over to cattle, worried about the future. I kept sheep alive by feeding them on turnips from Narromine—5 pounds a load—it filled them up.

'To put tucker on our table, I went rouseabouting in the wool-sheds—very energetic work, swinging a broom flat out on the shearing board, bending down picking up fleeces all day. After a while I thought, "I'm gonna get too old to keep this up." So I enrolled at TAFE to get my wool classing certificate. I'd always enjoyed working with wool, so I was keen, which is half the battle. I was lucky to have a first-rate instructor, a Pommie ex-Grazcos overseer called Andy Freebrain. He had broad experience of wool from factories in the UK and had the gift of passing on his knowledge. By then, the course was two not four years, one day a week, and was combined with learning the trade of "expert" in the shed [maintenance], plus shed management, so I'd be qualified for three different jobs.

'During those years, we survived by "making do" and "doing without". If you can do that, you can make it. It's hard when you're rearing kids—young people don't realise how much that costs. When I was a kid, I used to overhear my mother telling her friends and neighbours, who all had too many children, to get their tubes tied. She was a schoolteacher, well educated, and had read about it in a book and insisted her doctor organise it for her. Now that was a long time ago, but it was the best advice those women could have received back then, before contraception. When I was old enough to understand, when I was struggling to rear a family myself, I appreciated and admired how smart she was, and how she had helped so many other females take control of their lives. In the hard times of the early 70s, I remember welding the floor of the old car so it'd pass for rego, then the next year the last kid was off our hands and we could afford to buy a new car, for cash.'

Life became easier, Pat says, once he got his stencil, which allowed him to get work wool classing. He sold one of his blocks and easily managed what was left. Then, in 1978, he sold the farm and moved into town, to class full-time. 'Most of my classing has been done in the Brewarrina area, out west, for a very good contractor, Peter Orcher. You meet some funny characters in the shearing sheds, have a lot of laughs. I once met a Chinese cook, a real wag, who introduced himself as "Chris Mostyn—call me Mossy", which sounded pretty funny, coming from a Chinese bloke. Then he explained his surname was shortened from Mostoupoulopolous, a Greek name. He reckoned that as a newborn baby he'd been left in a basket on the corner dividing the Chinese part of the city from the Greek part, and a Greek lady adopted him. He kept a straight face the whole time, then he grinned, lifted up his fringe and said: "So I got this big Greek name, but look, mate, I reckon there's a little bit of Chow here, don't you?"

'Another memory that always gives me a laugh was the day a young stationhand who was about to get married confessed to me that he was still a virgin. He was worried that he would be okay at doing what you do on your wedding night. Gawd, he was naive. I said, "You'll be right, young feller. It'll just come naturally to you, don't worry." Well, on Monday, back in the shed, I asked him, "How'd it go—alright?" With a sort of relieved grin, he said, "Yeah, we had a whale of a time. I didn't know what to do, but thank goodness she did."

'At smoko and lunchtime in the sheds, when everyone's resting, stretched out on the floor or the bales, you hear some bloody funny stories, true yarns and jokes. You think to yourself, this is a bloody good life.'

Pat says that every shed is different, just as every mob of sheep is different. The wool varies depending on the age of the sheep and what they've been feeding on. It's always interesting, and satisfying doing a good job. The amount of a wool grower's cheque is very reliant on a wool classer's skill. Nutrition affects the quality of wool just as it does the shape and appearance of a person.' Looking at Pat, he is indeed a living testimony to his beliefs about a healthy lifestyle. He dominated veteran swimming events all over central and western New South Wales for fifteen years, through the 1980s and 90s, and still looks like he could swim across the Channel.

'When overweight people ask my doctor, who's pretty straightforward, how they can lose some of their fat, he replies, "Starve". When I was in the UK during the war, I heard a funny story about Field Marshal Montgomery, who was very fit. He went to inspect a camp and as soon as he arrived there, he shoved his finger into the commanding officer's gut and said, "You are relieved of your command until you lose that." Should be more of it. People in the police force and services should be fit. When I went into the RAAF you had to be perfect—not even a crooked fingernail.'

When he isn't swimming, socialising or wool classing, he's busy working for his son, Lindsay, who owns a car dealership. 'I'm the "gofer"—I buzz all over Dubbo and roundabout, to windscreen and tyre people, the RTA, you name it. This mobile phone is the greatest invention ever—Lindsay can "steer" me all over the place to do whatever he wants.

'It's good to be busy, but you also need time to enjoy yarning with your friends, and to read. I read everything—there's so much to learn and discover. Life's what you make it, and my life is pretty good. But you've got to look after yourself, and have healthy interests and friends. I've never drunk much grog. When I sold my property and moved into town, I avoided getting into the rut that many people get into of heading for the pub, seeking company of their own kind. You see farmers who retire and the first thing they do is make a pathway to the pub. In no time they've lost their colour, gained a gut, and they're on the downhill run. The RSL club is my second home, but that's mainly because the swimming club is there. I mix with the swimmers, not so much the drinkers and gamblers. We all value our health, and have a common outlook on life. Fit people are always attracted to each other.'

I reckon Pat Mumford was a 'life coach' before the term was even invented.

LADY FLORENCE BJELKE-PETERSEN

A genuine lady

The words 'lady' and 'gentleman' are often loosely used these days. You sometimes hear the worst type of criminal being described by a policeman or a news reporter as a 'gentleman', or a woman who is anything but a lady described as such by her boyfriend or the media. Those two descriptive nouns should only be used in the truest sense, or they are meaningless and false. Long, long before her famous husband was knighted, Florence Bjelke-Petersen, nee Gilmour, was a lady, in the genuine sense of the word. She is also one of the most loved people in Queensland, by those from both sides of the political spectrum, from all walks of life, for she has strived all her life to set the highest standards and help humanity in every way she can. She is a true Christian and a true lady.

So, what was Lady Bjelke-Petersen up to when I called to see if we could have a yarn? No surprise. Yes, the pumpkin scones were going in the oven as I arrived. A hundred of them, for a busload of tourists arriving that morning to tour Bethany, one the most famous property names in Australia, along with the Packer family's Ellerston and the Northern Territory's Victoria River Downs.

Naturally, the tourists all want to see 'Flo'—more than the beautiful rolling, red-soil countryside near Kingaroy. As the buses roll through the gates to the two unpretentious homesteads on the hill, Queensland flag flying out front, the visitors are all hoping to actually meet the famous lady. Both Flo and son John, who conducts the tours and loves telling people about the history of the property and district, are obliging and genuinely warm and welcoming hosts. At 90, she strolls out to greet them, smiling, looking healthy and happy. The 'Queen of Kingaroy' poses for photos with at least 50 people, chatting and shaking hands—a scene that has been repeated twice a week for the past twenty years. The delight of the crowd is tangible.

Florence Gilmour grew up in Brisbane, never dreaming she would one day be a farmer's wife, let alone a senator, married to the state premier, and known officially as Lady Bjelke-Petersen. With her sister Margaret, Florence had a happy and comfortable childhood at the riverside suburb of New Farm, several years before the landmark Story Bridge was built nearby to join the north and south sides of the city. Their mother was also named Florence, their father was an accountant, and the sisters went to meet him every day as he walked home from William Collins and Son at Petrie Bight. The girls also walked up a high hill to the local primary school, and to the Fortitude Valley Presbyterian Church. A tram ride after church to Granny's at Ashgrove for Sunday lunch, and occasionally a horse and sulky drive to her Uncle Rob's dairy farm at The Gap, completed the family's entertainment. It was a stable, if unremarkable, start to life that would serve Florence well in her challenging future.

After passing her junior high school years at Brisbane Girls Grammar, Florence was allowed to leave and attend the public service course at the commercial high school, where she excelled in the subjects she loved, gaining straight As in English, history, shorthand, typing and bookkeeping. In 1937 she began a long career with the Main Roads Department, firstly as part of the typing pool, and finally as secretary to the Main Roads Commissioner which was as high as a woman could go in her field in those days.

'I started off carrying huge files around the building; every vehicle registration number had a file, and if people came in to pay their account, I had to find the right file then lug it to the right counter. It was hard work. There were mainly men working there and I remember the shock when, for the first time in my life, I heard swearing. In the engineer's department during World War II, we typed estimates for road and bridge works, which was interesting. My contribution to the war effort was to work back at nights, long hours, then I'd go home on a late tram, which was quite safe back then. When I was the commissioner's secretary he took me on his tours of inspections, mainly to keep his wife company I think, but I met a lot of people and that was valuable later on when I entered public life.

'I met Joh when he came in with deputations from local authorities. He was already in politics then, believing he could do good work to help Queensland grow and become prosperous which, of course, he achieved. One of my workmates said to me, "If he asks you out, say yes, because he's not married and he has lots of money." He seemed a nice chap and I was pleased to find out he was a Christian man. That was important to me, even though we were from different churches. Joh was a Lutheran but was happy to marry me in the Valley Presbyterian Church, in 1952.

'Until then I was a career girl and Joh had been busy establishing himself, and neither of us had met anyone we wanted to marry. He was 41 and I was ten years younger. Joh's brother-in-law was his best man and he told Joh in the vestry that if he wanted to change his mind, that was his last chance, but Joh just laughed. We had a nine-week honeymoon in New Zealand. It was very cold but the warmth of our affection overcame that. We were happy together since the day we met. Every day was Valentine's Day to us.'

Although, Flo adds, even the fondest couple can have words when the husband attempts to teach his wife to drive! 'Joh was a patient, kind man but, like all husbands, not so patient when he tried to teach me to drive our car. He got a little bit testy. Luckily, he had to go away—he was always very busy—and his sister taught me to drive with infinite patience and good humour. We drove around the paddocks and I had to pretend that clumps of grass were policemen watching me. We couldn't help giggling when I bumped into them. Anyway, Joh came back and was so impressed when he saw me driving across the paddocks to meet him.

'When Joh brought me here to Bethany, I was a city girl and was scared of cattle, but he said, "Well, Florence, you just have to overcome that and learn to milk the cow, so you can do it if I'm not here." I was frightened, but I had a go. Then I let the cow go without untying the leg rope and, oh goodness gracious, that was a bit of a muddle—the cow was kicking and struggling—we were both upset! But I learnt, eventually. A farmer's wife has to learn to do many things, and a city girl must be prepared to adapt to a very different life in the country.

'I went from doing an important job assisting the commissioner to an even more important role in life, that of being a good wife and mother. When Joh would come home I would always ask, "Now, dear, what happened today?" Joh often said to journalists, "A good wife is above rubies." I would have found it a very hard job to go into politics with young children. No one should ever criticise a woman for choosing to raise their family in preference to another career, for we can gain a feeling of great satisfaction from training our children properly and watching them develop as sensible adults. I have always believed that if you can bring your family up with Christian faith and values, then that gives them a good standard to live by. The family who prays together, stays together. Joh left the disciplining of the children to me; I never used a strap, only my hand, and it hurt me more than it hurt them, but children must have discipline and standards to live up to. I don't believe in wasting money on luxuries; I always told journalists that I actually had four dishwashers—three daughters and a son.'

After Joh became premier on 8 August 1968, the people of King-aroy were immensely proud, but household life at Bethany didn't change much. The premier's wife was quoted as saying: 'You have to take an interest in your husband's interests and job, no matter what that is. Now and then he asks me what do I think about this or that, but he always makes up his own mind. Naturally I get upset with people who criticise him but never praise his good work.'

During that first year many people hadn't seen Flo, which led to an amusing incident at Julia Creek when they were invited to a function. Mrs Bjelke-Petersen (as she was then) had to attend a meeting in town first, and arrived late for the function at the town hall. As she tiptoed down the aisle during a lull in the proceedings, she knocked some ashtrays on the floor, causing everyone to look around. The hall was full so the shire chairman, hosting the evening, called out from up on the stage: 'There's a seat up here. Come on.' When Flo sat down, the chair shot out from underneath her on its castors, causing her to hang on in a rather undignified and embarrassing manner, with all the guests watching her. Then the chairman said to her: 'I don't know you, but I'd like you to meet our premier, Joh Bjelke-Petersen. He's here to speak tonight.'

Flo replied, 'Oh, yes, he's my husband—hello, dear.'

Although Joh was already in politics when they married, Flo never dreamt she would become as involved as she did. 'For many years I was very happy just supporting him in every way I could. I said back in the early days, "Joh, we must look after the people in your electorate or you can't expect them to vote you back in next time." What I meant by that was, if he couldn't go to any of the constant functions and duties he was expected to attend to here, I would. It was impossible for one person to keep up with the invitations that flowed in. Many of them may have seemed like insignificant occasions, but they meant a lot to the little communities that were holding them—school fetes and the like. I'll never forget the laughter at a function in Murgon when councillor John Kreggs introduced us to the crowd as "the premier, Joh Bjelke-Petersen, and the member for Barambah, Mrs Bjelke-Petersen". I was often referred to as the member, because I did so much to help the electorate.

'To give you an example of what I did back then, which I must say was a pleasure for me, I went on three big tours of western and northern isolated regions back in the depressing Whitlam years of the early 1970s. Because of Whitlam's attitude towards primary producers and rural people in general, they were having a very hard time. Joh received a call from Lady Pearl Logan, who urged him to visit the west and see how hard they were doing it out there, due to Labor policies, coupled with drought. Joh was so tied up with other very important issues but wanted to go, so I said I would go and represent him. Well, when I arrived, the first function was an Isolated Children's Parents conference and a television interview had been set up with Andrew Olle on the ABC and I had to carry it off, for Joh, and the National Party. I was so nervous, having never been on television before, but I got through it alright, and soon I was visiting other isolated regions, representing him—so people throughout Queensland were getting to know me personally.'

In 1983, there was a Federal election with a double dissolution. The Liberals wanted to snatch a Senate seat from the Nationals. The media started speculating that Joh was going for it, to which he replied with just one word: 'Hogwash!' Then suddenly the headlines started reading: 'It's not Joh—it's Flo!' Many journalists wasted no time publishing and broadcasting their ridicule at a 'pumpkin-scone housewife' running for Senate. Liberal member Yvonne McComb was going for it, too, and a National Party executive was quoted in the media as saying to the Libs, 'Our grandmother can beat your grandmother, any time!' Then more positive press reports started appearing, as journalists realised how savvy and composed Flo was. One report read: 'The pumpkin-scone politician will bring common-sense to the Senate chamber, for behind her motherly, homespun, God-fearing exterior, there's a lot of steel.'

Perhaps the most intriguing description came from author Hugh Lunn, then Brisbane-based editor of *The Australian*:

> *The Queensland Premier's wife is as homely as a sponge cake with passion fruit icing, as comforting as a squatter's chair on a shady verandah, as straightforward and practical as a yabby pump and as wholesome as a plump ripe mango.*

Even a Melbourne journalist, not known for kind words about the Bjelke-Petersens, commented:

> *Flo is now one of the six best-known women in Australia. She's a media natural. Behind her ordinariness, there's a star factor. She*

*is shrewd and determined but lacks that streak of cruelty . . . the
time has come to stop laughing.*

In response to many interviewers asking if entering politics at
her age, 59, was daunting, Flo would reply, 'Age is a state of mind;
experience counts in politics.'

Looking back at those amazing times, Flo recalls: 'National Party
president Bob Sparkes did not want me to get in and tried hard to
keep me from reaching my goal, but I got in by one vote. After
that I enjoyed twelve wonderful years in the Senate, achieving a lot,
and always got a wonderful vote back in. I wasn't comfortable with
certain situations, but the "boys" were always good to me. Then
came the Money Bill, trying to push through a tax on essential
commodities. I got up and said, "The people don't need more taxes
than they already have to pay," and I crossed the floor against it.
To people who accused me of disloyalty, I'd reply, "The Senate is a
house of review, not a party house." I was sent to Coventry for that,
and look what happened—the same tax was brought in by Peter
Costello and John Howard.'

One of Flo's finest moments came when she visited Ipswich
coalminers who'd been sacked but were having a sit-in down in the
mine, refusing to come up to negotiate. After getting up early to
prepare her 'secret weapon'—a basketful of pumpkin scones—she
walked to the shaft, where the desperate and angry miners' wives
were on guard, in support of their men. Even the most anti-Joh-and-
Flo voters or journalists had to admit that took guts! She told them:
'I'm here as a messenger from Joh, but don't forget I'm a senator

too, so I belong to you as well as the other side. I've brought some scones for the men.' They allowed her to approach the sit-in and she soon had the grim-faced, hard-hatted men eating out of her hand, as well as her scone basket. She promised them she would convince Joh to meet them and talk with them, if they would promise to come halfway up the shaft to meet him. They did, and the matter was soon resolved.

'I did a very good job as a senator—I know that—but I was well aware certain people in the media always tried to denigrate me by making out I was just a simple country housewife whose main accomplishment was making pumpkin scones. My name became associated with them. Well, all I can say about that is, I never became upset about their snide remarks. I'd say to people interviewing me, "Pumpkin scones appeal to the men who eat them, and the women who make them, and that's all the people in Queensland, so I regard my ability to make and promote them as an asset." Even Prince Charles said in his speech to open the Brisbane Performing Arts Centre that my scones must have helped keep Joh strong and in power for so long—that was a bit of fun and we all, including Prince Charles, enjoyed a good laugh. My recipe has been printed on everything you can think of and has raised a lot of money for charity. George Negus paid 430 dollars for the recipe at a charity auction and has it up on his kitchen wall.' In a newspaper report from the early 1980s, the Senator's scones were directly attributed to Defiance Flour Mills Ltd's record profit of 1 560 000 dollars the previous year.

'There were people in the media who chose to ignore what I achieved in the Senate. Apart from anything else, I was the chairman of many committees, and nominated as whip, and was the deputy leader for the National Party in the Senate for six years. I will say that I was fortunate to have very good secretaries, and I also had a capable girl at home looking after things as well. Joh and I didn't see each other a lot, as we were off in different directions much of the time, but I have to say about that situation, "Absence makes the heart grow fonder". We would try our best to spend time together at home, and enjoyed going to church together. We were always happy in each other's company.'

Even at the height of their power, the Bjelke-Petersens never lost touch with the 'ordinary people', remaining accessible to everyone. There was no silent number at Bethany—anyone could ring them for a yarn or a whinge. Although they were regarded almost as Aussie royalty by the majority of Queenslanders, it was still 'G'day, Joh!' or 'G'day, Flo!' from people of all backgrounds in the streets all over the state. When asked why Joh, then in his mid-70s, didn't retire, she'd retort, 'Sir Winston Churchill was still going strong in his 80s—why not Sir Joh?'

But it wasn't to be. Flo explains: 'The Victorian people were the initial ones, in 1986, who wanted Joh to go to Canberra, because Labor kept getting voted in, and Joh had had such a wonderful triumph in the Queensland elections the year before. [The year when, contrary to widespread predictions, he won in a landslide, emerging from the tally room to famously quip to the waiting media: "Shouldn't all you people be down at the hardware store buying scrubbing brushes, to scrub all that egg off your faces? And that Quentin Dempster—he'll want a very large scrubbing brush indeed, to get all that egg off his face!"] All these powerful people were urging him to run for Canberra, to try to save Australia from Labor, who just can't manage the economy. Well, Joh eventually agreed to try, but when Bob Sparkes tried to take over the campaign and establish a headquarters in Melbourne, all the big Victorian supporters pulled out and the campaign was finished.'

Despite his enormous achievements for Queensland and his equally overwhelming popularity with the people, it was those in Joh's own party—the party he had taken to heights beyond their wildest dreams—who forced him to retire early. How does Flo feel about the back-stabbers who brought the party down?

'They have had a long time watching the prosperity he created for Queenslanders disintegrate since then. They know they were silly. All he wanted was to be allowed to resign and retire from politics on the date he chose: the eighth of the eighth of eighty-eight, after exactly twenty years as premier. But they couldn't wait— certain people wanted someone new, and look what has happened since. They thought because he'd decided to have a go at Federal politics, they'd teach him a lesson that they could do without him. That was plain silly.

'It was bad. His many supporters were shocked at what they'd done to him, and many people resigned from the National Party in protest. The party was split and in disarray. The new leader had no charisma. Joh wanted me to also finish with the party and be an independent in the Senate, but I said I couldn't do that to the people who had voted for me only a year before. He wasn't pleased but accepted my decision with good grace.'

Then came the Fitzgerald Inquiry.

'The case came about because they tried to insinuate Joh had granted the Stamford Plaza development to a businessman called Mr Sng, but Joh didn't have anything to do with that decision. It was a committee which decided Mr Sng was the best person to give it to. Joh actually wanted Barry Pauls to get that development decision, because he thought he was the best man to carry it out, but the committee said no, they believed Mr Sng was a better choice. Well, the court never called that committee to give evidence. The jury was full of Labor people. Luke Shaw, who believed in Joh's innocence and stuck up for him, was, I believe, called up onto the jury by mistake because of his appearance. He was on his way to uni that day and dressed very casually, so they didn't think he was a Nationals supporter.

'Everyone knows who was behind the "Get Joh" campaign. It was a long time ago, and I have put it behind me, in the past. Joh was the most honest, honourable man God put breath into and I am so proud to have been his wife. They tried to "get" him for corruption, but of course there was no corruption, so they then tried to get him for perjury, and Joh did not tell lies, so that witchhunt failed also, but the legal fight to clear his name cost us very dearly. At the time it was literally shocking for us. We had to sell our son's property, and two other properties, to pay the astronomical legal fees. That fight, which was so unfair, nearly cost us everything Joh had worked so hard for in his younger years. Most people these days couldn't even imagine how hard he worked—physically—on the land, with his machinery contracting business, and later on the long hours he worked in politics. That trial dragged on and on—they were determined to jail him, humiliate him—and with one week to go, we had run out of money to keep pouring into the law firm we were using. They said they would pull out of the case if he didn't come up with the final quarter of a million dollars straight away. Joh had a friend in Tasmania who lent him that money against my superannuation. All we had left was our home here and my salary as a senator. We lived on that then, and after my retirement in 1993, on the second half of my super which is paid in small instalments. It hasn't been easy, but the income from tourism helps.

'I have had to put all that behind me. I have even stayed at the Stamford Plaza several times when people book me there for public speaking engagements, and I have to say it is a very elegant hotel. My attitude is that it's not healthy to keep feeling bitterness—even towards the people involved who were out to break Joh, or the media who wrote and broadcast such biased reports and opinion pieces at the time. The Christian way of life is to forgive your enemies, and—as they say these days—"move on". Hatred and anger are not good for you. We all have to face our maker one day. I'll leave it at that.'

Flo prefers to 'look to the future', and seeing her grandchildren every day helps her to focus on the future rather than the past. 'Many people ask me if I think my son John will eventually bring the Bjelke-Petersen name back into the political arena, and the truthful answer is, I'm not sure. He might, and if he does, John would be like his father—a very successful politician. He topped the primaries when he last ran but lost on preferences, which is, in my opinion, an unfair system. People should just be voting for the party they think can best run the state or country. John may run again but his wife Karen has another baby on the way so that might affect what he decides about a political life, because it takes up a lot of your time, and your children sometimes hear nasty and untrue things said about you in the media. For example, a television presenter once put a microphone in my daughter Helen's face, when she was very young, and asked her what it was like having a dictator for a father!'

Flo loves having Karen and John living at Bethany beside her, even though she says 'it's very sad and unfair' that their place in Central Queensland was sold to help cover the costs of the legal battle. 'I've been able to enjoy seeing their four sons growing up, and with another baby on the way, well, who wouldn't be excited?' John and Flo both enjoy meeting the tourists, and John is very proud to be able to tell them the wonderful stories about his grandparents and great grandparents who pioneered Bethany. Joh's grandfather arrived there in a horse and sulky, built a hut and left Joh's mother, who was only thirteen at the time, to look after the cattle on her own. 'She was a wonderful lady,' Flo says.

'God has been good to me—given me a 90-year lifespan. I feel good and strong. As well as my children and grandchildren, of course, I have many interests. I love reading. I play the organ at three different churches around Kingaroy, as well as at retirement villages to entertain the old people. [!!] I receive more invitations to launch books, attend functions, speaking events and public meetings than I can say yes to, because I have to keep two days a week free to meet and greet our visitors as they get off the buses. I enjoy shopping twice a week in town. It's just lovely to hear, everywhere I go around town, and literally everywhere I go all over Queensland, people calling out "Hello, Flo!" "Good on you, Flo!" That's wonderful. At Joh's funeral, as we were all leaving the church, a man called out, "We all love you, Flo!" I am blessed.

'Once I reached my mid-80s, people started asking me for the secret to looking so well. I have always tried to eat the right things and live a happy, healthy life. I've kept busy. I have young people in my life to challenge my thinking and keep me fresh—not stagnating and getting stale. I have mastered a computer. I don't let past griev- ances get me down. My church means a lot to me. I do worry about what God thinks now, about us, as a society—the anti-Christian attitudes which are prevalent. Not just young people, but everyone who has turned against the Christian way of life, will, as I said earlier, all have to face their maker one day. We all have a chance to believe in God or not. I choose to believe, and that is what helps make me strong, healthy and happy.

'I admire the way Tony Abbott stands up for the Christian way of life. The level of immigration now worries me. We are top-heavy with immigrants coming in to Australia who do not respect our Christian way of life and who will not assimilate. Islam will be a big problem here. I worry about this aspect and how it will affect my grandchildren and great grandchildren. This is the best country in the world to live in—I was always so glad to get back here after trav- elling overseas. What can we do to make these immigrants respect our Christian attitudes?'

Unfortunately, there's no easy answer to that, so I ask this wonderful lady what she considers to be her proudest or greatest achievement in her long and eventful life. She answers without hesitation: 'Being married to a man like Joh, having the happy family life we had, was a wonderful thing. If someone has a loving, lifelong partner and loving, happy, healthy children, then God has blessed them.'

JOHN LUNDHOLM OAM

Racing and rodeo legend

In the old timber roundyard, a horseman's ready to spring up into the pigskin.

The powerful chestnut thoroughbred colt, unbroken, might take the sudden, unexpected weight on his back calmly, or he might explode like a keg of dynamite. The rider has fought many a battle in this private arena, usually riding his snorting, squealing challengers to a standstill, with a small grin of triumph.

But not always—occasionally he's been catapulted into the sand. Today could be one of those rare days. Today he might find himself lying on the ground, gasping for breath after that awful *thud!* . . . mentally going through a checklist to see if there's any broken bones. And if not, climb back on, to teach the animal respect for the human on its back. That has been this man's life.

He swings on board in an athletic 'blink of an eye'. This colt, full of oats, full of nervous energy, hates the weight on his back. He goes to town with a series of sunfishing, twisting bucks like the son of Curio. The weight, the legendary Johnny Lundholm, is still there, winning, looking like he's got superglue on his saddle . . . very pretty to watch, the style of a saddle bronc champion. Suddenly, the wild-eyed chestnut rears, overbalances, then crashes to the ground, backwards.

Half a tonne of horse lands on one human leg. 'Oh, goodness gracious me!' yells John—or words to that effect. Trapped under the colt, he's in more strife than Flash Gordon as the horse struggles to its feet then bucks around the arena, flying hooves capable of smashing a human skull. 'Stand up, yer bastard! STAND UP!' The horse has learnt respect for the man's voice and stops, staring at him, ears pricked in amazement. Maybe he doesn't connect that the man on the ground, the man who has been kind and gentle to him, is the thing that was on his back?

What John knows, by then, is that his immediate mortal danger is over, but that horrible pain in his leg is not good news. 'What a jolly nuisance!' he comments—or words to that effect. Now, a busted leg can be a bit of a nuisance at the best of times, but doubly so when a bloke is aged three score and ten, plus nine . . . It was, in fact, just six months off his 80th birthday.

Just three weeks after the chestnut colt reared over backwards, there's a bloke riding trackwork on the Coonamble racetrack with his leg in plaster—yep, bloody Johnny Lundholm! As it turned out, the leg miraculously wasn't broken, but badly crushed. Of course, since the accident, he'd been whizzing about on his crutches, supervising and helping with the usual chores around his stables. When he turned up at the track mounted up with his leg in plaster, one of the trackwork riders said, 'I hope you don't come off and land on that leg, John,' to which he replied, with his almost permanent grin, 'Well, I reckon that'd be the best leg to land on, because the plaster should protect it!'

Tough as a gidgee limb, here is a man with no fear of any horse, no fear of suffering pain from the inevitable injuries that occur to people who constantly deal with horses: large, temperamental, powerful, potentially dangerous animals. Revered all over north-west New South Wales as a living legend, here is a bloke who rose from teenage trackwork rider to top racehorse trainer, with equal success on the rodeo scene. His trim horseman's physique always neatly dressed, John is a disciplined man of high standards, a quietly spoken, modest man who never boasts about his skills or his lifetime of achievement, but he's also a loveable, laughing larrikin who enjoys life to the max. He's doing what he loves doing, and that keeps him young.

Born at Euchareena at the tail-end of the Roaring Twenties, to parents who weren't interested in horses, John inherited his keenness and talent from his grandmother, giving proof to the old saying 'blood will tell'. As a youngster growing up in Dubbo, he was breaking in Shetland ponies for the love of it, with a cunning, tight-fisted breeder profiting handsomely from John's natural skills with the little hairy beasties. By his early teens, he had graduated to thoroughbreds.

A competitive streak saw him chasing ribbons and prize money at shows in a big radius of Dubbo. 'I'd ride in everything except the lady riders' class! I even rode trotters in races at showgrounds back before gigs were used—you had to be keen to do that!' As his reputation grew in horse circles, he was in demand to ride in the 'Number Nines' races. 'They were amateur events not recognised by the Australian Jockey Club. Pretty wild, Rafferty's rules. The shenanigans and dirty tricks that went on out of sight of the crowd and judge were great fun.

'When I turned fifteen, Randwick trainer George Gorrie invited me to Sydney to ride trackwork. His main client was W.J. "Knockout" Smith, owner of famous St Aubins Stud, and a great horse called Tribal. "Knockout" took a bit of a shine to me, encouraging me to be a trainer as I was too tall and heavy to be a jockey. But I felt I should heed my mother's advice to get a "proper" trade so I spent five years as an apprentice farrier.'

One of the most important tradespeople associated with racing, a farrier can make or break a horse's career. A really skilled farrier can even correct a leg problem or faulty gait. John still shoes his own horses and with 60 years' practice behind him, he reckons he's 'just about got it right'. Shoeing a horse is hard yakka for most people, but John makes it look easy, even at 80 years of age.

Spare time during his apprenticeship was spent breaking in thoroughbreds. John's skill at using a whip, gently, to make a horse face you, therefore respect you, impressed city-based racing people and he was given many valuable horses to educate. But the call of the bush was always in his heart and at last he was free to head west and become a trainer. 'I intended to set up stables in Brewarrina, then a busy racing hub in the north-west of New South Wales, but I was advised to go to Coonamble.' John and his bride Colleen arrived in the go-ahead town on the Castlereagh River in 1954. He set up his stables a short trot from the picturesque racecourse and, after enduring an initial lean time, soon made a name for himself. By pulling their belts in during those hard early years, and having faith in John's ability to become a successful trainer, the rewards to him, and Colleen, were eventually realised and enjoyed. The next 40 years were to be the golden years of country racing, and John Lundholm was up there with the most successful trainers.

No fewer than 33 times, he won the Trainer of the Year Premiership for the central west and western New South Wales—an amazing record. But he's no 'Johnny-One-Note'—featuring in the *Coonamble Times* and many other publications just as often for his achievements in rodeo as he did in racing. Immediately on arriving in the district, John was largely responsible for starting the Coonamble Rodeo and Campdraft, now the biggest in the southern hemisphere.

For more than half a century, he's toiled behind the scenes, or out front as a pick-up rider, as well as competing. At the first rodeo in 1955, he won all three championships—saddle bronc, bareback and bulldogging—and continued to compete until retiring from the arena at 77. 'To give the younger fellers a chance!' he laughs. John is proud that their rodeo has been chosen to host the Australian titles twice. The entire region was proud in 2001 when 'their Lundy' was awarded a Medal of the Order of Australia (OAM) for services to racing and rodeo. As a Rotarian, John has helped out with countless community projects, despite being such a busy bloke. Naturally, he is featured in Coonamble's Hall of Fame of local legends, cartoons and entertaining stories adorning the walls of various buildings.

A bloke who loves a joke, he enjoys the company of colourful characters. 'There was a real larrikin I often saw at the races and rodeos, a trainer called Dan Edwards. I'll never forget the answer he gave to a young rodeo competitor who asked him if he liked Arabian horses. Old Dan replied, "Well, they can't be any bloody good, mate, 'cos whenever you see an Arab bloke, 'e's ridin' a bloody camel."

'When Dan was 97, he went to the Tumbarumba rodeo to watch me ride in the old-timer's buckjump. Most of the so-called "old-timers" were about 35, which I s'pose *is* considered old by a lot of buckjump riders. I was 71 then and drew this big grey ratbag—he was a bloody demon. Dan said, "I wouldn't get on that bloody lunatic for a million dollars, mate." I told him, "I wouldn't either if I was 97!"

'That horse gave me a lively time and old Dan a bit of entertainment. He was still riding when he was 103—a great old character, but, oh boy, when he had racehorses, he got up to every trick in the book. He was a bugger for getting jockeys to pull horses up that were supposed to win, when he'd backed a different horse. One day he said to famous jockey Robert Thompson, "I might get yer to ride a horse for me." Well, I always laugh when I remember the horrified look on Robert's face as he replied, "I hope not!"'

In a game notorious for dodgy characters, John Lundholm has a reputation for being as straight as a gun barrel. Former chairman of the Western Racing Association, Bob Ridge, has, like John, been part of the scenery at the same race meetings for more than 60 years. Bob says: 'John's record is immaculate. He's also second-to-none at re-educating badly broken, bad-mannered horses that other trainers have given up on. One outlaw came to John's stables about five years ago—a big baldy-faced bay, mad as a meat ant. No one could control him in the saddling paddock, or get him near the barriers. When the horse was barred from Sydney racecourses, Jim Coxon from Come-by-Chance bought him because of his breeding, and because of his faith that Lundy could straighten him out.

'Well, that ratbag managed to do what most horses can't do—chucked John off several times, including twice in one day between the racecourse and his stables. But with that big grin and quiet voice, John said, "I won't let him beat me." Eventually he quietened him down enough to take him to a race meeting, but on the way to the saddling paddock, the horse suddenly went crazy. He wouldn't stand long enough for the jockey Greg Ryan to be "legged up", so John ran, leading the horse onto the track, while Greg ran, too, and vaulted on at the trot. Lundy would've been at least 75, but ran like a teenager. That big smile of his stretched literally from ear to ear when the ratbag flashed past the post at the front.'

Another stand-out character on the western tracks is the official starter, 'Icey' Canham, who was a successful apprentice jockey in John's stables. He says: 'I owed that success to John's skill as a teacher. He could, and would, patiently pass on his knowledge—a lot of trainers can't do that.' John also taught Icey the secrets of balance on buckjumpers, which led to him winning the Australian Novice Championship at Moree in 1969. Icey, who received his nickname aged six when he rode a buckjumping donkey called Icecream to victory at Gill Brothers rodeo, says: 'I was bloody lucky to have the greatest horseman I have ever seen in my life as my trainer. During my apprenticeship, he always had around 50 to 60 horses in work and employed fourteen of us lads. John's a great believer in swimming horses, and we'd all take them to the Castlereagh. Some horses were reluctant to go in, and he'd flick his whip at them, but because he didn't wear his glasses to the river he'd often miss the horses and get us instead, which wasn't any fun when you're just wearing shorts. We christened him "Vanderbilt" after the blind bloke from [the TV series] *F Troop*—all the lads called him that.' When asked if any of them ever protested, Icey laughed, 'No use whingeing—he was bloody deaf as well!'

John Marshall, a wool grower from Walgett, is a client of John's and has had a 50-year association with him: 'He also trained horses for my father, and neither of us ever had a cross word with him. He's a man of exemplary character, and when he breaks in a horse for you it doesn't have a bad bone in its body.'

Like most outstanding horsemen, John Lundholm doesn't skite, happier talking about horses than himself. When asked to recall his greatest triumphs, he smiles shyly, then modestly, almost reluctantly, produces an answer: 'I s'pose my most thrilling win in rodeo was riding the so-called "unrideable" horse Booringal at the 1957 Bushman's Carnival in Orange to score 92 points, a close-to-perfect score, and take out the championship.'

What about the most memorable spill? He chuckles. 'Ha! Hafta be here at Coonamble, when I rode the "best" bull [the one that bucks the most] in the draw. I was only a youngster then, in my 50s. I stayed the time [8 seconds], but as I was getting off the bull tossed his horns, driving one through my arm, breaking the elbow in three places.' John's doctor warned that he would suffer terrible arthritis in that elbow. With a characteristically quiet but merry laugh, John says, 'I'm flat out remembering which arm it was now!'

'Tough—amazingly tough!' are words most people who know John use to first describe him. He celebrated his 70th birthday at a rodeo by riding a buckjumper while cracking a stock whip, for a cheering crowd, but he was later bucked off by another horse and hurt his neck. He had a horse, Scrivens, racing in Sydney the next day and had to drive there. Unable to turn his head to the left, he shanghaied a mate to go with him in the passenger seat, with these instructions: 'You tell me if any cars are coming on our left, and I'll take care of looking for cars on our right.' Away they went on their seven-hour drive, and not only did they arrive safe and sound but were rewarded with a thrilling win by Scrivens.

John's walls are chock-a-block with photos of winners at both Sydney and Brisbane, as well as the regional meetings. He points to a big frame containing three photos of a mare called Marlotta winning in Brisbane in late 1988. 'After the first win, the owner asked if I'd like a photo, 'n' I said, "No, I'll wait till she wins the three races I've brought her here for, and put 'em all in the one frame," . . . and there it is.' What a wall of proud memories! Near a large exciting shot of John bursting out of the chutes on a buck-jumper at the Sydney Royal Easter Show, there's a picture of Just Trixie winning the Coonamble Gold Cup in 1965, ridden by Ray Selkrig. 'It's always a huge thrill to see a horse you've trained win, but I can never forget the thrill of seeing Just Trixie storm home that day to win my first Gold Cup. I was so excited I jumped the fence and ran at least a furlong to meet her!'

Another extremely proud moment in his life was seeing his grandson Clint Lundholm win his first race at Gilgandra, riding John Marshall's Royal Chapter. Before the year was out, Clint was named Apprentice of the Year. Like his grandfather and father (also named John), Clint is too tall to be a jockey and has given up the constant and unhealthy battle to keep his weight down. He can still ride trackwork at Dubbo, where he's based, and in amateur picnic meetings. Naturally, John hopes that one day he will return to help him and Clint's father run the stables. John and Colleen's two daughters have also given them many wonderful moments, as champions in their chosen sports—Dianne in rodeo contests and Chris (married to Goondiwindi legend Terry Hall) in campdrafting. They proudly show me their grandson Ben Hall's photo on the cover of *Queensland Country Life*, winning the prestigious Warwick Gold Cup campdraft, for the third time. The love of good horses and winning competitions has been passed down through their bloodline.

'I've always had at least 40 horses in work, but these days I'm down to half that number—not because I'm slowing down, but because the way country racing is run these days has put many people off owning a racehorse. I'm afraid I've seen the best of country racing, and if the same people keep running it the way it is now in New South Wales, the good days will never come back. Some of these blokes just fell out of the sky into positions they haven't got the experience to handle, and they don't know what they're doing with programming. Consequently it's so hard now to get a start for your horses. When the horses are balloted out, the owners are so disappointed. A lot of previously keen owners or syndicate members have given up, because there's too much time between runs, with horses eating their heads off in their stalls waiting for a start. There are 30 to 40 horses nominated for each race at some meetings. We trainers have to drive our trucks all over the place—big distances from out here—to get races for our horses, and there's hardly time to clean the stables.'

The frequent, long trips John takes on, driving his truck himself, is an amazing example of this octogenarian's stamina. A typical week for him nowadays could include at least one midweek trip to Sydney, back to Coonamble, off to Mudgee or Newcastle and back the following day, followed by a drive way out to the far west on the weekend, always arriving home at an ungodly hour—and cleaning stables, feeding, grooming, shoeing and exercising horses in between. 'We country trainers have to work like that to survive now, thanks to the powers-that-be in Sydney. The country race meetings deserve more respect; they are the stepping-stones for both horses and trainers, and provide an opportunity for trainers to get new clients. None of us out here in the bush are happy about how things are run now.'

Still, this racing man, who's experienced the self-satisfaction of leading in more than a hundred winners in a season, could not imagine any other life. The most obvious question—does he have any plans of retiring?—brings a huge, incredulous laugh, as if that was the craziest damn thing he'd ever heard. His eyes are again drawn to the many rows of winning post photos and it's plain to see that racing is not just his living, it's his life.

Watching his eyes pause momentarily on this photo or that, it's impossible to refrain from asking the next obvious question: What was his best horse? 'Well, I just can't answer that. Because if I said Marlotta, or Will Go, or Shady Place, or named any one of all the good horses I've had, the others might look down from the wall and say, "Oh, what about me?"' He laughs, and you can see there is affection and respect for all of these winners on his walls.

Well, it's time to ask the third most obvious question: Is there a secret to his success? From John's formidable wealth of knowledge and experience came the sincere, thoughtful reply: 'You have to have respect for a horse—any horse.' And I dips me lid to that.

TONY DOWTON

The battler

'Dowto', as everyone calls him, is one of life's unforgettable characters: not just a wag and a fun-loving larrikin, but also a one-off individual. In a region where many people fit that bill he manages to stand out. He's the bloke who lifts the atmosphere when he arrives at a party, pub, club, church barbecue, saleyards—anywhere there's a group of people—for Dowto can always be relied upon to say something hilarious or outrageous. That's just the way he is—a master of leg-pulling, baiting and stirring, a bloke who loves life, loves people, and loves a good old laugh.

He featured in my first book *I've Met Some Bloody Wags!* thinly disguised as 'Battlin' Harry'. After its success, my publisher asked me to write a humorous novel about an outstanding, battling outback character. Dowto was the natural choice for the *Battler* series to be modelled on, for he was not only the funniest wag I had met, but also the hardest-working bush battler I'd ever encountered. I'd seen him slaving like most men couldn't even imagine, out in the western sun—not only to survive, but also to educate his five kids. At 79, he's still toiling from sun-up to sundown. The mad bastard should have a four-letter word as his middle name—two four-letter words in fact. His full name should be Tony Hard Work Dowton. Will he ever steady up?

Not many people can lay claim to the fact they held three jobs when aged nine years old! This wiry, lively, Depression-era baby has never had an ounce of fat on his body. All muscle and sinew, he is a walking prime example of Clint Eastwood's weight-loss tip: 'Move more, eat less.' If he was a dog, he'd be a kelpie—rather work than eat. As anyone on a property knows, there's always a never-ending list of jobs to be done, and Dowto has a history of trying to do the bloody lot—on his own . . . but that's another story in this battler's life.

Born on his father's Bugildie Station in the Warrumbungle foot-hills, he grew up on Bundawilla, still in the Coonabarabran district, riding his pony to the tiny Neilrex school. On a recent visit, he received a bit of a shock to discover that the 'huge canyon' he used to ride down was a mere gully, and the 'big river' he crossed, on the way to school, turned out to be a creek. When his father enlisted at the outbreak of World War II, he moved his wife and seven children into Dubbo for the duration of the war because, like most women back then, his wife didn't drive.

Little Tony missed life on the land, and from then on was focused on getting money together to buy his own property. He started out by catching rabbits for the rabbit-oh at threepence each. 'I soon worked out I could catch many more if I bought a ferret, instead of just trapping them, so enlisted my twin brother Peter to help me in my "bunny business". We'd spread nets over the holes leading into their warrens, let the ferret go down a hole, and—holy ghost!— mayhem erupted. You could hear the stampede underground, then they'd start flying out the holes into the nets. Peter and I would rush about, wringing their necks as fast as we could. It was really exciting, except when the ferret would have a feast of kittens [baby rabbits] and go to sleep down there. We'd call and call him—many names besides "Jimmy"—but we always just had to wait till he woke up and came out blinking and yawning, which was infuriating. We couldn't whack him because he might bite our earlobes off, which is what he did to the bloke I bought him from.'

As well as his rabbit dealing, and empty beer bottles scrounged and sold to the grocer for a halfpenny each (to be filled with linseed oil etc.), Tony, at nine years old, was hired by the milko to drive his cart and help deliver milk from 4 a.m., for threepence a morning—later doubled as he was such a reliable worker. 'On Saturday mornings, I did the round on my own, and he trusted me to collect all the money, which people left out on their steps with their billies—can you imagine doing that now? I was so proud of being in charge of his leather cash pouch. It would never have occurred to me in a million years to not hand over every penny when I took the horse and cart back. I was also very proud of my ability to pour the milk out from the cans into the billies without spilling a single drop. Those cranky old housewives would carry on like a pork chop if you did, I can tell you! It was just instilled in us back then, that to waste anything was absolutely wicked and sinful, but I was also proud of doing the job properly. The horse, Sandy, sometimes made that difficult, as he could occasionally be a cantankerous bastard, suddenly taking off. He was probably having a great old laugh to himself as I ran like mad to catch and stop him. Normally he walked under his own steam from house to house, but sometimes he just took off. At least the chase warmed me up on frosty mornings when my hands were so cold—so painful—I could almost cry.'

Tony was to find out what frozen fingers really meant, when he was offered an ice run on Sunday mornings. He ran from the cart with the blocks in a piece of hessian, into houses, and dumped them in their ice-boxes, the predecessors of refrigerators. By the time he was eleven he was doing the milk run before primary school and on Saturdays, the Sunday ice run, and a paper run after school on Wednesdays. While other kids were out playing, he was working, even making time, somehow, in between his jobs plus chores to help his mother, to catch bunnies and collect beer bottles as well. His bank account for his own property was building up steadily.

A good source of beer bottles was the late Saturday arvo band concerts in the park, where soldiers, billeted in the big army camp, would take a couple of quart bottles of beer in a bag. When they became half-cut, and were either fighting or snogging sheilas on a picnic rug, Tony would swoop on their empties to cash them in. When the Yanks hit town, he was on a roll. He'd stand with his head on one side, staring at them groping and pashing the local smitten females, until they would finally say, 'Scram, kid!' He'd reply cheekily, 'It'll cost yer, soldier!' and they'd toss him a florin or a crown, whereas the Aussie soldiers used to chuck him just sixpence to 'Bugger off!' When they were earning 6 shillings and sixpence a day, Tony was earning an average of at least 8 shillings.

At school he was bright at sums but always in strife for high spirits, frequently having his arse cheeks soundly caned by the Christian Brothers of De La Salle. In retaliation, the night he finished school there, he went back with the axe he used to chop firewood for his mum and ringbarked the big pine tree in front of the office. When he refused to attend the Catholic high school and went to the state high school instead, his devout mother was ostracised from her church by the bishop, a whisky-loving hypocrite who lived like a king and drove around in a huge flash Buick.

Naturally, he wanted to work on the land immediately on leaving school, but his mother insisted he get a trade. From a long line of hopefuls who applied for an apprenticeship at Skerman Motors, Tony scored the job. It was every young feller's dream to be working on the big beautiful American cars—Pontiacs, Chevs and Buicks. He earned 27 shillings a week there and still had his income from rabbits and bottles, plus his ice and milk runs. The mechanical knowledge he gained that year would stand him in good stead all his life in the bush, even though most people who know him would tell you his vehicle repair kit usually consists of lumps of No. 8 and tie wire.

When his father demobbed and bought a property at St George—Bidgonbar—Tony was off like a rocket, back to the stockwork he had loved as a child. Hard as nails, Fred Dowton extracted every ounce of sweat he could out of his keen-as-mustard, energised son, who

Bill Hammond with his brothers and fellow fishermen hauling in the catch.

With a jewfish.

Still going strong at 94.
(Photo: Linda Marney)

Sid Martin in World War II,
before Changi.

Sid at 94.

John and Dulcie Charman.

John, enjoying his 90th birthday
party.

Mary Barry, Queensland's most popular publican. (Photo: Dalby Herald /APN)

Mary with 1986 Harvest Festival Charity Queen, Kerri Jurgs.
(Photo: Dalby Herald/APN)

Kevin Hopkins with his first child, Robert.

Bringing back memories.

Des Morrison as a patrol officer in the Northern Territory in the 1950s.

Des after receiving his Canadian Special Service Medal, 2007. (Photo: Country Design & Print, Nanango)

Pat Mumford
(second from left) with
his bomber crew in
World War II.

Wool-classing back at
Mogriguy.

Flo and Joh's wedding
day, 1952.

At Bethany.
(Photo: Helen Cameron)

John Lundholm on Boomerang at the Sydney Show in the early 1950s.

John, snr, and John, jnr.

willingly slaved—ringbarking, fencing, yardbuilding—to improve Bidgonbar and the two nearby places he also bought, Peppercorn and Crescent Vale. When he cut fence posts at 22 shillings a hundred for his father, he realised the old man was rejecting many of them, to avoid paying him but still using them, so Tony started cutting the rejected ones in half! He earned a thousand pounds picking up dead wool, a dreadful job, and learnt to shear on dead sheep. His father then gave him a start shearing on a block he'd bought down near Moree, in temperatures up to 115 degrees Fahrenheit. While racing to shear his first hundred for the day after two weeks at it, Tony cut a sheep's jugular vein. 'Throw it down the chute, quick!' yelled the shearer next to him. When his father saw it, he sacked him on the spot and hunted him off the place without any pay for his two weeks' toil.

Still just sixteen years old, Tony was often out on the stock routes on his own, shepherding the mobs his wheeling-dealing father had bought. 'I was so tired once, I went to sleep on my horse and the bloody sheep got away into the thick mulga; took me ages to get them together again. I had no cover except an old buggered piece of tarp and I remember on one really wet night walking to a mailbox on the stock route and climbing in to try and get some sleep. Some nights I was bloody terrified because I'd seen too many horror movies when we lived in Dubbo. Even when a mob was so big that the old man would put Aboriginal drover Bossie McKewan on to help me, I still often had the breeze up 'cos old Bossie was not only deaf as a bloody rail but you could only see the whites of his eyes at night. The old man paid me the least amount he could get away with, of course, so for extra money I helped neighbours catch wild cattle that ran in the dense scrub around the Boatman Road area—a thrill a minute. Where all that really thick scrub was around St George is now all open buffel country, worth a fortune, thanks to those marvellous machines called bulldozers, and to my good mate John Beardmore, who started off the first buffel grass experiment there. Apparently dingoes are giving the sheep that are left around there curry nowadays, and are nearly impossible to trap.'

When his twin Peter left his building apprenticeship behind him, they pooled their considerable savings and bought Peppercorn for 5000 pounds from their father. The tight, tough old bugger didn't do them any favours, not only making a good profit out of them, which they found out later, but loading it up with his own sheep as part of the deal. They bought a saw bench and a highly dangerous Hargen saw, which had an unguarded spinning blade, to mill cypress they cut and snigged, for a house, woolshed and various sheds. Their father convinced them to also cut timber for new woolsheds for Bidgonbar and Crescent Vale and, typically, didn't pay them properly for their efforts. When they got completely fed up with their father loading up Peppercorn, they sold it and borrowed 7000 pounds from the bank to buy a far better property nearby, Bells Plains.

In the big shearers' strike of 1956, when shearers were black-balled by the Australian Workers' Union for 'scab-shorn' wool, Tony and Peter bought an old Bedford truck to cart their own wool to Moorehead's in Brisbane, a small wool firm. The truck could only carry 30 bales at a time so this entailed many long, long trips over the worst and most boring road in Australia—the road through

Westmar and Moonie—then the terrifying challenge of steering it down the treacherous Toll Bar Range from Toowoomba.

Until the Bells Plains house and woolshed were built more than a year later—naturally the woolshed came first—Peter lived at the comfortable Bidgonbar homestead with Mum's cooking, while Tony chose to sleep in the back of his utility at Bells Plains, to be 'on the job at first light'.

Since Tony had married in 1954, he'd found himself increasingly toiling by himself while Peter was in town chasing sheilas, and he eventually decided to go out on his own. The only country he could afford was in the Western Division of New South Wales, marginal, largely scrub-covered semi-arid sheep country. Rugby was a soldier-settler's block, cut from the massive Dunumbral Station, between Collarenebri and Lightning Ridge. 'The shiny-arsed dills in Sydney who cut the blocks off as a reward for our returned men made them far too small. They should've been 30000 acres, not 15000. I knew we'd have a struggle for a fair while, but I was confident I could make a go of it and eventually buy more country. We arrived at Rugby in our old truck on a freezing July night in 1960, with four little kids, only to find there was no power. The vendor's promise to fix the generator didn't hold up—neither did his agreement to destock the place a month before we arrived. The lying bastard had loaded up the place with 5000 sheep instead, and eaten it out. When I saw him in Collarenebri I went across the road to knock his block off, and he ran like a frightened rabbit. He dressed like a real mug lair and I can still see his highly polished shoes flying through the puddles on the road as he tried to get away from me.'

Tony's boxing skills were almost called on again when he was forced to take his sheep out on the stock route, due to the lack of feed. The sheep forced their way through a broken fence into a wheat crop and he and his dogs struggled for a fair while to get them out. When the wheat cocky roared up on his motorbike, furious, the resigned battler said, 'Before you take a swing at me, mate, hang on till I take me teeth out—I can't afford a new set.' He popped them in his pocket then shaped up, but he'd already knocked the wind out of the cocky's sails, and they ended up good mates.

Further down the track, he was forced to camp the night between two watercourses, in pouring rain. As he heard, and felt, the rain driving down onto the tattered canvas over his swag, he knew that if it kept up all night, his sheep could be trapped and, being near full-wool, possibly drown. In his precarious financial state, that would mean certain ruin for him. As the rain continued, Tony became so terrified, so distressed that all his mighty efforts to get where he had flogged himself to be might be washed away, so he prayed, then he broke down and cried with fear . . . something so alien to him, it shocked him to the core and he has never forgotten that terrible night.

The rain stopped. With his first-class dogs, his only helpers, he managed to get his sheep out at first light, after cutting a fence (which, of course, he repaired) to get them up onto a ridge. Another furious cocky, another removal of the precious dentures, and, eventually, another friendship made. Dowto's personality would always win the day for him. It was also plain for anyone to see that although he was obviously a battler, he was a decent type.

He drove his sheep, alone, for fourteen months until it rained at Rugby. During that time he'd return home for a day or two whenever possible, to attend to chores at home and see his family. His first year had been a pretty accurate introduction to the drought-stricken area he'd moved to. His life from then on was to revolve around managing drought, a skill few, if any, men could match him at. Tony has always started feeding his stock as soon as they look like they're getting a bit hungry, not waiting till they're getting poor, as many graziers do. Feeding sheep out in that western country back then meant cutting scrub. Those early chainsaws were heavy to hold up for hours at a time, but he was fit for that sort of work from swinging an axe ringbarking to clear Rugby, mostly on his own, sometimes with a team when he could afford them. 'A good stockman looks after his stock. Blokes who let stock starve to death instead of feeding them, or moving them to where there's feed, shouldn't be allowed to own animals. I rarely lose a beast in a drought. I make money in droughts.'

By 1962 Tony had five kids to feed and educate. ('Well, we didn't have TV, remember . . .') That was a mighty challenge for a man on 15 000 acres in the Western Division, but he was just the man to battle on, survive, and succeed. A master of improvisation, there was no waste on the property or in his household, but they ate well and were a happy close family. All his daylight-to-dark slaving was for them. His plan was to gradually buy three more properties for his three sons, and operate as a family company.

Like many bush kids, his children were happy galloping their horses around their scrubby domain. 'They used to always want to be out in the paddocks with me, rather than doing their school-work. Their mother had a hell of a job sometimes getting them back inside. The little buggers'd pelt rocks at the mailman so he couldn't get out of his truck with their correspondence lessons.' They also loved to hear their father's imaginative stories at night. ('A giant wild boar attacked me at the bore drain today.' 'Yeah! What'd yer do, Dad?' 'I had to stab him in the throat with my shears.' 'Yeah! Geez, Dad, wish we'd seen that!')

He did come very close to death once, when his horse fell at the gallop. Tony's foot was caught in the stirrup, and when it got up the horse took off, dragging him and kicking at him. Sure he was going to die, Tony mentally took stock of his insurance situation. Three times the horse stopped, but as soon as he tried to undo the girth or get his foot out it would bolt again. Eventually the stirrup leather came off and he lived to tell the tale. Three weeks later, when his neck was still sore, an X-ray revealed he was a hair's breadth from a broken neck, and he wore a brace for several months.

Over the years many men, even experienced stockmen, tried but failed to meet the challenges of that harsh Western Division country, but Tony understood it—what it could do, and what it couldn't. In the mid 70s he was able to lease a neighbouring place from a bloke who had no hope of making a go of it, giving him another 16000 acres. Shortly after, another neighbour also got himself into severe strife. Both blokes were from Sydney and hardly knew which end of a sheep the grass came out, but had dreamt of being graziers. 'Their solicitors and accountants should have been shot for letting them buy out there.'

In 1976 Tony went back into debt to buy Bendeena from one of them, after the poor bloke finally let go of his impossible dream. Typically, a drought immediately set in and Tony drove 7200 sheep for ten months on the routes around Warren, smoking a tin of Log Cabin a day. A doctor advised him to give up the 'coffin nails', as he was skin and bone and would surely cark it if he became ill. He was hypnotised in Dubbo, and never smoked again. Shortly afterwards, when he had at last kept a bit of beef on his bones, Tony contracted the debilitating Q fever. If he'd still been a bag-of-bones smoker, he wouldn't have survived.

After 25 years of doing it tough, in 1985 the chance he had been waiting for finally came up—the opportunity to buy some really good country. Although next door to Rugby, Burranbaa sits on a plateau of quality grazing land, attracting more rain and therefore running more sheep per acre—beautiful safe country that he had admired through his boundary fence since arriving in the district. The Western Division produces top-quality medium wool—even on the rougher, scrubby country which Tony had bought earlier—but Burranbaa's pastures produced huge, magnificent sheep.

Tony had always been proud of his family, and proud of his sheep, looking after both and getting them through droughts and floods, with great skill, devotion and, of course, endless toil. Now he was even prouder, if that were possible, for owning a property like Burranbaa had been his life's dream—the vision he'd had in his mind for more than 40 years, during his countless hours of hard, hard yakka. At last, Tony Dowton, the battler, had made it! He was on top of the world, running 25 000 top-quality Merinos, the third-biggest wool grower in the Walgett shire—no mean feat—and getting half-million-dollar-plus wool cheques.

In the halcyon wool days of the late 1980s he was paying an average of more than 95 000 dollars tax per year. Even though two of his sons had not inherited his love of stock and the land and chose to work in town, Tony and another of his sons easily managed his four properties. The family company, Rugby Grazing, was a success, due to Tony's management skills, and was able to ride out the rough times to come. But old habits die hard. He still slaved from dawn to dusk.

'Hindsight's a wonderful thing. I know now I should have been paying blokes to do a lot of the labouring type work, but it never occurred to me not to try to do everything myself. Instead of trying to crutch thousands of sheep on my own, fixing fences, cutting scrub, etc. I should have been out on my bulldozer, clearing my scrub country nonstop, to make it productive. Now the greenies are in charge of every tier of government, it's too late. They've locked up thousands of acres of bloody useless scrub that produce nothing— no produce, no income, nothing. Those ratbags reckon bandicoots are more important than men trying to make a living, to feed and educate their families and feed the country. I'm 79 and I have to ask a 22-year-old girl straight out of university for permission to clear some of my own country. I have to do a time-wasting, expensive chemicals course every few years or I'm not allowed to buy the sheep dip and drench I need and have been using for 60 years. Australia is now being run by unproductive people who are hell-bent on preventing productive people being productive.'

When wool crashed overnight in 1990, Tony's hair literally turned grey, but that was nothing compared to the shock that was in store for him a few years later. Burranbaa, his proudest possession, the jewel in the crown of the little empire he slaved to build up, was sold from underneath him. 'Yes, if I could undo anything I've ever done in my life, it would be putting Burranbaa in my son's name. Hawke, who like all Labor prime ministers hated primary producers, was talking about bringing back probate when I was buying it, that's why I did it. One piece of advice I can pass on to other men on the land is this: you might be able to control your sons but you can't control the girls they marry. Keep everything in your own name and make sure you've protected yourself and your property. These girls arrive with just a bag of clothes and a second-hand bomb, and leave a couple of years later with half of a man's lifetime's work. That is so wrong and it's happening all over the bush. What they did to me put me back 40 years. I lost half of my life. I've ended up back with just the scrubby battler's blocks, still working my guts out to survive, when I should be taking it easy. I've been trying to get back on my feet since my mid-60s. That place was part of our family company, to benefit the whole family, not just them. The first thing they did when they sold Burranbaa was buy a new flash expensive car—I was 50 before I bought my first Fairlane. They've wasted the lot now. I don't know how they sleep at night. I never dreamt of the treachery that was going on behind my back, in their house and mine.'

Despite this crushing blow, Tony's unquenchable spirit of a true battler has kept him sane, and focused as always on looking after his sheep to the best of his ability, and producing the best quality wool he can. His pride in his stock and his wool ('150 bales now instead of 600, buggerit!') keeps him going. He can't afford to employ a stationhand so he still toils all day every day, still cuts scrub during the regular droughts, still saves every flyblown and bogged sheep he finds.

Most importantly, though, he still enjoys life and laughter. 'I nearly went mad, nearly did a couple of desperate deeds while all I thought about was revenge. Being terrified of going to jail was the only thing that held me back. My anger and frustration at losing Burranbaa was hard to put behind me, but a good mate helped me to look forward instead of back. You can't undo the past. When I'm buggered from hard work and look back at what happened, my mate's advice snaps me out of my "hate sessions" and keeps me going. That advice was to focus on remembering that I still have a lot more than a lot of people: I have my land, such as it is, and my sheep, good dogs to wheel the buggers in the bloody scrub, and my sense of humour. A good feed of chops whenever I want, and plenty of good mates. I have to be grateful for all that, and get on with life.'

Tony Dowton is one of life's achievers. His greatest prize might have been taken from him, but he can look back on a life full of satisfying milestones. A popular personality in the Ridge, he can take much of the credit for the establishment of the town's famous, impressive bowling club. 'A few of us back in the early 60s wanted to build a place where we could take our wives for a drink away from the rough language, brawls and wild shenanigans at the pub, the Diggers Rest. Plus, as cockies, we wanted to do something for the town, our town, such as it was. We all guaranteed a thousand pounds each to kick the club off, held working bees, and built our club. The publican tried every dirty trick in the book to stop us getting a licence, but we eventually made it. There were plenty of big drinkers in the Ridge to keep both bars busy, I can tell you.'

As the first president Tony astounded the district by inviting the governor-general to open the club. Lord Casey's visit was a huge, memorable milestone in changing the rough-as-guts opal-mining settlement into a proud, progressive community. 'I wanted to show we weren't all hillbillies out here, that we could put on a really flash turnout, so I decided we should have a roast pig with an apple in its mouth at the governor-general's luncheon. My neighbour Steve Thorne and I shot sixteen pigs between us along my bore drain, and kept measuring their snouts, trying to get one with a shortish snout, so they wouldn't realise it was a wild grunter they were about to tuck into. If only the old G-G had known what we'd been up to! He and Lady Casey, who was a real stuffy old sheila, were most impressed, so I think we got away with it.'

Dowto tells a good yarn and loves making people laugh with stories of the wild, rough old days of the Ridge. Let's hope he's around for a long while yet, to pass them on, and keep enjoying life.

Postscript: Since this chapter was written, 'the battler' has had the last laugh: he sold his most recently acquired property for a handsome profit and is finally enjoying freedom from debt—every battler's dream. He still runs Merinos on his 10 000-acre 'hobby farm'.

PAUL CALOKERINOS

The last dinki-di Greek cafe owner?

His hands move swiftly, confidently, for he has constructed this fantastic masterpiece many, many times. To watch him at work is to enjoy his art . . . the art of feeding a hungry human. Not with a stir-fry, pasta, tapas, omelette or quiche, for the person waiting to demolish his devoted effort is a bloke from the bush, and he wants a 'proper feed'. He has put his trust in the professionalism of the cafe owner, to meet, and perhaps exceed, his appetite's expectations, for he knows the Greek man will know—as so many of his countrymen have known for more than half a century—exactly what an Aussie country bloke wants on his plate.

Half a bullock is sizzling on the hotplate. The smell of the onions frying around it is torture to the waiting man, whose sweat-stained Akubra sits on the floor beside his well-worn RM Williams work boots, like an obedient dog. The Greek man knows what that heavenly fragrance will be doing to him, and represses a small, knowing smile as he gets on with his work.

From the corner of his eye, he sees the customer demolish the bread roll like a king tide devouring a sandcastle, and again he enjoys a little private smile, which this time is slightly sad. His magnificent homegrown olive oil sits unwanted on the table—the man has naturally opted for the butter pats. Only city visitors seem to appreciate the significance of the choice offered. One day, maybe not in his time, but one day, all Australians will go for the product he is so proud of. Still, the puzzled expressions of the bushmen, when glancing at the bowl of oil, always brings a little humour into his day.

On an oval plate that would hold a fair-sized dog, he deftly arranges the salad—traditional, of course: lettuce, tomato, onion, beetroot, corn kernels, grated carrot. He pushes all that closely together before patting a generous serve of mashed potato nearby— the edible bed that the sizzling bullock will soon recline upon. Bewdiful! A match made in heaven. But wait, there's more . . . A cloak of golden brown onions for the gorgeous beast, a perfect fried egg placed reverently on top—bright yellow yolk the hue of happiness. Then the jewels in the crown are finally added: at least 53 fat, golden chips—proper chips—proudly positioned on the fourth floor of this culinary edifice. A big piece of baked pumpkin stands to attention, glued to the beef, half a pannikin of peas are pushed into the mash, while six mushrooms take up the opposite side, like bollards at the edge of the plate. Every centimetre of crockery surface is covered. It's quite amazing, but it's not finished . . . Ah, the *pièce de résistance* . . . a fried pineapple ring—for 'something sweet'—is put into place with the skill of a CWA cake decorator.

No brand-new father, no Olympic gold-medal winner, could outshine the expression of immense pride on this architect's face, as he carries the tray bearing that splendid meal to the hungry bushman. Is that a tear in his eye as he looks up at his lifesaver? Generosity—the pleasure of giving—radiates from the Greek man's face, savouring the spellbound expression of his guest as he gazes in sheer wonder at the sight before him. Naturally, he grabs a chip first, but before consigning it to its 'interior decorating' career path, he manages a heartfelt and eloquent: 'Thanks, mate. That'll shut the old tapeworm up.'

With those poetic, beautiful words threatening to overwhelm him, the Greek man gives a small bow, saying, 'Enjoy your meal,' and returns to his beloved hotplate. At this point he often enjoys a little speculation as to whether the customer will manage to consume his entire construction, but seeing this chap is big enough to hold a water buffalo out to pee, he has a pretty good hunch that his plate will come back almost clean enough to put straight back into the cupboard.

Paul Calokerinos glances around his cafe. The other customers are all happy with their gigantic hamburgers, generous toasted sangers, gorgeous cakes, pots of good coffee or delicious malted milkshakes. He doesn't do so many of the traditional 'Greek cafe' big meals lately. Except for his customers who are on the land, still doing hard physical work, he's found that most people eat less these days, because they work less.

Like so many of the migrants who came out to Australia after World War II, Paul knows all about hard yakka. Hard work put him on his feet, and took him to well-deserved prosperity. The Greek post-war migrants, in particular, saw a business opportunity in feeding meat-hungry Aussies, out in isolated rural regions where many others did not want to settle. They had the guts and enterprise to go out to places like Bourke, Hay, Walgett, Cunnamulla, Longreach and Moree—places that were hot as hell, with flies, dust, dirt roads, almost no entertainment or cultural life—and they provided a service for the bush people. They set up their cafes to feed them when they came into town, and to cater for travellers—staying up till all hours.

It's hard for anyone less than 50 to try and imagine what it was like back in the 1950s and 60s, travelling out west, driving for endless hours over rough-as-guts dirt roads in a basic sedan with no air-conditioning. Just put yourself in that picture, if you can. You hope to make a town like Bourke or Longreach or Katherine by dark, but you might get a flat tyre, or the radiator keeps boiling over, or you hit a roo and are limping along at 40 miles an hour. There's no mobile phone, of course. By the time you crawl into town, everyone's in bed. The pub's shut, there's no motel. But wait . . . there's a light on in the main street. The Athena, or the Paragon, or the Rose, is still open—oh joy! It's 10.30 at night in Woop Woop, but Nick, Con or Dimitri are still there, waiting to feed the lonely, exhausted traveller. The lifesavers of the bush, they were . . . nearly all gone now. But Paul is a stayer, giving people who visit his Canberra cafe at Manilla, near Tamworth, a glimpse into the past. Memories flood back as you walk through the door, of Saturday nights before or after the flicks, or a great, memorable meal after a long journey on dirt roads.

'Back then most cafe proprietors came from the island of Kythera—my birthplace—whereas the cinema owners and hoteliers nearly all came from Lesbos or Kasterlorizo. There was a lot of migration after the war, because life was so hard in Greece. Relatives who came to Australia wrote home to their families about the wonderful opportunities out here and sponsored family migration. Most, if not all, Greek people did well because they were prepared to work very long hours.' [Before World War I, most Greeks migrated to the US. Eight of Paul's grandparents' children emigrated and they never saw them again.]

'Greece had been dragged into World War II when the Italians attacked in 1940, and we were winning, but then the Germans invaded us through Serbia and Bulgaria and occupied our country for four years. They treated the Greek people extremely harshly. I was twelve when the war ended, and I remember it all very clearly, especially the joy we felt when we saw the British parachuting in to help us. Then their navy sailed into Kythera and their guns kept the German planes away.

'My father had been fighting for six years. I was lucky because we lived on a farm and always had plenty to eat, unlike a lot of other people during those terrible years. We grew olives, vegetables, wheat and grapes. We had goats and sheep, and bullocks to plough the fields. We made everything, from olive oil, to bread and cheese. As a boy I always helped with the work, including building stone walls and topping up our clay roof. When I left school at fifteen I took on more of the farmwork.

'My uncle Bill had emigrated to Australia and started a cafe in Tamworth, the Golden Bell. Then he bought a taxi and the Post Office Hotel. In 1948 Uncle Bill sponsored me out here by paying my fare, which was 400 pounds—a lot of money back then. I was very sorry to leave my homeland, but by then there were many Kytherians in Australia, and my uncle painted me a dazzling picture of what could be achieved here, through hard work. There were plenty of jobs, but naturally he already had work for me.'

Paul's journey Down Under became an even bigger adventure than the fifteen-year-old had imagined. 'I stayed in Athens for three nights with my father before catching my plane. It was a 30-seater four-engine aircraft which only flew in daylight hours. Because it had engine problems, what should have been a seven-day journey to Sydney ended up taking 30 days! Our first stop was Karachi, where I saw a mozzie net for the first time in my life, then to Calcutta, where I stayed in a huge hotel of 400 rooms which amazed me even more than the mozzie nets. I tasted beer there for the first time in my life. Next stop was three days at a British hotel in Singapore, where I was surprised by barbers working in the street, and tasted my first apple. Funny how the impact of those first impressions stays with you throughout your life. Then on to Java where, because of that dodgy engine, we experienced an emergency landing on a jungle airstrip, then waited for two weeks for another plane to collect us.

'We were taken to an army camp, and the women passengers were not happy when they saw the big tents with hammocks. Meals there were a complete mystery—you wouldn't know what you were eating. At last, a plane collected us and we were finally up, up and away . . . to Australia—the land of opportunity. How exciting it was to land in Darwin, first port of call at our new country. Best of all, we were taken to a Greek-owned hotel and were so happy to eat Greek food again. We waited there a week. Fortunately it was June so the weather was lovely.' The impression Paul gained during his look around Darwin was summed up in one word: 'rough'.

To Brisbane overnight, then to Sydney, which he didn't get a good look at, as he'd been booked on a five-seater commuter plane leaving that day for Tamworth. His first impression of Tamworth: 'a nice place'. He had his uncle's address on a piece of paper in his pocket to give to a taxi driver—Paul did not speak English then. As it turned out, the taxi he caught was owned by his Uncle Bill, who soon had Paul learning English from a book, and from enforced English conversation.

Less than a month after he arrived, in July, Paul was sent up to Walcha to work for Bill's brother-in-law, who owned the cafe there. It was freezing on the forbidding New England Tableland and Uncle Bill lent him 25 pounds to buy warm clothes, of which he had none—no long trousers, no jumper, no coat. The energetic teenager was 'generously' allowed to warm up during the bitter cold of each early morning by chopping wood for the stove that created the hot water. There was no hot water until 11 a.m.—an icy experience very new to the boy from the Greek Islands.

It was a busy cafe and Paul was immediately thrown in at the deep end, learning everything about the business—even how to cook. He was only supposed to be preparing the vegetables, but at really busy times he would be told to throw a steak and onions on the hotplate, with intermittent instructions on how to cook it to the customer's liking. Nearly everyone ordered steak, which was cheap at the time—around 2 shillings (20 cents) a pound. He was fascinated with the Indigenous customers, who came in to buy vegetables. And he loved the sight of the beautiful array of cakes. Everything was a new experience.

While working in chilly Walcha, Paul's grasp of English was improved greatly by an old Greek man who worked in the cafe, and a Syrian man who ate there every day. After eighteen months, he was sent to Uncle Bill's new Ritz Cafe in Tamworth, to complete his 'apprenticeship'. Saving most of his wages, the teenager was already planning to buy a business of his own.

'In 1950, another brother-in-law of Uncle Bill's sold his two cafes to him, the Canberra and the New York in Manilla. I was sent to run the New York and my cousin John Travasaros, who had travelled out from Greece with me, took over the Canberra. Uncle Bill came and went, keeping an eye on things. He had five cafes by then. His timing was very good—a lot of men moved to Manilla to work on the Keepit Dam, earning good money and reluctant to cook for themselves.'

When the dam was completed in 1961, business plummeted and Uncle Bill closed the New York cafe. Paul and his cousin John continued to run the Canberra for him and soon managed to save enough to buy him out. They quickly learnt: keep the customers happy and they keep your cash register ringing.

'The locals had previously been overcharged for cigarettes, and they certainly appreciated our fairer prices. Everyone smoked back then and cigs were hard to get after the war. There was a quota system. The brands were Wills, Craven A, Ardath, Capstan, Turf, 333's, and Champion tobacco, fine cut or a solid plug. In the mid 50s, Rothmans King Size came on the market and immediately took most of it. People loved that extra bit of nicotine for their 2 shillings [20 cents], which was roughly what a packet of smokes cost then. It wasn't just the cigarettes we sold for a reasonable price—John and I offered value for money with everything that kept our cash register ringing. Volume turnover is more important than trying to make big profits on some items and turning customers off.'

'Life was looking very rosy for me in my new country, and I had the confidence to fly back to Greece in 1961 for a holiday. I saw a very beautiful girl, Helen, who was eighteen. She had only been a small child when I left Kythera. I proposed, she accepted and we married in 1962. Helen settled beautifully into life in an Aussie country town, learning English very quickly. She liked Manilla immediately. We didn't waste much time producing three children: Kathy, Mary and John.

'Then my cousin decided to buy the Acropolis in Tamworth, and I was finally—at last!—the owner of my own cafe. I was pleased I had stuck with the Canberra, as I had no opposition and did very well. I didn't want to go to a bigger, busy town and I was confident I could have a successful business in Manilla. It's a very nice town, and the people were lovely, too—they had been very good to John and me.

'When I took over the Canberra on my own, I could make all business decisions myself, and immediately improved the business by offering a free cup of tea and free bread with all meals. I began selling fruit and veggies at the front of the cafe, and added a "milk bar", selling milkshakes, sundaes and hamburgers. That was what the young people wanted. A great night out for them was a night at the pictures or a dance. Their social life didn't revolve around the pub. The pictures were on four nights a week, always attracting big crowds, and during interval at 9 p.m. we would be swamped with people. It was all hands on deck, including the children, who were a great help to us in the cafe from when they were small. They enjoyed helping. The customers naturally made a fuss of them.

'The people were wonderful—happy, polite and friendly. The only time anyone said anything rude or caused trouble—and that was rare—was when the pub closed at 10 p.m. There was a golden rule amongst drinkers and fighters that you never hit the bloke behind the counter, but if I was worried about customers in the cafe who were drunk I would ring my friend Phillip Fearous, who could fight like a thrashing machine. He would come round and call them outside into the street—sometimes taking on more than one bloke at a time—then sort them out pretty smartly, bearing in mind that they were drunk and he was sober. In those days if the police arrested someone for being drunk, their friends or family had to pay 10 shillings and sixpence to bail them out next morning. There were four pubs in Manilla then.

'Boxing was very popular at school there. The rules were "no hitting below the belt, no kidney punches and if someone's down on the ground, don't kick them". A feller who was nicknamed "King" was a terrific fighter—no one could beat him. He challenged Phillip Fearous to a fight to the death—no rules—in the main street outside the Canberra Cafe. A big crowd gathered, but "King" didn't turn up. We sold plenty of soft drinks and ice creams while they waited.

'The Canberra Cafe was a big part of everybody's life, but by the 1980s the movie theatre had unfortunately closed down, which had an impact on our business. I bought a nice little farm out of town and started closing the cafe on Sundays, for the first time. Instead of living in town right near the cafe we were 5 k's out, on 135 peaceful acres. It cost us 1000 dollars per acre, which was a lot to pay then, but it was ideal to grow olives, which I'd always wanted to do, and it had a nice big house on it. I was very lucky to buy the 1200 acres next door in 1994, before prices went crazy.'

A qualified chef with a business diploma, son John, now 34, worked as an executive with Westpac then at the Sydney Stock Exchange, but returned to Manilla ten years ago to run the cafe with his father. Kathy runs high-powered business forums in Sydney. Mary helps in the cafe each day. Paul is also there every day, doing what he loves, talking to the customers and feeding them, or introducing them to his olive products. At 78, he still puts in the long hours, for that is the way of Kytherians. As Paul will tell you, they like to work for themselves, and it comes naturally to them to work hard in business—to make that extra effort.

He is sad that most, if not all, other Greek cafe proprietors in country towns have closed their doors now. 'Most of their Australian-born children did not want to work the long hours their parents did. The cafes in the bush are now run by Asians, who provide cheaper meals because they use less meat than the meals we Greeks used to serve. Times change. I guess I represent the end of an era. It was a great era, and I was fortunate to be part of it. We Greek migrants are all grateful to have the life we've had in Australia, but we have worked hard and contributed a lot to the country's development. Life in Australia, even in a small town like Manilla, is very different now, but I am happy with my olives and making oil and paste, and as long as I can keep working I will still be part of my cafe. My customers always seem so pleased to see me when they come in. There are three generations of locals and other regulars now who know me, and I enjoy seeing the children and grandchildren of my customers growing up. I'm proud of my business, my town, my lovely wife and family and, yes, I am proud of what I have achieved since I arrived in Australia with nothing but energy and ambition.'

Back in 1956, Paul and a local Dutch-born chap went to the shire council to be naturalised (in those days you had to have been in Australia for five years). From then on Paul was a 'local' and was sponsored into the Rotary Club. He became an extremely valuable addition to Manilla Rotary, generous with his time, money and effort for 54 years (and still going), his service culminating in the highest honour in Rotary—a Paul Harris Fellow (Paul Harris was the founder of Rotary).

President of Manilla Rotary Club, Scotsman Sandy Allan, businessman and another Aussie migrant success story, kindly contributed these comments: 'Paul's business interests extend a lot further than his cafe and farm, but I know he would be too modest to talk about just how well he has done. His admirable business acumen is matched by his generosity. He is a genuine humanitarian, and has done more to help people in this district than most people know about. A great and loyal citizen, he boosted and promoted confidence in the future of this town, in leaner years when a positive future for most small country towns was not easy for others to see. For more than half a century, he has contributed overwhelmingly to Rotary projects, and his catering for our club is the envy of many others.

'When I came here to set up my business, he took me under his wing, guiding and advising me. He predicted accurately that my "probation" would last about twelve months before I was fully accepted into the community. If you asked the people of Manilla to describe him in one or two words, "true friend", "mentor", "reliable confidante", "quiet achiever", "smart", "wise", "modest" and "generous" would be repeated many times. I am honoured to contribute to his story and proud to know Paul as a unique and true friend.'

Now that you know Paul and his family, there's no reason why you shouldn't stop and call in to the cafe next time you're within cooee of Manilla. A warm welcome awaits you.

TOBY GRANT

A life with trotters and Telecom

'Life's good here,' says Toby Grant about his hometown of Manilla in north-eastern New South Wales. 'We've got a nice quiet spot, we're near the river, plenty of room for the horses, and to grow our veggies. Plenty of friends—of course, we know everyone. Having lived here nearly 80 years now, I've learnt that the worst place to say "G'day, how are you?" is the doctor's surgery, where all the oldies are looking for a chance to tell you all about their aches, pains and complaints. They drive me bloody mad—I don't want to become like that when I'm old.'

I have a good long laugh at that last comment, because Toby is 79, and has more injuries than most of these 'oldies' put together. But he does admit that when he hits the cot at night, the old injuries start to 'talk' to him. So, I wonder, what are they saying? Well, they're actually telling the story of this amazing man's life . . .

'First the middle back starts to throb, like it does after I've been shoeing horses, and I remember the first horses I shod as a gullible kid, for a rogue called Monty. He sat back while I did all his work shoeing heavy carthorses; I was so grateful for the *experience* he was giving me. I thought he was so *generous* to let me be the first to ride the horses he broke in, while he sat back to see how hard they'd buck. Boy, what a mug I was, but at fifteen, keen as mustard on horses, I was ripe to be used—being pelted off again and again while that cunning Monty made out he was doing me a favour, helping me learn how to ride buckjumpers.

'I move around real steady in my bed to get in the best possie to manage the back pain, then try to doze off, but—bugger!—my hips start to ache, and I remember vividly the day racing at the Tamworth trots, when a drunk driver crashed into me to shove me out of my winning position. He hit me with such force, causing me to land so hard on the track on my backside, that I thought—when I regained consciousness—my back was broken. But the ambo gave me the all-clear, my wife and daughter helped me off the track and I went home, staying in a hot bath all night to ease the pain. I hobbled to the doctors, hobbled to the X-ray, then finally they saw I had a cracked spine and a cracked pelvis and told me not to walk another step. Six weeks on a board bed, before I could return to work.

'I turn on my stomach, trying to get comfortable. Ah, there goes the old neck pain, from that day way back when my daughter Julie was a toddler and a runaway horse and sulky went over the both of us. As it raced towards us, I only had time to grab both sides of the horse's bridle and heave it off balance. We both crashed to the ground and the last thing I saw was the steel-rimmed wheel about to go over Julie. After I regained consciousness, I was vaguely aware that I had probably seriously damaged my neck, but I was naturally panic-stricken whether she had survived. What a relief to see her in my brother Kevin's arms! He'd pulled her to safety just in time. A couple of days later I went to the doctor, telling him if I even slightly moved my neck I started to cry, which was very strange for me and extremely upsetting. He shocked me by telling me I was still in shock and that was a symptom. He said, "Toby, I've patched you up many times, but this is the first time that one of your family has been involved. You saw one of your children about to be run over. That has affected you more than you realise."

'I move over a bit in bed and—ouch! The arm that was the first thing to hit the trotting track when I was tipped out one night is giving me curry. I can still see my mate's horse stamping on the arm, as he flew past me, then see myself trying to curl in a ball as a couple of horses and gigs go over the top of me. Two steel plates and 21 screws mended the arm that Frank's horse smashed in three places. I'm grateful for the advancement in surgery, but I have to say I hope the "reminder" I experience some nights doesn't increase in volume . . .

'But the worst pain I ever felt has to be the busted collarbone. A young horse I was breaking in and cantering for the first time, outside the yard, started bucking when a cloud of grasshoppers suddenly shot up all around us. He was really into it, high in the air, when suddenly his front leg collapsed under him as he came down. His full weight crashed sideways on top of me. The off-side stirrup iron swung round and knocked me out—a free dose of anaesthetic. I've busted most of my bones but, I can tell you, a busted collarbone is very, very painful.

'The last crash a few months back, the biggie, that put me on a private jet—flash, eh?—to get me head cut off—weeell, close enough to it . . . That injury gives me the least of my worries now, funnily enough. Those doctors at John Hunter [Hospital, in Newcastle] are bloody amazing—they peeled me scalp back, hammered a steel plate on the old skull, then riveted it back over, like fixing a motor.

'If someone had been at the track with a video camera I could've ended up on TV—buggerit!—because it would've been pretty spectacular, with the gig tipping me out on my head when the colt shied violently at full pace, then me skiing along behind him hanging on to the reins, everything in a hell of a tangle. When you're 78, and you've been doing the trots for 60 years, you think you've had enough experience to see things coming, but that happened so fast, and next thing I know . . . no more trotting races for Toby.

'Horses can knock you about, but I had a lot of fun, thrills and adventures with them, in between trips in the ambo. Now I pay for all that enjoyment, when I try to get comfy in the burrow. Oh, well, at least I'm still above the ground.'

Toby Grant is a born and bred horseman, a real rarity these days. Both his father and grandfather were outstanding, all-round horsemen, and Toby's brother, uncles and cousins weren't short on skills either. It's in his blood—and his broken bones. But despite the lifetime of hard work, pain and injuries he has endured from 'mucking about' with horses, one thing is certain—he wouldn't have it any other way. Horses have always been the Grants' way of life.

'Dad's father was a Cobb and Co stagecoach driver, and later in life also had a local mail contract. I can still see old Pop trotting off in his sulky with a lantern swinging under it, to collect the mailbags from the night train.

'My grandmother came from a well-to-do family who were horrified that she was marrying a lowly coach-driver. Anyone who earned their living as a horseman—jockeys or horse breakers, for example—were looked down upon in those days. My grandmother worked like a slave from the day she married till the day she died, doing other people's washing and ironing all day and night—the hard way back then, of course. She'd light a fire under a big metal tub, "the copper", swirl the clothes back and forth with a special strong stick, wring them out by hand, rinse them in two big galvanised tubs of water, wringing them this time through the rollers of an old mangle, which wasn't easy to push, especially with large items like trousers or sheets going through, then peg them on the old clothesline held up by wooden forky sticks or props, as they were called. Anything white was dunked up and down, after rinsing, in a tub of Reckitt's Blue, which miraculously turned them even whiter, not bluer. Good clothes and items of household linen took even more time and effort: they had to be starched in a tub containing Silver Star Starch. It was heavy work. She would be absolutely exhausted, poor lady—all for a few shillings. My grandfather enjoyed a drink and she hated hoteliers because she said they take a man's money, get him drunk, then chuck them out.

'My grandparents were renowed for their hospitality—their home was like a coach depot and somehow she managed to feed many people in between her other toil. A lantern was always set outside their house every night for people arriving late to find their way in. My grandmother also reared my oldest brother. She must have had boundless energy.

'I was brought up in a completely different world from the Australia of today. I was one of seven children and we lived in a tin shed. Times were hard but we were happy. When I was very young, my dad, who was a self-taught saddler, made a little leather horse for me, and my mother sewed a little rug and nosebag for it. Dad even put a little bit of chaff in the nosebag. A gift that cost them nothing but was a priceless treasure, for it was made with their own hands . . . and love. You don't forget those things.

'My father could ride and break in anything on four legs; the worst outlaws would not beat him. As a child at the local show, holding my trembling mother's hand, I saw him compete on a very nasty horse he owned, jumping over 7 feet 5 inches, squealing in pain with a broken ankle. He could also build beautiful sulkies or improve other people's inferior sulkies.

'What they would now call "a legend", Dad was christened Donald after his father, but was well-known throughout the district as "Darkie"—a much-loved character. I am proud of the poem and song written about him—'Darkie Grant's Mail Run'. Jim Bignall wrote it and Stan Koster put it to music. Dad's mail run, which he held for 33 years, was known as "the Retreat run"—Retreat Station was at the end of it. As a little kid I loved to accompany Dad in his sulky, going from station to station, yarning and joking with the stationhands when we'd be changing fresh horses, plus the rabbiters and swagmen we'd see on the track.'

Toby will never forget the first time he tagged along with his father on a run. As usual, Darkie changed his horses at around 9 p.m. at Glen Barra, before heading off for The Springs and Atholene. (Atholene, incidentally, was the home of famous Australian June Dally-Watkins, nee Skewes.) 'It was such an adventure, trotting along the lonely dirt road in the bush, in the night-time. After dropping off the mailbag, bread and other groceries at The Springs, I noticed he carefully tied down everything that was left. As we proceeded through the night, he kept glancing around as though expecting something to happen. I sensed he was nervous or worried and asked, "What's wrong, Dad?" He said, "Just be quiet, and whatever happens, hang on tight." I started to become worried also, glancing about like Dad, trying to see in the darkness. Suddenly we could hear something crashing through the scrub. Dad pulled the whip and in two strides we were full gallop, with Dad yelling to me, "Hang on!" A dark shape soon emerged on my left, another at the same time on our right. Two horsemen were grabbing at our reins. We skidded to a halt. One said, "This is a hold-up, hand everything over." As Dad threw them a mailbag, I thought it was lucky we didn't have a lot of mail and goods left on board, apart from being terrified what they would do to us. Dad handed a bag of bread and a parcel to the other horseman, who growled, "Is that all?" Dad said, "Yes, you thieving mongrels." Then they suddenly all burst out laughing, fit to bust a gut. "I gave you a run for your money tonight!" Dad said. He told me later the wild young Skewes boys from Atholene often broke the monotony of life out in the bush by "robbing the mail".

'I was named after my dad's brother Gordon. Toby was my nickname 'cos they reckoned my head looked like a Toby jug. Once when Uncle Gordon was visiting from Forbes, he offered to take Dad on the mail run in his car. Because this would save a hell of a lot of time, Dad, who loved grog, took Gordon to the pub for a while, then they set off with plenty of "refreshment" to keep them going on the trip. Dad was excellent at presenting himself as a sober man when he wasn't, so he took the mail and goods into each homestead, leaving Uncle Gordon, who wasn't in good shape, in the car. Glen Barra had new owners who were a bit posh but they really liked Dad. While he was inside being polite, their dogs kept barking up a hullabaloo outside. Dad tried to stop the nice couple from following him out, but failed to do so. There was Uncle Gordon on his hands and knees, barking at their dogs through the fence. All Dad could say was, "I'd like you to meet my brother, Gordon."

'On Dad's one day off, he would repair harness and sulky, and shoe his horses if necessary. Naturally I learnt to do these things. I inherited my skills from Dad, and from an early age I rode all sorts of horses—stockhorses, showjumpers, buckjumpers, trotters and race-horses . . . you name it. My father always said a bad-tempered person can never be a good horseman or horsewoman. He'd say, "Horses are only animals and they get frightened, and they never forget bad treatment." That is so true. I've never forgotten his advice.

'Uncle Bobby taught me to ride buckjumpers and break in young-sters during my early teens. He'd been taught by my father. I rode a lot of young horses that could really buck and I'd think I was the best in the business, but there were quite a few that sent me flying over the rails and then I wasn't so sure. When I'd go home, Dad would notice a bit of bark missing off me, or dirt still on my back, and say with a grin, "What threw you today?" An old neighbour, an ex-rough rider, saw me have a hell of a spill one day, and advised me I was riding with my stirrups too short: "The saddle's throwing you, mate, not the horse." I let my stirrup leathers down and from then on I was literally on top.

'I rode in my first trotting race at a show in 1947. The starter would run backwards from the line-up for 20 metres holding a white hanky above his head, and if the line looked even drop it, hitting his stopwatch at the same time. Then he would walk to the finish line to act as judge, timekeeper and steward. We rode the trotters in races until the early 50s, when gigs came in.

'In those days you didn't have to have a lot of money to ride in shows. People gave you horses to ride if you rode well, because you were giving them experience and also making the horse more valuable if you won prizes. Like my father, I also jumped 7 feet 5 inches in the high jump, which was always the main feature of the Manilla, Tamworth and Barraba shows. I was so proud because, for the first time, my mother was watching. People would toot their horns and go crazy at the Manilla Show if a Grant won something. My brother Kevin, uncles and cousins all competed too, and we rode *hard* to beat each other.

'We all loved the great entertainment provided by the tent rodeos, set up at most shows. There were sharpshooters, whip-crackers, country singers like Tex Morton and Buddy Williams, and some marvellous lady buckjump riders—Violet Skuthorpe, Kitty Gill and Gwen Winter, to name three. Under an open roof, a roped sawdust ring was set up, and locals were invited to try and ride the "star" buckjumper. I first took up the challenge to ride the star horse Ginger Meggs, at Boggabri in 1953, and rode out the time [the full eight minutes]. The showman, Snowy Baker, challenged me to ride him again next night—double or quits—so I turned up and flew on board, full of confidence. Ginger Meggs threw me that high I could've read the newspaper while I was up there. My uncle Bobby saw a blue heeler fly in and grab the horse's leg. Old Snowy must've thought I'd won enough of his money and reckoned between me and his blue heeler, we'd give his customers a real good show.'

Toby left school at fifteen to get a job as a telegram boy for the Postmaster General (PMG), the forerunner of Australia Post and Telecom (later Telstra). He then discovered that if he switched jobs to working nightshift on the telephone exchange, he had all day free to ride horses either with Uncle Bobby or at old Monty's place. 'I didn't get much sleep during those twelve months.'

Working at Monty's—'which was a "do drop inn" place with constant visitors'—was certainly educational, Toby says, recalling a 'blow-in' he met there: 'This young feller was asked to help me lift timber up to the saw bench. He wasn't strong but tried hard and didn't talk much. Turned out "he" was a fourteen-year-old girl, dressed like a bloke. She had just murdered a drover and was trying to hide from the law. The drover had used her as an offsider, dressed as a boy with short hair. When his advances became too insistent, she shot him as he slept in his tent. Fortunately, the Salvation Army took over her welfare after her trial and she eventually married and settled down in Queensland.'

Toby moved on from the exchange job to work for Stoddart and Hayward's big general store, as a pushbike delivery boy. One day the bloke who had the 'cushy' job of driving the store's delivery van around town did his block with the manager and knocked him arse over head. Toby, who was seventeen, asked if he could have the job. In reply to the obvious question 'Can you drive?' he replied, 'Too right I can!' Toby figured he'd been driving horses for years so a van couldn't be all that different.

'The boss's son was a mate and gave me a few lessons in the delivery van down at the town dump. The first time I managed first and second gears, then he taught me how to do a racing change into third. We were heading for a big pile of boxes and I was leaning back, pulling on the wheel and yelling, "Whoa! Whoa!" It felt like we went through the boxes at about a hundred miles per hour, and the boss's son pulled on the handbrake. It was a pretty exciting lesson. Luckily, the local copper had a galloper which I'd ridden for him, so he gave me a driver's licence. Then I learnt to drive on the job, so there were quite a few dents and close shaves.'

While Toby was in the store collecting parcels, he'd 'sneak glances' at Judy, the lovely girl working above in the cashier's office, receiving the cash sent up on the wire and sending the change and docket back down. 'I plucked up courage to ask her out—to the races, of course. Well, I rode four winners, which you'd think would impress any sheila but she didn't seem that impressed! That day an illegal bookie told me that I had a natural talent to prepare winners and I should train racehorses full-time—and many people there agreed. But I already thought that Judy might be the girl I would marry and so I should stick with the steady job I had at the store—for a while at least. There's many men who take on training full-time and come unstuck.

'Judy and I had a three-year courtship before we married. During this time the local PMG line foreman, for whom I'd broken in and worked many Shetland ponies, suddenly sacked his entire gang— all footballers who'd turned up drunk Monday morning—and was looking for replacements. I was terrified of heights but the money was better than at the store and Jude and I were getting serious, so I decided to put my faith in a safety belt, and have a go. I started on the bottom rung, digging the 5 feet deep holes in all sorts of terrain for the telephone poles. Then I'd help to erect the poles, after cutting slots for the crossarms. Everything was done the hard way back then and success relied on teamwork. At the yell "All together!" five men would strain with every ounce of their strength to lift those big poles up into position. Then came the tricky bit— climbing up the 10-metre pole, hauling the crossarms up on a line and bolting them. Nothing was easy.

'When the foreman, Col, had to go along the lines inspecting for poles that needed replacing—usually due to whiteants—he would drive his sulky to give his Shetlands a run. I'd follow in the truck pulling the float. One day some pigs jumped up and startled his pony,

Tony Dowton and Lord Casey in 1967.

610 bales—not bad for a battler. (Photo: Kristin Williams)

Paul Calokerinos behind the lolly counter at the New York.

On the cover of
The Land newspaper
in 2008.

Toby Grant with Coolamon Lass in 1956.

Toby with wife
Judy—a great team!

Hayden Kenny (left), winning the National Iron Man, 1966.
Son, Grant (right), winning the National Iron Man, 1986.

Hayden with the Energex rescue chopper, 2004.

John William Stewart and ringers at Ivanhoe, Kimberley.

John today.

Janie Marshall with her team of toilers. (Photo: Kristin Williams)

Janie on Giggle.

Malcolm McCosker after being
inducted into the Rural Journalism
Hall of Fame in 2010.

Ron Canlin with his underground sculptures.
(Photo: Paul Mathews/Fairfax Syndication)

Sheila Ross during
World War II.

Sheila and her husband,
former Royal Scots
Guard, Graham.

Peter Venables in his jockeying days, late 1940s

Peter driving his beloved team of Clydesdales.

Lesley Webber rescues an orphaned calf at Go Go Station in the Kimberleys, early 90s.

who leapt in the air sideways. Col, who was a very big man, ended up stuck upside-down, headfirst, in the well of the cart, where you'd normally put your feet, while the pony bucked around in circles. Col was yelling, his feet kicking in the air, and I was laughing so much I wasn't much help for a while. Col was not pleased with me.'

A main attraction of Toby's job was having Saturdays off to compete at race meetings. Trotting was starting to become popular, and Toby's aunt gave him a pacer as a reward for handling year-lings at her stud. 'I began to succeed in the trotting game as well as at the gallops. There wasn't time for both so I chose to focus on trotting, as I knew that a bloke of any age and weight could always enjoy the thrill of driving a horse in a gig, whereas once your weight puts you out of riding gallopers, you're out on the side-lines as a spectator.'

He bought a filly called Coolamon Lass and had great success with her. She won 28 times—seven of them in a row, including the mile-and-a-half [2400-metre] Northwest Derby at Broadmeadow, in 1956, worth 200 pounds, by 2 lengths. The *Newcastle Herald*'s report stated:

Coolamon Lass was in a hopeless position in the early stages and it was a real treat to see this reinsman from Manilla show all the skill and judgement required to win against the more experienced drivers of Newcastle and Sydney.

Toby says: 'I certainly felt proud reading that. Judy and I were married by then and I used the money to furnish our house. My wage at the time was 4 pounds a week. Coolamon Lass went on in the next fortnight to win the Gunnedah Cup, and a 100-pound free-for-all at Inverell Show—bloody fantastic it was!

'You can imagine how I was tempted then to train full-time, but with a wife and a mortgage, I felt I could not take the risk of giving up my job and going for it, much as I'd have loved to. My marriage and the thought of becoming a parent one day made me focus instead on giving my job 100 per cent at all times, in the hope of improving my position. So I trained horses in the dark before work, and in the dark again after work. It was worth it. Our four children Graham, Alan, Julie and Debbie were all keen riders when young, but typically of modern times the boys lost interest after discovering cars, while Debbie continued with dressage and Julie with trotting. I am so proud of my children and grandchildren. Judy and I have been blessed, not with monetary wealth, but a happy healthy family which is worth more than all the gold in Fort Knox. I am also proud of what I achieved in my career with Telecom, which I stuck at for them—my family.'

Over the next three decades Toby worked his way up from labourer, to linesman, to cable joiner—a job requiring great precision—to being in charge of an aerial gang. When he was overseeing the changing from manual to automatic lines throughout the district, it didn't really sink in what an historic chapter that represented. He also witnessed the PMG splitting into Australia Post and Telecom—another turning of the tides.

'After twenty years in the job I noticed that young blokes I'd trained were eventually being promoted over my head, so I complained about that. Telecom sent me to do an estimating course, so I could be promoted. I'd never used a calculator in my life and the course was a big challenge, especially when the instructor told us that if we failed the first exam we were out. I felt I shouldn't risk taking that exam and failing, which might give Telecom an excuse to knock me back for advancement in the future. I told my daughter Julie this and she said, "Dad, you always told us to have a go—that's what you should do now." So I had a cup of tea, a big think, and gave it a go. I made it through, and ended up travelling all over the north-west of the state estimating the cost and what is now called "logistics" of jobs. I was also put in charge of a 30-man task force.

'Next step up the ladder was a course to learn "lines recording", which involved reading topography maps, using a compass, and recording all cables as they were installed. This led to my appointment as an A-class estimator. I was then in charge of installing radio communication towers at places like Cumborah, Come-By-Chance, Collarenebri and Lightning Ridge.

'I loved going out to those western places, but on a job at Walgett I was disappointed to see all the beautiful Mitchell grass plains being ploughed up for crops—what a waste of first-class sheep country. At Pokataroo, I was intrigued to hear from an old-timer that in its heyday, it had two barber shops and a picture theatre. An unforgettable experience was being confronted at a Collarenebri homestead by a character pointing a .45 revolver at me and my offsider, demanding to know what we were doing there. Trying to stay calm, I remarked I'd never seen a .45 up so close before. He fired the revolver into a tree with a noise like a cannon and my offsider nearly fainted. Then he invited us in for a cool drink. The western people are very different to the people "down inside", as they'd call our neck of the woods. A lot of them are a bit wild, but all are hospitable.'

After 34 years with Telecom, Toby retired at last, to work full-time with horses. He says that although he has always enjoyed his share of wins on the track, there isn't a lot of money to be made. 'It's a costly hobby. He knows he made the right decision sticking with a regular job while responsible for his children.

'After the wonderful run of success I had with Coolamon Lass, I had a lot of good horses, but it was 40 years—a long wait—before I found another champion. I bought Sunbelle Emily, named after my granddaughter, for just 900 dollars as a yearling because I liked her breeding. She gave me many proud moments but none prouder than when she won the 10 000-dollar New South Wales Sires Stakes at Tamworth Paceway in 1996. As owner-trainer-driver, I was so chuffed to hear the roar of the big crowd cheering me home. You can't describe that thrill to anyone who hasn't experienced it.

'Most of the public attending trotting or race meetings cannot even begin to imagine the huge amount of expense, work and preparation that has gone into getting a horse right for the day. So many things can go wrong after all that work. You just have to accept these big disappointing knocks, get over them, and keep trying.

'Judy has been a most wonderful backstop. In 1964, 40 feet of floodwater from the Namoi flowed through and over our house. Judy was home alone and managed to save the horses and dog. Like all couples we had our ups and downs but we were a great team. For fifteen years, the two of us ran trotting gymkhanas in Manilla for various charities. Many good people helped us—we were all like spokes in a wheel, all pulling our weight, and because of that we never had a dud. Judy and I were invited to a special dinner at the RSL and, to our great surprise, awarded a shield of appreciation for our charity work, with the RSL emblem and our names engraved on it.'

It is amazing, and inspiring, that—as well as his dedication to his work, his horses and above all his family—Toby has also managed to give something back to his community and his sport. He is a life member of the Manilla Pony Club and still enjoys helping out at pony club camps as guest instructor. The Tamworth Harness Racing Club elected him as the first recipient of their 'Outstanding Contribution to Northwest Harness Racing Award'. As well as competing, he has been a racecaller, timekeeper, steward and judge many times throughout the years around the region, and is very proud to have helped a lot of young people get into the sport and succeed.

Amongst his most treasured achievements was being presented with Manilla's Citizen of the Year award in 1997, and when he was honoured by the Manilla Show Society for 50 years of service on the committee with a life membership. 'I was so pleased to be given the opportunity to experience receiving that recognition—many people don't receive recognition for their efforts and achievements until after they're dead, when it's too late.'

The obvious final question to Toby had to be about all those broken bones, all that pain, even almost getting his head cut off— was it worth it? He gives me a wry, thoughtful grin as he thinks about it. 'Yeah, mate,' he says. 'The good times always outweighed the bad. I'm a lucky man.'

HAYDEN KENNY OAM

Our first Iron Man

Part of Australia's great sporting history—one of its most exciting and notable pieces of memorabilia—are the identical photos featured in the picture section showing Hayden and Grant Kenny—father and son—running their way to glory as Iron Men, two decades apart (1966 and 1986).

A household name in Queensland for many years, Hayden Kenny, like his equally well-known son Grant, could easily have been a 'heart-throb' movie star. They both chose to save lives instead. Hayden passed on not just his good looks and passion for the surf, but also his natural desire to want to help people. Australia's lifesavers are all truly magnificent people—Hayden is no exception. Imagine yourself suddenly swept out to sea, out of your element, out of control, the terror of being sucked under the waves, the horror of realising you are helpless and going to drown. This is it, your life is over. Suddenly, there's a blur of red and yellow as a bronzed angel appears by your side, strong arms are holding you . . . you're safe, you're going to live. Often the person saved never sees the face of their hero. The ambo carts them off and the lifesaver returns to duty, the satisfaction of a good result their only reward. Hayden has experienced that happy feeling countless times.

So was this brave ocean man born on a fishing boat? An island? A lighthouse? No, he's a boy from the bush, born at Maryborough, Queensland, in 1936, raised at nearby Granville, a little country village with no power or town water supply. There were no luxuries to speak of, but life was good—free and easy and healthy, in true Queensland style. Children walked or rode ponies to the little Granville school. As a boy Hayden's idea of a terrific time was to go down underground into the nearby coalmine with his father to work alongside him. Part of the attraction was the ride back up in the skip. (Imagine that happening today . . . not bloody likely!)

Hayden's paternal grandfather, also a coalminer, had emigrated from Scotland. Although he'd been attracted to the Maryborough district by the number of coalmines in the area, he soon decided to go for a better life working for the Queensland railways, but his son—Hayden's father—followed the family coalmining tradition.

It was a marvellous area for children to grow up in, with the mighty Mary River and nearby Hervey Bay for fishing and swimming, and miles of bush to explore. Occasional trips to Fraser Island were precious memories from Hayden's teenage years. It was pristine then, mainly because it was so difficult to get there. In later years, when four-wheel-drive vehicles became common and barge services to the island increased accordingly, the long, magnificent beach on the eastern side became a hectic highway, putting locals off revisiting what had been 'their' peaceful island.

'Maryborough was a good solid town. It had always been a thriving river port and was once considered the best choice as Queensland's capital. Although it was a prosperous-looking place with gracious stone buildings, including a customs house, it was still essentially a country town, surrounded by cane and cattle farms. The popular mode of transport, as in many other big Queensland towns, was pushbikes. Many men didn't own cars—people didn't buy anything then unless they had the money for it. When Walkers Engineering and the brickworks men knocked off, the roads were chock-a-block with bikes. The coppers walked the streets and crime was almost nonexistent. Everyone had a father who worked and a mother who was home when you got home from school. There was discipline and respect in the vast majority of children's lives. You worked for your pocket money and valued it.'

While at Maryborough High School Hayden became well-known as an outstanding swimmer, and during the 1950s won every state title he competed in, from 200 to 1500 metres. A keen member of the Maryborough Swimming Club, and one of its champion competitors, he was invited during a carnival at Nambour's Memorial Pool to take part in a race in the surf nearby, at a carnival held the next day.

'I jumped in the ocean and just loved it. That was a turning point in my life. I began to compete in surf carnivals regularly, as well as racing up and down pools. It was only natural to become a lifesaver. As well as the tremendous satisfaction of saving people, I loved the camaraderie of the lifesaving movement. It was all blokes then, even though females had patrolled beaches during the Second World War. When I joined, everything was set up for males. We all took pride in keeping our clubhouse neat and tidy when we stayed the night [an untidy bunk brought a shilling fine] and you could leave your wallet and watch on your bunk. No one would dream of touching someone else's gear. At the end of the day when the public had all left the beach, we'd set up a 5-gallon keg of beer under the trees and enjoy our mateship. Juniors were strictly limited to one glass of beer each. By the time my son Grant joined, he had missed out on experiencing the all-male discipline and the very different atmosphere I'd been lucky enough to enjoy.' Little did Hayden know then that his working life in the future would revolve around water and the family name would become synonymous with surf carnivals.

During the Korean War, from 1950 to 1953, the armed forces weren't attracting recruits, so the first National Service Act was brought in, requiring every male over eighteen years to do three months of full-time army training at a base. (The second National Service Act introduced a ballot system.) After training it was compulsory to return for occasional weekend bivouacs, attend annual army two-week camps and a weekly night parade in a regiment nearest to their place of work or residence. In Hayden's case, that was the 47th Wide Bay Regiment.

Hayden enjoyed his stints at Wacol and Canungra, then Maryborough, staying with his regiment for five years. Like many of his generation, he wishes national service was compulsory again: 'The discipline was so good for you. Everything had to be perfect— not just your barracks, uniform and rifle, but also your physical fitness and mental attitude. Everything was about personal pride and teamwork. I can vividly recall how proud I was taking part with my 11th Battalion in the Royal Review parade at Victoria Park opposite the Royal General Hospital, 13 June 1955. It was held in honour of the Queen's birthday, with 5500 riflemen assembled. It was an impressive sight.'

Hayden's natural desire and ability to do things properly saw him promoted to corporal. Things hadn't changed much in the military since World War II. He recalls shooting massive artillery weapons in the Canungra jungle without any ear muffs. It's a different world now. He also laughs at the memory of travelling home on the train every week with all the other high school cadets, each one with a .303 slung casually across their young shoulders; most were country boys who'd been brought up with firearms.

During his time as a 'Nasho', he noticed many men's attitudes changed when they were drinking, and made a conscious decision never to allow alcohol to control his behavior. Self-discipline came naturally to him, hence his success as an athlete. Coming from a family where everyone was expected to be considerate of each other—a form of self-discipline—and cherish their good health, he has always found it normal behaviour to enjoy a few drinks with friends without giving his liver a complete caning. 'You had to be 21 to be served alcohol during my teenage years, but of course some blokes would find a way to get grog. Travelling back from Wacol

Army Base to Maryborough on the army bus, a few blokes were "into it", thinking they could drink like there was no tomorrow. They were sick as dogs before they got home—in a hell of a mess—and I thought to myself, "What's the future in that?" The army brought in a law that Nashos couldn't be served alcohol, even if they were over 21. The blokes who were being sent to Vietnam weren't happy that they could be sent to fight and maybe die for their country, but couldn't have a beer.

'Some Nashos went into their initial training with the wrong attitude and stupidly made it hard for themselves. The army is all about teamwork and obeying orders. You've got no choice but to fit in. You can't beat them. My younger brother Raymond liked the severe discipline of army life and went on to become one of the legendary tunnel rats of the Vietnam War. Those men were the toughest of the tough, without equal in their bravery and psychological superiority. I'll never forget the story Raymond told me about his regimental sergeant major bawling at an injured man who was reacting to his situation like a civilian: "Are you looking for sympathy, soldier? Well, the only place you'll find sympathy here is in the dictionary—between *shit* and *syphilis*!"'

Although he respected the army, Hayden didn't see himself as a career soldier like Raymond. Their brother Bryce followed in their father's footsteps to work in the mines at Torbanlea and Howard, but later left to work in the timber industry. (He died from lung cancer aged 57.) In contrast Hayden, after completing Year 10, followed the path their grandfather took in Australia, working for the railway department. He started on the bottom rung at

Maryborough as a porter, learning how to live very basically, in the corner of a goods shed. His childhood spent without power or running water helped considerably.

Hayden especially enjoyed helping to bring cattle in to be loaded at Ideraway siding, near Gayndah. He hadn't had any experience with cattle, so it was all a great adventure. 'I loved mixing with the drovers and farmers who brought the mobs in. They were such characters and so independent. They asked for nothing, and were prepared to camp the night on the ground near the cattleyards. I always invited them to camp on the platform. There were no comforts—just a thunderbox dunny—but there was a roof over their heads and the ones who took up my offer when it looked like rain were very grateful. In the morning I'd help them load 20 to 30 K-wagons and loved to hear the way they spoke—different men altogether from people who'd spent their lives living and working in town. The old saying "salt of the earth" is so true.'

At seventeen Hayden was trusted by the railways hierarchy to take control of small stations in the region while the stationmaster was on holidays. His duties included being in charge of loading and unloading goods and precious mailbags, and banking cash. Although he was a responsible young feller, he was still human and enjoyed a bit of a lark. When stationed temporarily at a little siding near Gayndah called Humphrey, he decided it would be fun to commandeer the 'trike'—used by railworkers to travel between stations—and whirl into Gayndah for a night at the movies. Highly illegal, of course! All went well till the trip home when, haring along on the noisy machine, he was suddenly illuminated in the ultra-bright glare of a loco steaming down on him, pulling a goods train. Holy hell! Somehow he pulled up in double-quick time, jumped off, and found the strength needed to haul the trike off the line. It tumbled down the embankment. In his good go-to-town clothes, he scrambled down after it as the train roared past, then spent ages working his guts out, in the pitch dark, long speargrass and rocks, getting the bloody heavy, bloody awkward machine back up the bank and onto the tracks once more. The driver didn't see him, or at least didn't report the incident, and not long after Hayden rose from porter to shunter.

In the thrilling era of steam power, the task held a lot of appeal for a young bloke. Hayden was put in charge of shunting the trainloads of sugarcane and coal out to the ships waiting at the end of the Urangan (now Hervey Bay) jetty—an extremely impressive, mile-and-a-half timber construction (now half demolished). It was a great job with many interesting moments, but after two years, in 1960, he spotted a business opportunity and went for it.

Hayden left the railways to take over the lease of the town's pool. He began coaching, helping many youngsters on to great success, and fundraising to build a 50-metre Olympic pool. A concert was staged—the Olympic Capers. His high-school sweetheart, Fae, also a swim champion, danced up a storm as part of the 'Maryborough Follies'. Her magnificent performance inspired Hayden to propose. Fae made him proud by winning the *Sunday Mail* Sun Girl Quest in 1958, aged 17. A natural beauty, she won the Siren of the Surf contest judged at Bundaberg in 1959. Married in 1962, they enjoyed a wonderful social life, going to the regular Wide Bay Rowing Club dances and glamorous balls all through the winter months. Life-saving and competing took up a lot of his time in the summer, but fortunately Fae loved the beach.

The surf belt race was Hayden's favourite contest in the early days. Back then the belt was the main equipment in rescue and resuscitation procedures. In 1961 he took part in the all-triumphant Australian team's tour of New Zealand, and also competed at the national carnival held at Moana Beach, South Australia—the biggest carnival in history, with more than 80000 spectators. In 1964 Queensland teams finally broke the hold New South Wales clubs had over the national competitions when Hayden, John Rigby and Gordon Jeffery trounced all-comers in their events at the Perth State Titles.

Subsequently Hayden was selected the following year to take part in an Australian team to travel to the US and Mexico, to compete against their lifesavers. Hayden made his country proud, winning the Iron Man contest at Carpinteria, near Santa Barbara. In August, during the US summer, events were held during the long twilight; Hollywood lights illuminated the beach for the night events. The Aussies brought back two great new ideas: one was the use of foam rescue boards, tubes and inflatable rescue boats, the other was the Iron Man competition. It was a significant point in Australian surf lifesaving history.

The US Iron Man contest comprised one leg of swimming, one leg of paddle-boarding, then rowing a Cape Cod timber dory. Normally a two-man craft, with no seats, these boats were designed to be solid and stable enough for two men to stand up in and fish the Cape Cod waters. In the Iron Man contest, the competitor sat at the back with sandbags placed in front for balance. This rowing leg, therefore, was extremely difficult—a real test.

In 1966, Hayden won Australia's first Iron Man contest, held at Coolangatta. The *Courier Mail* report read:

> The term 'Iron Man' is no misnomer. It calls for swim, board and ski races in immediate succession and this first event was held in very tough surf conditions, with a nasty chop, northerly sweep, and close-to-shore gutter. An all-round competitor, Kenny was also competing in several other events, not saving himself for the Iron Man. He had to complete in quick succession, a heat and semi-final of the Malibu board comp, a heat of the Iron Man, a Taplin relay, then with no respite, race straight into the final of the Iron Man.

Highly successful business people are frequently accused of having 'good luck', but that luck is often a result of hard work, and timing, plus the confidence to take the initiative with a new idea. 'At the 1956 Olympic Games Exhibition Surf Carnival, I had watched the Americans on their easy-to-manoeuvre boards and thought, "This is a thing of the future."' Hayden cashed in on his spot-on intuition by being the first surfer north of the Gold Coast to begin making boards. Joe Larkin on the Gold Coast was his only competitor in the fledgling business. Hayden began making his big Malibus—up to 9 feet 9 inches long—in his granddad's barn at Granville, between driving a bulk sugar truck for extra money. Both were great sidelines to managing the pool and coaching—a busy young man with energy to burn!

By the mid 60s, he was receiving so many orders for his boards he was confident enough to go into it full-time. The obvious place to do that wasn't inland Maryborough, but the Sunshine Coast, or North Coast as it was then called. With Grant just a baby, Hayden and Fae set sail with everything they owned in their Valiant stationwagon to a rented cabin over the road from the Alexandra Headland beach. Their palatial dwelling measured 20 by 20 feet, and Fae cooked their meals on one hotplate.

The shop he'd rented was opposite the Surf Lifesaving Club, of which he was an active member, and some of the lifesavers would give him a hand. Soon he had to move to a bigger building, business was so good, then an even bigger building, purpose-built, with a flat on top.

As well as surfing, Hayden had also discovered the joys of sailing. He and three mates had built their own 24-foot Quickcats out of flatply. Over a beer one arvo during the late 60s, they decided that there should be a yacht club at the river mouth, then set about making the Mooloolabah Yacht Club happen, with a 2-dollar joining fee, on a 1-acre block used by the pilot boats. From those humble beginnings, the club grew bigger and flasher, but by then Hayden was getting too busy to sail.

As the Sunshine Coast grew, the Department of Commercial Development established industrial parks, and Hayden built a big factory on an acre west of the beach village. He was also making surf skis (and is still making them under the Hayden Surfcraft label).

Back then, the Sunshine Coast was only busy on weekends. The rest of the time it was a peaceful, idyllic place to live.

'When I was down south competing or on business, and people from down there would start rubbishing Queensland, as they used to all do, I'd agree with them, and say things like, "Yes, it's a bloody awful place alright. You wouldn't like it, that's for sure. You're far better off living down here." I was a cunning bugger, trying to keep our beautiful bailiwick for ourselves as long as I could, but after Sir Joh wiped death duties, then put on World Expo 88 in Brisbane, they all started moving up here in droves. And they're still crowding into this south-east corner—the infrastructure can't cope with the numbers of people moving up here for a better life. We were so lucky to have 25 wonderful years living on the ocean front, but increasing traffic noise led to a decision ten years ago to move back a few blocks to a quieter area, on high land surrounded by bush. Naturally we miss our ocean views, but it's peaceful up here.'

While Hayden made his boards, Fae kept herself busy starting up and helping to run a kindergarten. Her focus was always on home and family, providing a secure, stable environment for their children—Grant, Melinda and Martin—like they had both enjoyed in their childhoods. The Kenny family had a wonderful life together, travelling to carnivals up and down the coast, with Hayden and the kids competing, and Fae—who Hayden, with a grin, refers to as the 'Silent Master'—supervising. Grant's role in the *Coolangatta Gold* movie was one of the many highlights.

A long life of major achievement, success and travel has given Hayden a wealth of treasured memories and souvenirs—many beautiful and interesting things. One very special memento is a letter to him written by a New Zealand woman—a belated 'thank you' for saving her life as a fourteen-year-old girl holidaying at Alexandra Headland in 1966. After getting her to safety, Hayden returned to save her father and grandfather. The grandfather was unable to be resuscitated. It's a cruel and traumatic blow to a lifesaver, to have to give up and accept that someone they are working on is dead—no longer a living breathing fellow man. When this happens, the disappointment clouds the euphoria experienced after saving another life, or lives, that day. Thus, the letter of heartfelt gratitude from the woman Hayden saved was appreciated immensely and touched him deeply.

A decade after that dramatic and traumatic incident, he was attempting to rescue a young man who'd fallen from a cliff onto a rocky beach. This lad died from his injuries and Hayden couldn't help thinking that his life might have been saved if a helicopter had been available. This thought plagued him for a while then, and as an action man, he decided to make it happen. He discussed it with other lifesaving friends, who all agreed it was a terrific idea, but there was a small problem—a helicopter rescue service would cost a lot of money. Local businessman and friend Des Scanlan (proprietor of the Big Cow, amongst other interests) chartered a Bell 47 for joyflights and agreed to make it available for emergencies. Hayden lobbied hard to get further assistance and eventually received help from the Wales bank [now Westpac], the Australian Guarantee Corporation and the state government. When a larger machine was acquired in 1979, with capability of handling a static line rescue out of the ocean, Des Scanlan and another mate, Roy Thompson, became guarantors to purchase the turbine Jetranger. Now sponsored by Energex, the service also rescues medical cases, as well as surf casualties.

The surf rescue chopper was a dream come true, and helping it become a reality is one of Hayden's proudest achievements. It has saved countless lives. While Hayden is not one to boast, many of the rescues have been due to his skills, plus his daring—jumping out of the machine into all sorts of tricky, terrible and dangerous situations. 'One of the worst situations to be in is when weather or terrain conditions are so dangerous, the pilot and crew are forced to weigh up the risks against the possible outcome. A winch rescue in difficult conditions is always full of tension. If a hovering chopper loses power, you can be in big trouble. When you've rescued a patient by being lowered down on a cable, there's a point when you are ascending with them where, if you fall, you will not survive, but all you think about is the patient. You just want them to live, with every fibre of your being. To save a person's life—there aren't words to describe how you feel.'

Hayden retired in his early 70s, in 2007, having been a full-time crewman in the Energex rescue helicopter for more than 25 years and involved in 156 rescues. He also rescued literally thousands of people during his 50 years as a volunteer with the Sunshine Coast lifesaving movement. His adage is: 'Putting something back into the community is the responsibility of everyone.' In 2006 he was presented with a Medal of the Order of Australia (OAM) for services to lifesaving and the community.

Health, family and community are the three things that Hayden feels are most important to care for, to nurture, for a rewarding life. Four years after his retirement he is still fit, but doesn't have the rigid regime he stuck to for years, which made him fit enough to put in the sometimes superhuman effort necessary to save a life. All those years of working with fibreglass fortunately haven't affected him, because he was used to looking after his health and always wore a mask. 'And I've still got my own knees, thanks to not being involved with sports that are hard on your legs.' As well as being 'superfish', he and Grant also hold black belts in karate. Nowadays Hayden enjoys a jog, bike ride, gym session and afternoon swim, shifting his exercise routine to fit in with the travelling he and his still-beautiful Fae enjoy. Snow-skiing in Canada is a favourite regular holiday; they're both first out on the slopes in the mornings. 'As Fae says, "While you can, you should." We do prefer shorter trips now, so we can return to be with our family, who all live nearby. When there are grandkids in the house, Fae's as happy as a cat in a fish shop!'

They are deservedly proud of their children's successful lives. Martin and Grant work well together in Grant's aviation business; Melinda, with degrees in tourism and teaching, also chooses to work in the aviation industry. Although Hayden and Fae take a great interest in all their grandchildren's sporting activities, including the 'Nippers', or junior lifesavers, they don't believe in putting pressure on youngsters to take competition too seriously. For this reason, they don't display photos of sporting successes on the walls of their home. If one of their grandsons was to win a third-generation Iron Man title, that would naturally make them proud, but the kids wouldn't have been pushed or pressured into that level of competition.

Lovingly referred to by family and friends as 'The Fossil'—because he is anything but!—Hayden can look at the photographs of himself winning that first Iron Man contest and rejoice in the knowledge that he wasn't a one-hit wonder. He not only went on to many more achievements in many spheres—great family man, great community leader, great businessman, to name just three—but also passed on his tremendous ability to succeed as well as his family values. Many people owe their lives to this brave man.

JOHN WILLIAM STEWART AM

Cattleman and fighter

When a bloke has spent several years as general manager of a major pastoral company running 220000 head, you can pretty much assume he knows a thing or two about cattle. John William Stewart, known throughout the industry, doesn't only know which end the grass comes out, he is up and well ahead on every aspect of producing great beef. From nutrition and breeding, to transport, pest and disease control—every bovine challenge—it would be safe to say he has 'more knowledge than a 30-acre college'. He is a world-wise elder who looks to the future, a fierce protector of the nation's beef industry, and a fighter for the rights of the man on the land.

In the blazing Brisbane heatwave of 1934, a truly committed stork managed to safely deliver him to his mother at Wooloowin Private Hospital. Either the heatwave or genetics put the character into the boy that would see him go through life as a leader, an achiever who makes his mark. John's early childhood was spent on Lyndley Station near Dalby, where his father was manager until he heeded the call to arms in World War II. While his father was away fighting, John lived at his grandmother's house in Brisbane, attending Eagle Junction primary school. After the war, the family all moved to Dilga Station, Glenmorgan, where John learnt horsemanship and stockwork under the capable guidance of his much-respected father, who, later on, would have been extremely proud of his son's sterling career.

It was only natural that the 1953 captain of Brisbane Boys College would swap his boater for a Silver Spur hat after matriculation, and head west. (He was also a lieutenant in the cadets, and captain of the college's rugby firsts—a fine and gentle bunch of gentlemen, to be sure.) On Caldervale Station, Charleville, then running 10 000 head of cattle, he started as a jackeroo for the Australian Agricultural Company. John's outstanding stock and 'people management' skills were noticed early on by management and after only a year there he was made head stockman, working with a camp of highly skilled men. One of them saved his life one day. Seven men were holding up the mob on the flat and John was campdrafting, when his big black horse suddenly plaited its legs, went down, then took off, dragging him through the pine and brigalow, which was full of stumps and pointed stakes. These things happen in a stock camp and you either live or die. Ernie Gadd managed to gallop up beside John's horse and save him. This is the type of event that breeds close mateship in the bush.

After two years at Caldervale, he was sent by the company to their Kimberley station, Ivanhoe, as head stockman. His experience hunting wild scrubbers in the Queensland brigalow would come in very handy out on the largely unfenced run. Once owned by the famous Durack family, Ivanhoe was then running 12000 head of cattle in difficult-to-manage, isolated country. John was only 21 years old, and put in charge of a camp of twelve Aboriginal stockmen, plus Johnny Walker the cook.

But first there was the six-day expedition to get there: by car, then truck to Brisbane, then five different aircraft (including a Dragon Rapide), to Mt Isa, Alice Springs, Katherine, and finally the Ord River—his destination. As the Connellan Airline's pilot approached the Victoria River he asked John if he'd ever seen a crocodile, and to oblige his young passenger with a new experience buzzed the water, sending crocs flying down the banks everywhere. It can be easily imagined what was going through his mind—a tremendous adventure for a young bloke, but there was plenty more to come.

Peter Ogden, the head stockman he was replacing, was staying on for a little while to show him the 'paddocks', but on his third day there, John saw rain like he'd never seen—torrential, flooding rain. The Aboriginal staff disappeared into the hills. Did they sense that the biggest flood in the Ord's recorded history was about to occur? In no time the water was a metre deep through the house, but fortunately it had two storeys, and the two men lived upstairs for five days, shooting crocodiles from the verandah.

As always, the flood eventually went down, the crocs left the house yard and went back to the river, the stockmen and Johnny

Walker returned from the hills, and away they all went mustering. The Australian Agricultural Company was certainly pleased with John's efforts. He managed to brand 3000 calves that year—100 per cent more than the previous year.

Typically, the Aboriginal men preferred to keep to themselves. To cope with his solitude, the gregarious young man from 'way over east' absorbed as much as he could of the landscape, the conditions and the peculiar challenges. Conditions in that prehistoric, 'character-building' region had not changed much since the pioneering days of the previous century. Bronco-branding, packhorses and mules were still in use, and they still walked the fat bullocks to Wyndham meatworks, a trip of six days, and the stores were handed over to drover 'Slippery' (so-called because of his penchant for 'slipping' into pubs) Pendegast, to walk for four months to Headingly, Urandangi (near Camooweal).

Kununurra didn't exist then, and to say it was a primitive and lonely life in the Kimberley in 55 and 56, with little entertainment or comforts, would be a great understatement (although John did break up his almost hermit-like year and enjoyed attending the 1956 Melbourne Olympics). That aside, John appreciated the responsibility that had been placed on his young shoulders, and the tremendous learning experience with both stock management and the erection and maintenance of improvements, in notoriously hard country. A galloping horse putting its hoof in a hole then rolling over him sent him off on a long journey to an orthopaedic specialist, whose most excellent advice to him was: 'Don't ever let anyone operate on your back. You are a "time-healer"—you will heal in time, if you look after yourself.' No more galloping through the rugged ranges after scrubbers for young John.

John's next posting, in 1957, was another challenge—Manager of Tremere Station, Aramac, western Queensland, running 12 000 sheep. Extremely proud of this promotion, John took it as an opportunity to expand his knowledge and experience by learning everything he could about the sheep industry (even though the woolly buggers nearly drove him mad!) and property management in a vastly different environment. An English girl working as a governess in the district, Mary Mansfield, caught his eye and they married at Barcaldine in 1959.

After three years running a sheep station he was still very young and felt like having a go at something completely different. He tried a year as a sales representative for Sunbeam Shearing Machinery (also selling cattle and sheep dip), then spent 1961 as a trainee auctioneer with the New Zealand Loan (later Dalgety and NZ Loan Limited) company in Rockhampton. He regarded both these interludes as valuable opportunities to acquire self-confidence in dealing with and assessing people. After a very brief time practising to be an auctioneer by pretending to sell trees, gates, dogs, etc. as he drove past them, John was chucked in the deep end when the manager of Dalgetys at Rocky, Jack Stevens, sent him straight in to auction several pens at Eidsvold saleyards, with: 'You're here to learn, now go and sell!' John took to the skilful occupation like a duck to water but left after a year, partly because of the heavy drinking culture of the job, which didn't appeal to him, and partly because he was a horseman and cattleman and wanted to return to what he did best.

CATTLEMAN AND FIGHTER

A chance to begin a new adventure in northern Western Australia was irresistible. He was soon on another marathon trip across the country, to Halls Creek, to manage Turner River Station, running 15 000 head of cattle for Vesteys (the Vestey Brothers company, owned by Lord Vestey, one of Australia's biggest land-owners at the time). On this second trip to the 'wild west', he was accompanied by wife Mary and baby son Alex. Daughter Wendy was born five years later.

Turner Plain was the subject of a huge regeneration project by the Western Australian Department of Agriculture for the Ord River Scheme, and by 1964 John transferred to the company's Limbunya Station near Katherine, running 20 000 head. When the famous 'Wave Hill walk-out' by Indigenous staff occurred next door in 1966, the ABC's *Four Corners* television team landed on Limbunya to interview John, whom Vestey's general manager Peter Morris judged to be capable of remaining cool-headed and a little more discreet while being interviewed than Wave Hill's manager, the redoubtable Tom Fisher. John acquitted himself well, and was featured recently on the ABC's show about the 40th anniversary of the walk-out.

After the interview the *Four Corners* presenter told John he wanted to finish off the segment by galloping off through some dust, into the sunset. A teensy bit fazed because the city bloke had never ridden a horse, John nevertheless managed to get the quietest horse on the place, leg the fellow up, showed him how to hold the reins, then with the aid of a bucket containing stones, sent the old plug cantering off. The TV man, arms up in the air, immediately fell off . . . then fell off again . . . and again! The cameraman still wasn't

191

happy and asked him to have another go. To his credit the presenter gave it a fourth shot, by then decidedly dusty and minus quite a lot of bark and hide. John warned the cameraman not to buggerise around—he would only have a few seconds to get the shot of his mate still in the pigskin, and if he kept missing it they might be calling the flying doctor. Between the three of them they got the take and the battered presenter lived to tell the tale.

During his six years with Vesteys, John was largely responsible for the pleuro-pneumonia eradication program, the first of the two major cattle-disease control programs in Australia. This experience whetted his appetite to become heavily involved with cattle disease prevention on a grand scale.

On to even bigger things. In 1967, he was recruited by Queensland Stations Ltd to run Vanrook, in the Gulf of Carpentaria, in charge of 40 staff and 36 000 head with brandings of 7500 on average a year. Within five years, John's management strategies had increased that to 11 000 a year, due to purchase of better bulls, supplementary feeding of cows in the dry season, and cleaner mustering, eradicating cleanskin bulls. He also streamlined the delivery of fat cattle to the meatworks, saving time and money. He was rewarded in 1972 with a directorship of the company and a new title, pastoral inspector and manager. From then on, John was based in Townsville to manage all the stations and flew to Melbourne seven times a year for board meetings. Somehow he also fitted in time to contribute to the Gulf people by becoming a Carpentaria shire councillor, attending meetings in Normanton.

For the next fourteen years, he planned and oversaw the tuberculosis (TB) eradication program on the company's seven properties, during which more than one million tests were carried out. The scale of the job was so immense—every beast on every station *had* to be found, brought in and yarded—that he decided to try the then-radical idea of mustering using helicopters. This eventually led to a revolution in the northern beef industry, at a time when the big mustering camps were becoming a thing of the past, due mainly to higher wages. John was invited to sit on several state remote area TB committees and, although very busy, was happy to give others the benefit of his experience. His increasing interest in pasture research and development eventually resulted in an invitation to join the CSIRO's Division of Tropical Crops and Pastures Advisory Committee, to which he contributed for 25 years.

The early days of helicopter mustering provided John with more than a few challenges, as well as fond memories. He recalls one of the helicopter pilots, a bit of a lair nicknamed 'Captain Marvel', put his machine (unintentionally) into a waterhole. John was not pleased, but received a bonus when he managed to haul it out. As the chopper emerged from the drink, water pouring out of its doorways, a 14-pound barra was found wedged in the bubble. Headlines in the next Normanton newspaper read: 'We Found the Biggest Lure in the Gulf!'

John has seen many changes in the Top End over the years, but one thing is constant—nature is a force to be reckoned with. During the third week of January 1974 the Gulf of Carpentaria received 54 inches of rain in four days, resulting in the largest recorded flood since 1956. Water was flowing 3 feet deep through the house on Vanrook. The Cessna 310 was tied down on the highest point of the airstrip, while the helicopter (a Bell 47) was put down on a trailer tied to 44-gallon drums. John had to radio the Flying Doctor Service in Cairns every hour just to let them know they were all okay. At one point he was wading into the office to do this when a huge black snake swam in through the door beside him, then disappeared. Nervously John radioed in on schedule. The radio operator asked if all was okay and he replied: 'Yes, but I'm a little worried about the black snake that swam into the office with me. Over and out.'

John flew over the five Gulf properties assessing damage. It was a shocking, unforgettable sight—cattle were floating 20 miles out to sea, some still alive and swimming. Fences flattened and washed away was a major problem, especially the new paddocks built for the TB testing. An enormous clean-up lay ahead, plus bangtail musters to assess losses. The company lost a staggering 65 000 of their 220 000 head.

But there were more troubled times to come. Three months later, cattle prices plummeted—and didn't improve until nearly five years later. From then on, the directors all agreed to put away one year's working expenses on the short-term money market as a safeguard against future disasters.

During this terrible time, when many beef producers crashed and all were struggling, membership of the United Graziers Association (UGA) dropped dramatically and John was asked in 1976 to try and revive the Gulf branch. This was his introduction to agri-politics. When a big job needs doing to benefit a community, it seems it's always the busiest person who takes it on. John was, by then, responsible for the breeding properties Vanrook, Strathmore and Miranda Downs, and fattening properties Wandovale, Dotswood, Glenprairie and Bluff Downs (two others, Iffley and Rutland Plains, were sold in 1978 to the Mcdonald family)—a total of 25 000 square kilometres. These operations included several studs, breeding Santa Gertrudis and droughtmaster cattle, and Australian stock horses. Of the 700 replacement bulls required each year, 600 were company-bred. John was in control of the company's twin engine Cessna 310 and three Bell helicopters, which were serviced by the company's own aircraft engineer. It was a massive enterprise.

In 1979 Mary wanted to go back to England, and tried to convince him to try life over there. John couldn't see himself as a farmer managing 'piddling pocket handkerchief paddocks', and stayed in Australia. Three years later he met Margaret, a fine arts lecturer, whom he married in 1983.

After Queensland Stations was sold to Coutts Brothers, John resigned in 1986 to form Glenlyon Pastoral Management, a consultancy advising major clients such as the Queensland Department of Primary Industries, Herron Todd White (valuing properties to be resumed for the Burdekin Dam), the United Graziers Association, the Cattle Council of Australia, Posgold Ltd and Normandy Mining Ltd, and Jagheda Pty Ltd (owners of Dunbar Station in the Gulf). He also supervised the operation of Dunbar, and ran his own cattle on agistment country near Cardwell.

Amid growing concerns that the Meat Research Corporation was ignoring the concerns of producers, John played a large part in establishing the North Australia Beef Research Council (NABRC) in 1991 and was appointed inaugural chairman. Representing the NABRC, he sat on the board of the Co-operative Research Centre for the Tropical Savannahs for three years. A driving force by then in the UGA, he became a councillor on the Cattle Council of Australia (four years later, he was vice-chairman) and was appointed the council's brucellosis and tuberculosis eradication campaign consultant.

Somehow he also found time to organise the Townsville-Thuringowa Landcare Committee and chaired the committee for five years before leaving the area. Then there were his fundraising activities for charity (primarily the famous Bush 'n' Bay Muster for the Royal Flying Doctor Service), plus his highly active memberships of the National Farmers Federation, James Cook University Experimentation Ethics Committee, the Perc Tucker Regional Gallery Advisory Committee, and his government-appointed position on the Queensland Aboriginal Land Tribunal.

If life had been hectic up till then, the next twenty years would see him stretched in many directions, but all linked to the beef industry. In the mid 1990s he was invited to help set up the Australian Animal Health Council (now Animal Health Australia), became an original board member and was elected vice-chairman for the next three years. He left Townsville in 1996 for Brisbane and bought a small cattle property at Maleny, running Charbrays (Charolais–Brahman cross). He became pastoral supervisor for Newmont Pajingo Pty Ltd, with whom he had worked previously as a consultant.

Australia was declared free of TB in 1997 and John rightly felt extremely proud of his enormous contribution. The following year he was chuffed, to say the least, to be made an honorary member of the Australian Veterinary Association.

The Cattle Council of Australia presented him with their award for services to the Australian cattle industry in 1999—the same year the United Graziers combined with the Grain Growers Council to become a united lobby group titled Agforce, to work for the rights of Queensland's primary producers. John was elected vice-president, to represent the state's biggest primary industry, cattle. His first major achievement for Agforce was to acquire two beef cattle research stations that were going to be closed down and sold off—so they would not be lost to the beef industry. It was such a crucial deal that the CEO of Agforce promised John, a lover of good red wine, a bottle of Penfolds Grange if he could pull it off. It took four years of patience and negotiation from John before Agforce was finally able to buy the research stations for 4.3 million dollars. (Agforce was able to raise 1.6 million dollars, and it fell to John to somehow raise the balance. This he managed to do, although it wasn't an easy task, and it undoubtedly contributed to his being honoured with the Member of the Order of Australia for 'Most Outstanding Contribution to Primary Industries' in 2004.) John now chairs the committee which oversees the operations of these two prized assets, which were recently valued at more than 10 million dollars.

John suffered from a stroke in 2000, during this dragged-out deal, probably brought on by the pressure of trying to save the two research stations and at the same time struggling to raise money to set up Rangelands Australia, a national education, training and research concept. He'd also been battling a bad cold and was really ill. His normal doctor was away and the one he finally saw didn't take his blood pressure. That night he fell over in his bathroom. His blood pressure was 200/150 and he loafed around in intensive care for six days. (At the time, John was also handling a large and highly contentious Native Title case, and the new financial manager from Agforce came in to the IC ward wanting John to run him up to speed with it all, in case John carked it!)

The stroke meant John lost the use of his left side and couldn't speak clearly. Thanks to two wonderful women in St Andrews Rehabilitation Unit he went home right as rain after just five weeks. While there he charmed an Irish nurse into allowing him to monopolise the fax machine so he could continue running his campaign to raise the money needed for the two projects.

Having recovered from his stroke, in 2001 he was part of a delegation exploring the cause and effects of foot and mouth in England and Ireland. His next major project then involved helping to develop an Exotic Animal Disease Response Agreement, a major milestone for Animal Health Australia, in 2002. Shortly after, he was invited by the CSIRO to join the Australian Animal Health Laboratory Advisory Council, and in the same year became a member of the new Queensland Biosecurity Advisory Council. It was no surprise to see him listed in the next year's Australia Day Honours, as a Member of the Order of Australia (AM), for services to the beef cattle industry.

What a doer! And there's still plenty to do, so John continues all his activities, though scaled down slightly in recent years. He still enjoys it all—the challenges, the human interaction, the rewards gained from helping others—so why, he says, stay at home and loaf about? To spend his so-called 'golden years' fishing or playing golf is unthinkable. His energy is reserved for more important things. Thankfully that means his wealth of experience isn't consigned to the scrap heap, as is the sad case with so many people of his age. With a spring in his step, he heads for his Brisbane Agforce office every day, researching solutions and fighting battles for the men and women who are out there where he used to be—toiling in the heat of the paddocks and the dusty stockyards.

He considers his most significant achievement to be the part he played in eradicating TB. What else stands out in his memory as a truly great thing he has done? Without hesitation, he replies: 'Giving up smoking. I used to roll a tin of Log Cabin a day like most stockmen did back when I was a young bloke, and one morning I looked at the tobacco and thought, "This is a really stupid thing to do," and I never smoked again. That most probably helped me to survive the stroke.'

With his eyes always on the future—the future of the cattle industry—he moves with the times, committed to taking 'his' industry forward. He cannot help himself because he is driven to continue to contribute—that's what makes John William Stewart tick.

JANIE MARSHALL

Contract musterer, completely one-off character

There's no one else like Janie Marshall. Once met, never forgotten. As well as being a one-off, this tall, tough, capable 'stockperson' is also a *mystery woman*. When you first meet her, you could be shocked by a torrent of swearwords flowing from under her 10-gallon hat and a voice gruff as a cattledog's bark, snapping questions at you like, 'Who th' f . . k are you? What's your f . . kin' claim to fame, eh?'

But . . . here is a female who constantly uses swearwords, in a very loud tone, no matter where she is, that would honestly make a bullocky blush—yet she'll put on perfume and lippy and take the local nuns out to dinner. ('Give the poor buggers a f . . kin' good feed, mate—they f . . kin' deserve it, eh?') Here is a musterer who swears and roars at her dogs all day, calling them 'useless f . . kin' dimwit arsehole of a dog!' and every other curse she can lay her tongue to, but she absolutely, unequivocally adores them. Here's a bloody tough cookie who frightens hell out of most ordinary men and women, yet her generosity, and her kindness to those who need help, are legend. Here is a woman who has always worked like a man out in the hard, hot, far north-west, who knew every dirty trick in the book in her time as a shit-hot amateur jockey, who will knock you arse over head quick-smart if you insult her family or friends (including her dogs), but who thoroughly enjoyed her time at one of Sydney's poshest girls' schools. As the Yanks say, go figure . . .

Janie (pronounced Jenny) was born in the early 1940s, and spent a wonderful childhood on Boorooma Station, between Walgett and Brewarrina, where her father, Jim Marshall, was the boss. He was a big man with a big job. Boorooma's half-million-plus acres of good-quality country ran 95 000 sheep and 3000 to 5000 cattle, depending on the season. It wasn't a lonely bush childhood, for there were always at least 30 staff to yarn with and learn from, plus Janie had two sisters, Vicky and Chrissie, and two brothers, Joe and Jim.

For the sake of avoiding repetition, I won't put in Janie's favourite word where she is speaking during most of this story, but it starts with 'f', ends in 'g', and punctuates approximately every half-dozen words of her normal conversation. Bear in mind, too, that Janie doesn't 'speak', she yells like she's permanently in a stockyard. With her dulcet tones that could strip paint, her remarks and observations are always colourful, always entertaining, and often repeated around the district by many, usually with great delight. ('Have you heard Janie's latest?') What would seem totally outrageous if spoken by anyone else—particularly a sheila—is accepted by those who know her and, indeed, is relied upon to provide occasional entertainment out west where that commodity is really valued . . .

'Dad thought the sun shone out of my arse. I'm not sure about that—haven't looked. I was his favourite offsider, his shadow. There was none of this la-de-da bringing-Janie-up-to-be-a-lady bullshit with him. It was unusual for a man in those days to allow his daughters to work with the stock and the men, but Dad worked us like brown dogs because he thought it was good for us. Didn't want us to be spoilt, as we easily could have been, by the people who worked on Boorooma. He was a hard taskmaster; everything had to be done properly, as it always is on a big well-run station. I did everything with him in the stockyards, as well as mustering out in the paddocks, even had a go at biting the nuts out of ram lambs like he used to, but I hated the taste of blood so left him to it. Thank gawd they use rubber rings now. What a terrible job that was! Biting the nuts out of lambs all bloody day. I loved helping Dad drafting [channelling the stock through a race into different yards, by swinging gates open and shut]—he was pretty to watch. Fast! We drafted big mobs, so you couldn't buggerise around. My youngest brother Jim dobbed me in to Mum one day, that I was swearing my head off over at the yards, so I got a dressing down from her when we went in for smoko. Dad and I looked at each other sideways and sneaky, grinning. He'd been encouraging me. I could tell he appreciated the fact I didn't dob him in to Mum.

'One of my earliest memories is of sitting up in bed suffering from whooping cough, which is murder to experience. When I'd start coughing, Dad would rush into my room and put his big hand across my forehead and say, "Lean on that, Janie, lean into it!" That used to help and relieve me so much, having Dad's hand supporting my head while I coughed uncontrollably. I was so lucky to have a great dad who loved me. Mum was lovely too, but I was dad's girl. He taught me how to fight—how to drop a bloke fast—and how to fight like a cat and dog together if you couldn't get that big surprise punch in straight away. He was a good mate.

'We could never, ever be bored on Boorooma. Our favourite, most-used "toys" were a hessian chaff bag, a tomahawk, and a bridle each—that's all we needed to go rabbiting, which was our favourite pastime. We'd let off a heap of dogs, catch a horse, jump on bareback, and away we'd go. When we were little, Dad gave us a baby billygoat for a pet—Nankypoo, we called him. Dad made us a little cart and set of harness for Nankypoo when he was fully grown, and didn't we have some fun and spills teaching him to pull us around in the cart! Bark and hide off us everywhere. Dad also made us a cricket bat. The things he made for us with his own hands impressed us more than anything that was bought in a store.

'My mother Elizabeth—or Betty as she was known—was a saint, a great horsewoman and bushwoman, but a lady, from that other era. She wouldn't say "shit" for sixpence. She had her work cut out trying to rear us—we were five wild kids! Dad kept us in line, especially when we were in the house. Dining room rules were strict—speak only when you are spoken to. The men all ate in their own dining rooms, but during that era the jackeroos, who were training to be managers, ate with us. Mum wouldn't serve the meal if they weren't all very neat and tidy. The offender had to go and comb his hair or put a clean shirt on—whatever he'd forgotten to do—knowing he was keeping everyone waiting.

'Mum was the boss in the house and within the house yard, which was about 3 acres of nice garden and veggies. There was a gardener to help her with all that. When we'd been naughty she would make us go and wait in the big old linen press until we'd decided to be good. We'd be in there in the dark, pretending to cry—"Wah! Wah! Boo hoo!"—but she was up to our tricks and was probably killing herself laughing listening to us. If she was really cranky with us and we'd run away, she'd wait and flick the stockwhip up our bums all the way inside from the gate. Gawd, that hurt. Sting! As well as being an expert rider, she was also an absolute expert with a whip. Once she even flicked her whip at a jackeroo who had annoyed her and was hiding from her in a big kennel. Dad's weapon of choice in the kid-controlling game was his razor strop—frightening if you were waiting your turn, because the two pieces of leather made a hell of a noise.

'Dad had to be tough, with a lot of staff to control under often difficult circumstances. He really knew how to pull anyone into gear—including us—if we played up. The station had to run smoothly, no matter what. When Joe and I were about nine and eleven years old, we told the cook that we'd heard Dad saying to someone that he was a cantankerous bastard. Cooks are usually cantankerous bastards, because it's a bastard of a job, especially out in the heat of the west. But the truth often hurts. He got in a huff, rolled his swag and shot through. Dad was bloody ropable when he found out what we'd done. With 30 staff needing three big meals a day plus two smokos, it was a catastrophe to be suddenly left without a cook. Dad told Joe and me we'd have to cook the dinner. He told us what to cook— three legs of lamb, a big mob of veggies, and gravy, plus pudding. We didn't dare whinge, just got stuck into having a go. We didn't know anything about the ovens, so we boiled everything—legs 'n' all. No way to make gravy, in those pre-Gravox days, as there were no pan juices to stir flour into, so it was a pretty ordinary meal as you can imagine. For pudding, we opened a heap of tins of peaches and tins of cream. It was bloody hard yakka, but we did it. Next morning we had to do the breakfast, and I can remember making 70 pieces of toast—that was what was required—on the old Aga stove. Luckily we were rescued by the arrival of a Chinese cook, who was a good bloke and loved to entertain us when he had a spare minute, flying his box kite for us.

'Another time, I remember the cowboy or groom—who was the bloke employed to milk the cow, chop the wood, feed the chooks, kill, and do general jobs around the homestead—left in a hurry, and Joe and I were deployed to take over his jobs till a new bloke arrived. We earned a hiding on the first morning, via a decision to only milk the cow half out, then topping the bucket up with water. It seemed like a good idea at the time . . .

'Poor Mum tried to teach us correspondence school lessons but could only stand it for a year. Trying to keep all of us inside was not easy—we'd bugger off and go rabbiting or riding as soon as her back was turned. So along came our long-suffering governess, Miss Tavanah. On our first morning with her, while she was trying to find out what schooling we'd kept in our brains, and I s'pose make friends with us, she said, "Would you like to ask me any questions?" So I replied, "Yes, Miss Tavanah, what's f . . k mean?" I got a flogging from both her and Dad, but I'd simply heard someone say it, and it's such a bloody funny word—the neatest word I'd ever heard—so I was just being curious, fair dinkum. I admit, I had a fair idea it was a swearword, and the reaction of Miss Tavanah pretty much confirmed it was *real bad*! Not long after, Mum was entertaining some ladies with a posh morning tea. I egged Joe on to go in the sitting room and ask Mum, "What's f . . k mean?" The silly bugger did it. There were scones and cups dropped and old sheilas waving their flamin' hankies 'n' nearly fainting. Poor Mum, that would've been the talk of the district for ages. Joe had a sore arse after the visitors all left.

'Our lives revolved around horses. Joe and I, when we were small, double-banked everywhere bareback, on an enormous ex-racehorse, 17 hands high, called "Giggle". We climbed up his leg to get on, if there wasn't a stump or rail handy. Naturally I got on like a house on fire with both Bobby, who trained our racehorses, and Hollywood George, who was our breaker. After Mum's tea-party episode, I still didn't know what the word 'f . . k' meant, so I asked Bobby. He nearly bit the end off his rollie, then roared laughing. He gave me a vague explanation about what I'd seen mares and stallions, dogs and bitches, bulls and cows, etc., doing—that they weren't piggybacking each other, they were making baby animals. But it wasn't a word for girls to say, he said, which of course encouraged me all the more to say it, and I've been saying it ever since. It's a terrific word!'

'Hollywood George was the best horse breaker in the west. He used to have his own travelling show and was an expert stuntman, sharpshooter, whip-cracker, you name it. He liked life on Boorooma so much he stayed for years, and we were bloody lucky to have him. He could get horses to do anything for him. If he said "Jump in," a horse would jump straight onto the back of a truck. It was amazing. He could take the bridle off a horse and send it home—away they'd go, jumping gates—they'd do everything he told them to do. Mum bred palomino ponies and he taught them to bow, count and do other tricks. We would all clap. It was our own private circus.

Another memorable character who worked for Dad was "Big Tony", the Spanish cement man. ("Little Tony", also Spanish, was the gardener.) Big Tony could build anything out of cement. His cement loos, with their flat Spanish roofs, were always cool. They had proper pull-the-chain dunnies inside—flash! The several sets of stockyards all featured Tony's cement posts. Boorooma was famous for the wonderful red and white wings he made either side of the ten grids on the road, which featured kangaroos and emus that he'd taken ages to create. Idiots gradually shot them up or wrecked most of them, but an identical set can be seen on a gateway north of Bendemeer [towards Uralla], on the right-hand side of the road. Tony must have made them for the owner of that property.

'Like all big stations, we had a big store, but Boorooma's was larger than most. Neighbours could call in and buy anything, from a carton of condensed milk to sets of horseshoes. It was a long drive to Walgett or "Bre", over dirt roads. We were also the post office and telephone exchange, so there were always people coming and going.

I learnt to operate the exchange, which I enjoyed, but of course you wouldn't catch me inside if there was stockwork on, or horses to be worked.

'When the time came for Joe, Jim, Vicky and me to go away to school [Chrissie was too young], we were sent to the Glen Innes convent first, so they could knock the rough edges off us before we went to secondary school in Sydney. We were wild scrubbers. Dad paid the nuns extra to keep our shoes on. They straightened us out with the cane plus, sometimes, a violin bow. Most of the nuns were nice, but we tested their patience and their authority, big time. Then I was first to be sent to Mum's posh old school in the Big Smoke. She said, "Janie, you'll come back a lady." Hah! I thought there was a fat chance of that. Elocution was one of our subjects, and the first time the teacher tried to get me to say—with a plum in my gob—"How now, brown cow"—I couldn't resist saying, "Pretty full, red bull!" The class pissed themselves—most of them were from the bush. But I surprised myself by actually enjoying being in that school and meeting girls from all over the world.

'Even so, I could never imagine myself doing anything else but riding horses and mustering. That was all I wanted to do. After I finished school, I got a job training polo ponies for the Campbells at Quirindi. Mr Campbell put me on a toey ex-racehorse first, to see if I could ride. That horse could buck, but he didn't throw me. I rode him alright, and Mr Campbell told me I must have had chewing gum on me bum.

'After a while, I was homesick for the west—that's the country that's in my blood, and it's very, very different to that soft country down "inside"—different people too. When the polo season finished, I went back to Boorooma, mustering there and on other places for a living. I also loved going back to riding my own racehorses in the "Number Nines", or unregistered meetings, where amateur jockeys could ride. I had a lot of success, especially with a horse called Chunderloo, named after a good old black swaggie Mum had fed and looked after on her family's property, Mulga Downs, at Goodooga. All the black kids knew old Chunderloo the swaggie and loved him, so they loved my horse too. They'd go apeshit whenever he won a race. He was a bloody good galloper and had his fan club cheering him on at every meeting in the Western Division. People brought horses up from Sydney to try and beat him, and some even brought up professional jockeys, thinking they could outsmart this girl from the backblocks with their slick tricks, but me 'n' Chunderloo sent the dust flying into their smug little faces. We won many cups, and the one I loved winning best of all was at Coonamble, where it had been won the previous few years by the newspaper owner's son. The trophy for the main race—the cup race—was always a canteen of silver cutlery. He was so confident of winning it again, he'd asked the committee to provide a different trophy, as he already had so many cutlery canteens. Chunderloo 'n' me took the wind out of his sails, good an' proper!'

At Goodooga one year, Janie won the prize for top jockey after a sensational tussle. She had won five races and a male jockey, with the romantic name Tangletooth Thompson, had also won five. There was only the ladies' race left to run, so Janie asked the judges to allow Tangletooth to ride against her to decide a clear winner of the top jockey contest. The judges agreed, but Tangletooth declined, preferring to let her have the trophy rather than ride in a ladies event, the silly bugger.

'Not long after that, I was mustering for a bloke near Walgett, when I got bitten on the ankle by a big brown snake. Luckily we were at the house at the time. I stood on the bastard in the garden and whack! Bloody hurt! The boss was working in a shed nearby. He'd warned me earlier that his wife couldn't stand the sight of blood, so I yelled out to her through the gauze door at their kitchen, "Chuck me out a tea-towel". She was a bloody bitch as well as being a ratbag, and yelled back, "Whaddaya want it for?" I replied, "Just chuck it out here, NOW!" Again she yelled "What for?" So I pulled open the door, stuck me leg in front of her with the blood running from the fang marks, saying "Cos I've been bitten by a bloody snake!" Holy hell, didn't she go right off her flamin' rocker! You've never heard such a performance. Her screams carried to the shed where her old man was working and he raced over, drew his fist back and knocked her out cold. Straight to the jaw. Bloody beautiful it was. That shut the mad bitch up. "Only thing yer can do with her when she's like that, mate," he explained.

'Then he sliced open the fang marks with a razor, sucked the poison out for ages, spitting it out, of course. He put a tourniquet on, rang an ambo, then set out for Walgett. We were nearly there before they found us. The doctor was as handy as an ashtray on a motorbike. Wouldn't do anything for me, he said, till I started "showing symptoms". So I cast aspersions on his qualifications in no uncertain terms and bellowed at him to stick his surgery up his arse sideways—then commandeered his phone. I rang Mum, who told us to head for Brewarrina hospital—two hours' drive away. The patients and receptionist in the waiting room at Walgett had all cleared out when I did my nana with the doctor. They were out in the street looking terrified. To cut a long story short, I chundered all the way to "Bre", was given anti-venene, and was crook there for a long, long time. Because we didn't know the tourniquet should've been released regularly, my leg went black and there was a chance for a while that I could have lost it. I was lucky to live through that and return to normal health.'

If you're getting the impression that Janie doesn't suffer fools lightly, then you're pretty much right. Even as a young woman living and working in the all-male domain of stations out west, she could look after herself.

When she was riding bullocks and buckjumpers in the local rodeos, she would always instruct the pick-up men beforehand: 'If you blokes pull my flamin' shirt up when you lift me off, I'll f . . kin' kill yer!' And there's the story of her flying instructor, who was notorious for expecting certain favours from his female clients in return for their pilot's licence. It was a well-known fact that when he landed his Tiger Moth on a claypan in the middle of nowhere, he was hoping to show the girls what his 'joystick' could do. He soon realised his eyes had made appointments with Janie's trim figure that his body definitely would not get a chance to keep. Her reply to his (imagined) seductive suggestion left him in no doubt. Not being keen to experience having his joystick broken off and inserted in his rectum, he shrugged off his naughty thoughtsand, to calm her down, taught her flying aerobatics instead. She continued to fly for the fun of it, for several years, but racing horses would remain her number one passion.

'Like all young people in the bush, we mostly made our own fun, but occasionally went into the open-air theatre at Walgett to see a cowboy movie. At home we fished and played tennis and cards, but riding horses and talking about horses was our main form of entertainment.'

It was a very sad day for Janie, her brothers and sisters when Boorooma was sold in 1970 and they had to leave the place that had been their home all their lives. 'Dad and Mum were sad, too, but owned a couple of blocks further "inside" and went to run their own show, on a much smaller scale. Boorooma had been a good base for me to contract muster from, but all good things must come to an end.

'Then began my colourful career of doing just about everything you can think of. People think I should be 115 years old to fit in what I've done, but a lot of work out here in the bush is seasonal— you put in a few months doing this, a month or two doing that, so you fit in a lot of different jobs.

'I was opal mining out at the Grawin field with a female mining partner, Cathy, back in the 70s when it was a bloody wild west show there—blokes dropping sticks of gelignite down other blokes' mines, that sort of thing. We never camped there at night—too bloody dangerous. If they thought you were on to opal, anything could happen. The greed of some people on the opal fields is terrible—a man might kill his best mate. There would be a lot of bodies down the bottom of abandoned shafts out in that area. People say these days the Grawin, Glengarry and Sheep Yard fields are like Lightning Ridge was 40 years ago. Well, when we were there, it could have been the early 1900s—there was no copper for miles and everyone was a law unto themselves. The two brothers mining the claim next to Cathy 'n' me kept an eye on us, sort of protected us. They were wogs but good wogs. They hunted any men who came anywhere near our claim.

'I built a camp for myself in the scrub and was proud of what I'd achieved with my own two hands, but decided I'd finish it off by building a dunny, instead of going behind a tree with a shovel all the time. I put a thunderbox on a frame over an abandoned mine-shaft, put in four posts, and got the roof on, all before dark. The walls would be on next day. I felt the call of nature and decided to christen my masterpiece. There I was perched on the throne, nice and relaxed, when suddenly I could hear voices. Yer wouldn't read about it—out in the middle of nowhere, and two flamin' tourists, big cameras round their necks, were wandering towards my camp. They saw me sitting on my dunny with no walls, at the same time that I saw them. I yelled out, "Take a photo if yer want, then piss off!"

'Cathy and I hadn't had much luck but I got the brainwave of digging up the "floor" before we abandoned our claim, and wacko! There it was, under our feet all the time. We didn't make a fortune but we bloody enjoyed spending the money we made there, and you can't describe the thrill of finding opal. Since then I've always had a claim on one of the fields, and mine in between doing other stuff. I find enough to keep me interested. I mine with my brother Joe these days. He comes over to have a dig around when he's sick of the Big Smoke [Tamworth].'

Janie's 'colourful career' included a stint pulling beers at Lightning Ridge—in both the old Diggers Rest and the bowlo—back in the days of the really big drinkers. 'The Ridge was a wild west town—anything could happen. People make bloody idiots of themselves on the grog. I've never been a drinker. Probably seen too much of what grog does to people.

'My mother, as I mentioned earlier, was a real lady, and would have been horrified to think that I'd work in a bar. When I was young, I was keen to learn bar work because I knew you could always get a job if you knew how to pull a beer. My opportunity cropped up when Chrissie and Vicky went to Sydney to a sort of finishing school—learning elocution, deportment, all that stuff—and Mum and Dad asked me to go to Sydney and keep an eye on them. A mate of mine worked at the Menzies Hotel—flash as chain lightning—and I got her to teach me how to pour drinks. I ended up with a job there in a nice quiet bar where the men were well-dressed and behaved themselves. I liked it, and the customers liked me. I've always been able to have a yarn with anyone—especially blokes—probably because I'm interested in people, where they come from, what they do.

'There was a public bar downstairs and in those days only men worked down there. When I told the bar manager I'd work there, he was shocked. "No, we don't have girls working there, because there's quite a bit of rough language," he said. Of course, he didn't know me that well, and I'd minded my p's 'n' q's at the flash bar upstairs, so I had to convince him. "Listen, mate, these city blokes couldn't come up with anything to shock me. If I can sort out f . . kin' jockeys trying to slap a whip across me arse in a race, or tryin' to see me tits in the changing room . . . If I can knock a drover arse over head because he's put the hard word on me out on the stock route, I reckon I can handle anything these pansy bastards down here wanna try. Give me a go. You'll see. I'll get 'em to f . . kin' behave themselves."

'His eyes stuck out like dog's balls, but he was desperate for someone to work downstairs so he reluctantly gave me a go. Well, the first bloke that dropped the "f" word in that bar got the rounds of the kitchen from me. I said: "Now, listen here, mate! There will be no more bad language in this bar. If you, or any of you soupy-eyed lookin' pricks, use the "f" or the "c" word here, I'll knock you arse over f . . kin' head and have you barred from this pub. Right? Now, just mind your language and we'll get on good as gold, okay?" You should've seen the look on their faces! That was in the early 60s so they'd probably never met an assertive female. Did them all the world of good; I trained them all to behave themselves, and the management thought I was f . . kin' Wonder Woman. A bloke asked me one day where was my tip jar. I didn't know what he was talking about. He said, "It's a jar you have here so anyone who wants to give you a tip can put some change in it. Grab a middie glass—that'll do." I said, "Bugger the middie—I'll use a schooner." I did bloody well out of tips. I couldn't get over people wanting to give you extra money just for doing your job. The old sheilas working the upstairs bars with their painted-up faces got a bit jealous of how well I was doing.'

Janie says that working and living in the city was good for a change, but she was soon 'yearning to get back to the bush'. As well as contract mustering, she did a few droving trips on her own, out around Bourke and Brewarrina, from time to time, and spent two years driving semi-loads of roo meat from the chillers at Bollon to Sydney. She's also run teams of lamb-markers and cotton-chippers. 'Like Dad, I'm good at organising people. I taught a lot of previously bloody useless young people how to work hard, how to be punctual, and to take pride in doing a job—even a menial job—properly. Parents used to beg me to give their kids a start and get them off their arse. I'd get them off their arse alright!'

Janie did quite a few seasons in the cotton fields in the early days of the industry in Australia, around Narrabri, Collarenebri, Moree and Bourke, organising teams of chippers. At one stage she was at a big show where it seemed money was no object, and they had just taken delivery of the first 'moon buggies' to be seen in Australia. These buggies were crazy-looking machines that towed the big bins around that were used to build modules, or enormous bales, of cotton in. To back them into a module took skill as they had no brakes. Janie reckons, 'Even the bloody mosquitoes'd get out of their way!' From the time she clapped eyes on one, she was keen as mustard to drive it, but was told by the boss that women weren't allowed anywhere near them. Having backed trucks, trailers and horse floats all her life, she waited for her chance to have a go. One day, to everyone's shock, she just jumped in and had a test run. 'Yes, it was a bastard of a thing to manoeuvre alright, but I had worked it out in no time and set about showing the boss what I could do. There were several big bosses there as well that day and they couldn't believe their bloody eyes. I gave them a real good demo, handling the buggy better than any of the blokes on the place, and they *had* to give me a job driving it. That was a good day.

'Working on an emu farm near Walgett was something different, and interesting. We'd gather the eggs to be incubated, from the mothers, who were often cranky as hell. It was a lively exercise, to get as many eggs as you could from them without getting killed. They can rip you open, kick you to buggery or peck your eyes out in a flash. You haven't lived until you see emus mating—snakes are funny enough—people are even funnier I s'pose—but emus . . . Streuth! The female squats down, shaking her tush to attract a male. He stalks around with his stupid-looking head darting this way and that, then his pea-sized brain finally twigs what's going on, so he sorta squats down too, 'n' sort of crawls along the ground up behind her—a truly ridiculous sight!—then somehow launches himself on board, 'n' into it!

'Emu meat's good for dogs, and they love it. A bloke had built a big processing works over near Collarenebri—put a lot of money into it—and bugger me dead, this greenie bastard put in a protest and because councils these days actually take notice of these green ratbags, the project was stopped, the bloke lost his dough, and the district lost a source of employment. They're useless stupid bastards these greenies! With nowhere to process them locally, the bloke who owned the emu farm I was working on opened the gates and let 'em all go. If greenies had their way, there'd be no industry of any sort, and everyone in Australia would be on the dole.

'I've always been able to find work, because I'll have a go at anything. People who say they can't get work aren't trying hard enough. There's always plenty of work if you make the effort to look for it. Learning to operate the Boorooma exchange as a kid paid off when I was at a loose end once, and there was a job going running the exchange at Goodooga. That was still back in the party line days. Seeing I knew everyone in the district, it was good having a confab with everyone and keeping up with all the news and gossip.

'I even ran a cafe once, for a lady who was sick of it and needed a break. I'd never made a hamburger in my life, but I soon got a reputation for the biggest and best hamburgers in the entire west. I did so well the lady who owned it handed it over to me permanently and I was there for a couple of years—but you get sick of dealing with the public. I was there during the shearers' wide comb dispute, so I bought a heap of those plastic rake things women put through their hair, had them hanging on the wall with a big sign "Wide Combs On Sale Here"—the tourists bought bloody heaps of 'em. Gave them a good laugh and me a good profit.

'I was making more than I do working with stock, but I was glad to get back to mustering. I muster all over the district. People can't afford permanent stationhands any more—everything's done contract or casual. I still work as hard as I did 40 and more years ago, and even if I won Lotto and bought my own property, I'd probably still go mustering for the blokes that I enjoy working with, because I love the work. It's hard and hot and dusty, but it's my life.'

Janie's forte, which makes her valuable to stock owners, is finding stragglers—sheep hiding in the scrub. She's a bloody whizz at it. Her skill is not only due to her ability and stock sense, but also her absolute determination to never leave any stock behind—a clean paddock—just like her dad taught her, way back. The heavily timbered and sandalwood scrub country in the district gives sheep plenty of places to hide . . . but not from Janie. When everyone else is sitting on their arse having afternoon smoko, she will ride her motorbike into the blazing sun for hours, searching until she runs out of light. If she finds any, she returns in a vehicle—in the dark if necessary—to retrieve the stragglers she's left tied down. Or in Janie's case, tied up, for she has invented her own method. When she sends her dogs around to put a straggler on the ground—it might be sick, or just a rogue—she, in her words: 'Puts a f . . kin' collar round its f . . kin' neck, mate—I keep a bunch of 'em on me bike— then tie the bastard up to a tree. That way it's on its feet, fightin' th' f . . kin' rope till I get back, but the f . . kin' crows can't peck its f . . kin' eyes out, like they do when you leave them tied up on the f . . kin' ground. I go back with the f . . kin' trailer to get 'em. It's not easy loading the bastards onto it, 'n' I knock shit out of me vehicle bashing through the scrub to get to 'em, but it's worth it—it's me f . . kin' pride, yer know. Doin' th' bloody job properly. Yer leave a straggler behind, it might have lice, it gets back in the mob when its mates come back, the f . . kin' lice gets onto all the sheep that have been mustered and f . . kin' treated—thousands of dollars worth of f . . kin' chemicals f . . kin' wasted.'

Why does she keep working so hard—dare I say it—at her age? When she's not mustering for other people, she's working her opal mine—also hard yakka. 'I gotta f . . kin' keep goin' or I might drop dead, mate. I've made it past the Marshall deadline—we all die of aneurisms of the brain by 65. I had two, but got the bastards cut out. That's why I keep me hat on me head, even in restaurants. Got a bloody big scar on me f . . kin' forehead. Those bloody doctors are f . . kin' marvellous! They cut the top of me f . . kin' head orf, put it on a table, cut th' f . . kin' aneurisms out, 'n' sewed me f . . kin' head back on again. F . . kin' clever, 'eh?

'I never had kids but that doesn't worry me. I've always had pups 'n' foals 'n' orphan calves 'n' lambs to look after. Bloody kids can be a disappointment to you. At least if a horse is bad, or a dog keeps letting you down, you can shoot the bastards. I got married once— the less said about that the better. Too much grog and gambling, like a lot of blokes in the bush, especially a couple of generations back. We're all entitled to one mistake.

'My dogs mean the world to me. I look after 'em 'n' they look after me. They work their hearts out in the heat and the burrs, but they love working. I feel sorry for some of those "turners" in town—that's dogs that are only good for turning tucker into turds. They're bored stiff! Then there's the owners who let them wander—don't even tie them up at night. I've shot a lot of the sheep-killing bastards. It's not just the sheep they kill, it's the dozen or more they leave with their guts trailing on the ground or their rump half-eaten that makes you really hate them. I've even choked one to death with me bare hands. This big Alsatian-cross sheep-killing mongrel attacked me when I was out "specking" [looking for surface opal glinting after rain]. He went straight for my leg and was ripping a hunk out—shit, that hurt—so I grabbed him by the neck with both hands, dug my thumbs into his neck, saying "Die, you hairy bastard! Die!" while concentrating all my strength on digging those thumbs in. It was self-preservation—the bastard could've gone for my throat next. He took a while to die, and a bloke happened to see the whole thing happen, so that gave the town something to talk about for a while.'

Janie's pretty good at giving people something to talk about. A story that did the rounds for quite a while concerned her search a few years back for a new vehicle. She phoned a Toyota dealer in Brisbane (as usual, in decibels equivalent to a chainsaw). 'Now listen, mate. I'm looking for a f . . kin' good deal on a f . . kin' Land-cruiser. You phone me when you got a real f . . kin' good one, with a f . . kin' good deal, 'n' I'll come up 'n' try the bastard out. If you get me up there to look at crap, y'll f . . kin' regret it, right, young feller?' Well, how could any salesman resist an opportunity to deal with such a charming, interesting lady from the wild west? In due course he phoned her about a spot-on Cruiser wagon just traded. She got herself up to Brissie, took one look at the beautifully presented vehicle, and said: 'Yeah. F . . kin' looks alright. I'm gunna take it for a spin. If she runs alright, I'll be back in three days to pay for it.'

'Three days! Where are you going?' asked the horrified salesman.

'Ter see me mate up in Bundy,' replied Janie. 'Now, get that f . . kin' look off yer dial. I'll look after the f . . kin' thing. I'm from Lightning Ridge. Me word's me f . . kin' bond. Give me the keys— good man. See yer Monday.'

Can you imagine the look on his face as she drove off? True to her word (of f . . kin' course!) she was back Monday and paid in cash.

Another colourful exchange involved a newly arrived constable who was foolish enough to pull her over, and was treated to a dose of Janie's earthy language.

'What th' f . . k are yer pullin' me up for, mate?'

'Random breathalyser test, madam.'

'Shit, mate! I don't even drink! Havn't yer got anything more important to do, like go and catch some f . . kin' mongrel opal ratters?'

'Please just blow into the tube for ten seconds, madam.'

'I just f . . kin' told yer I don't drink . . . what's the f . . kin' point? Yer not telling me yer think I look like a f . . kin' pisspot, are yer, eh?'

'Madam, are you refusing to blow into this breathalyser tube?'

'Argh, for Christsake! I'll *shit* in the bloody thing if yer want me to . . . Give it here . . .'

She might be the embodiment of the quintessential outback woman, but there is absolutely no one else like her. To use an old saying, they broke the mould after Janie Marshall was born, fair dinkum!

MALCOLM McCOSKER OAM

Rural journalist and editor

For as long as I've been reading the *Queensland Country Life*—for more than half a century—there's been a familiar face smiling from its pages. Malcolm McCosker has covered every type of rural-based story imaginable and held many different positions in the organisation, since he started as a cadet way back on Armistice Day in 1961.

Malcolm (his middle name, which he preferred to Robert, which was his first name) had a hard-working but enjoyable childhood on his parents' dairy and banana farm at beautiful Mapleton in the Blackall Ranges. One of seven children, he is now brother-in-law to Queensland's governor, The Hon. Ms Penelope Wensley. After passing an agricultural course at Nambour High School in 1953, Malcolm returned to work on the family farm and during those years became heavily involved in the Junior Farmers Organisation (later called the Rural Youth). A welcome break from the grind of dairying and the hard yakka involved in banana farming was a three-month study tour of New Zealand farms.

Feeling like a change, Malcolm applied for and secured a job as a trainee journalist with the Queensland farmer's 'bible'—*Queensland Country Life* or QCL—and took to the job like a duck to water. Within a year, he was appointed its northern representative, based at Townsville for two years. He covered a massive area, including south to Rockhampton, in a basic Holden sedan with narrow wheels, no frills and no air-conditioning, along mostly rough dirt roads. He recalls travelling from Julia Creek back home to Townsville when a mob of Ampol rally cars flew round him, hurling a rock up that shattered his windscreen. He could have done without the hold-up that caused, because his wife Joy was due to have a baby that night. At the next servo Malcolm bought a pair of sunglasses to help prevent the wind in his face causing his eyes to water. The servo staff couldn't do anything about the windscreen, of course, but told him to help himself to a feed in the kitchen—anything he liked. It was a kind gesture that Malcolm has never forgotten, perhaps because of the circumstances. Nor will he ever forget the sandwich—the beaut big thick hunk of cornbeef with plenty of yellow fat on it, between two buttered slabs of old-fashioned high-top 'dodger', was just what the doctor ordered, to stick to his ribs on what was going to be a bloody long, bloody awful drive home. Replenished by the Queensland country hospitality, away he sailed, with the burning wind in his face, bits of glass flying everywhere, eventually arriving at Townsville at 2 a.m.—just in time for the birth of his baby.

Malcolm feels fortunate to have experienced—during his first years with the newspaper—the early expansion of the Brahman breed into the Queensland cattle industry and regards that as the most memorable development in the beef cattle industry. They may never have caught on if it wasn't for stories in *Country Life*, informing resistant cattlemen who loathed the sight of them of their proven tick resistance, ability to walk further to water, etc. Malcolm, and the handful of people involved in importing and buying them, could see how they could transform the running of stations in the tick-infested regions of the coast and far north. The part he played in this historic era was to provide concrete, factual information.

When the Brahmans first arrived with their strange appearance and snorty attitudes, the bitter resistance of the diehard British breeds' loyalists to the 'lop-eared yaks' often made for lively copy. For example, Malcolm remembers one of the Brahman breed pioneers, Lionel De Llandelles from Cherokee Stud, Yeppoon, who was the first to show them at the Brisbane Royal, arriving with his hump-backed curiosities at the Stud Beef Cattle Pavilion to disgusted looks from other exhibitors. The stewards actually refused to allow them in the pavilion with the other 'proper breeds' (such as Herefords and shorthorns) and sent him to unload them at the rodeo yards. Eventually, of course, Lionel had the last laugh when the breed caught on, and Malcolm was there to write up all his successes at shows and in the sale rings.

In 1964 he was posted to Toowoomba, as the Darling Downs representative, for four years. An unforgettable experience was a big trip to the western regions during the terrible drought of 1965, to gather inspiring stories of isolated primary producers coping with tremendous hardship. In 1967 he undertook a study tour of the US and Canada, to compare grain growing and cattle lot-feeding there with what was happening on the Darling Downs. The feedlot industry was in its infancy in Australia then, and primary producers could rely on *Country Life* to deliver up-to-date information. In 1968 he transferred to the Brisbane head office as assistant to the editor, Wallace Skelsey, who was a much-respected figure in Queensland. Wallace would have a profound influence on Malcolm's career.

After six years in this high-profile role, travelling all over the state, Malcolm was appointed editor of *NSW Country Life* based in Sydney. Originally the parent company of *QCL*, the New South Wales operation was in a rundown shape. 'When I accepted the promotion in 1974 to run *Country Life* in New South Wales, I knew the paper was in financial trouble but I hoped to turn it around. Unfortunately, I couldn't save it.' Malcolm did manage to lift its quality and profile—until the disastrous beef slump that year ripped the guts out of the paper's revenue. This resulted in a forced sale to its opposition, *The Land*, the following year.

Malcolm returned to Brisbane to take over as editor of *QCL*, from the retiring Wallace Skelsey. The newspaper was going well but, as a result of several takeover bids, *QCL* was bought by *The Land* and the papers were soon working together under the umbrella of the newly formed Rural Press Ltd. For Malcolm, however, 1978 brought the 'most memorable' highlight of his career—breaking the news in the *QCL*'s June edition that the beef industry's dreadful woes were over. 'Many cattlemen had suffered, many went broke during the previous four years. I received reliable information from the US that they had ordered 80 000 tonnes of beef from Australia. It was an exhilarating experience to put out the front-page headline of that issue: "Beef Slump Turned Around".'

Having travelled around Queensland reporting on literally thousands of shows, field days, conferences, property sales, political rallies and bunfights, Malcolm is known and welcomed throughout the state. He's seen three generations of youngsters from all over rural Queensland grow up. Along the way, there have been count-less memorable and entertaining incidents, especially out in the far-flung areas.

As well as judging and compering many showgirl contests, in-cluding the Brisbane Royal for years, he also traditionally judged and compered the Queen of the Outback at the North Gregory Hotel in Winton. 'There was always a big blow-out after the announcement, everyone really kicking their heels up, western-style. After one particularly huge party, I realised I'd left my key locked in my room. As usual at those sorts of affairs, I was dressed up like a pox-doctor's clerk in a dinner suit. At some ungodly hour, I was legging a giggling female, who was an entrant and also in evening dress, up through the skylight above my door, when along came—of all people—the main organiser of the contest. To say she was surprised would be an understatement. Girls were expected to be very ladylike back then. I hasten to add that the young lady was merely being kind enough to help me get into my room.

'Another incident that sticks in my mind happened in the dairy cow shed at the Atherton Show. I was interviewing a competitor, a real scrubber, whose overworked missus was making his lunch on a bale beside the cows, in less than hygienic circumstances, to say the least. She had shit stains all over her old frock, broken shoes and teeth, hadn't seen a hairdresser in years, and it was extremely doubtful if she'd washed her hands before making the sandwiches. In fact, it was fairly obvious she hadn't, so my stomach lurched when she handed one to me. I took it to be polite. Then she noticed a cow lifting its tail, left us to it, grabbed a shovel, and caught the very spattery manure as it came out. Naturally it was spraying off the shovel, over her, but she didn't flinch. Munching into his sanger, the husband drawled, "She mightn't be much of a looker, but by cripes, she cin work!"'

Over the years Malcolm learnt many valuable lessons about rural life, such as when he accepted a lift from a bloke who owned a property near Nebo—where he was covering a story—to Mackay. He'd thought the bloke was very kind to offer, but soon found out why. 'I always take a shortcut,' he said, and foolishly, as it turned out, Malcolm replied, 'Oh, good.' The bloke's shortcut was rough as guts, through many properties, and the gates were mostly big heavy timber, c.o.d.—'carry or drag'—bastards or difficult-to-infuriating barbwire 'cocky's gates'. When Malcolm eventually started counting them, there were 52 more. Plus, they laboriously crossed rivers and creeks at least 30 times. It was a nightmare trip he would never forget.

Now, if this next yarn from Malcolm's huge store of anecdotes doesn't make you laugh, you must be dead. It's my favourite, maybe because I have a vivid imagination. Many years ago he was staying on a central Queensland station to cover their annual bull sale.

The host was one of those larger-than-life characters who made sure there was a full bottle of Scotch on every table at the pre-sale dinner. He was also famously fond of the fairer sex and frequently in strife because of his habit of 'riding one and leading one'. The night Malcolm arrived there, it became obvious that his host's wife had just found out he was having an affair with the governess—an oft-repeated scenario in the bush. The wife, dressed to the nines, was awash with Scotch at the dinner table, having been hitting it all afternoon. When the governess walked into the gracious old dining room to join them for dinner, the wife hurled a bottle at her. The governess ducked in time, it smashed against the wall, then the wife launched herself at the governess. It was on, with the two females—the old and the new—punching and abusing each other full-bore on the floor, chairs flying everywhere. Malcolm's a pretty quiet, reserved sort of feller but whenever he recalls that night, he says he can't help grinning: 'All I can see in my mind is the amazing sight of the two women rolling around amongst the antique dining furniture, the wife kicking her legs in the air, revealing her corsets and suspenders, while in the background her beloved husband was at the sideboard calmly carving and sampling the beef.' Stupefied with embarrassment, Malcolm said, 'I think I better go to bed, mate, I'm pretty tired,' to which his genial host smilingly replied, 'No, Malcolm—stay up and enjoy yourself.'

'People think all country people, especially women, are glorious cooks, but I've had some shockers of meals in the bush—and it always *is* a shock when that happens, because you're expecting something delicious, fresh and wholesome. A woman at Biggenden—a beef producer—amazed me by actually serving a frozen quiche for dinner—bloody incredible! I was expecting a big juicy steak.

'Another time I went out to do a story at a huge station, privately owned. The bloke had about 20000 head of cattle, his own twin-engined aircraft, road train, etc., but served up for lunch a loaf of frozen bread, tub of margarine (yuk!) and a tin of Camp Pie, made—as every rural person knows—from lips and arseholes. I should've picked him when I saw he was wearing a woman's white belt! Either too tight, or too strange, to know what a decent feed is.

'An occasion when the big slab of fresh beef that you are naturally looking forward to on a beef property was not only forthcoming, but tasted even better than it smelt, was cooked for me over an open fire in the freezing desert by David Brooks from Birdsville. It was the most delicious beef—turned out to be the organic product they are so proud of out there. David got it out of an old canvas mailbag, and cooked it up with onions. Bloody beautiful.'

It's no surprise that Malcolm has met more than a few unique characters over the years. 'I have a bit of a chuckle whenever I remember that great identity, Sandy Kydd* from Windorah—the man who saved the Cooper—using an old bag from the back of his Toyota to rub the crap off a steel barbecue plate before chucking the tucker on. We were roaring round Mayfield, his country, thrashing his Toyota through high fresh feed. Sandy kept bellowing now and then: "Look at this wild sorghum! Fatten a f . . . in' crowbar!" What a character—one of the last of the larger-than-life one-offs.

---

* Sandy led the campaign to stop cotton-growing being allowed along Coopers Creek.

'When I was sent to write about the Humpty Doo rice project, I met the bloke whom the Crocodile Dundee character was based on. I was invited into his humble abode, and suddenly there was a huge buffalo coming inside, right behind me. That was something different! He was turning his huge head and horns sideways to get through the door, which he'd obviously done many times. Turned out it was the bloke's pet and they ended up using it in the movie.'

'One of the most impressive women I've met was Maudie Fraser, who did a tremendous amount of work organising fundraisers for the Flying Doctor. She helped organise the Queen of the Outback contests, and put a lot of work into preparing Aboriginal girls to enter the quest. Apart from finding it hard to make some of them, particularly from places like Kowanyama, wear shoes, it was also a challenge to get them to talk when the judges were questioning them about themselves. "What do you like doing?" was one question they'd resort to, to get them to open up, but the answer was nearly always "Fishin'". "What do you fish for?" "Barra." "What do you do when you're not fishing? Do you like books?" "Can't read." Maudie would try very, very hard to give these shy girls confidence. The quest was probably the highlight of their lives.

'Apart from meeting many wonderful people in my roles with *Country Life*, I've also been lucky to go to many interesting places. I love the Territory. Alice Springs annual show runs for four days and everyone makes the most of it. The locals love it. I was sent out to cover the story of the show's carcass competition, which is hotly contested by the Territory's cattlemen. I had a bugger of a job finding the abattoir, about 50 kilometres out of town, but was rewarded by a memorable sight when I drove in. It was about seven degrees below zero, and outside the abattoir there were all these people standing around fire drums, all pissed, the women drinking champagne, the men rum, having a great old time. I thought it was the oddest sight until I realised they were the competitors, out there waiting for the results. I reluctantly went inside to introduce myself to the judges, and I swear to God the chiller rooms were warmer than it was outside. My next surprise of the day was to see camels hanging there on hooks. Weird! I was interested to hear an expert opinion that the steaks from a camel—t-bone and fillet—are quite good. You never know what to expect in the Territory.

'When I did a story on the Wyndham meatworks, I thought it was a really spooky place, so isolated, and outside, in the river, massive crocs were chomping on barras that were feeding on blood. A truckie fell in there once and all they could retrieve was his left foot and right arm. Inside, there was a surreal scene—a sewing room, where calico bags were being sewn. The low-grade beef was put into the bags to be sent frozen to British institutions—reform schools and jails—while the better beef went to the US. An abattoir is not an attractive place to be, but that place was horrible. I remember the cattle waiting in the trucks, terrified. I was glad to get away.'

Malcolm says he's proud to be associated with a paper that has always been known as 'the bushman's bible'. 'Some writers work for newspapers that don't command any respect. *Country Life* readers all love their *Country Life*.' However, it did take its toll on his marriage and Malcolm and Joy divorced in May 1986, due to the pressure of his work. They have three children. Sadly Malcolm and Joy's third child, Ian, born in 1966, died in 1969 of a heart condition. In 1989 he married Christina Miller, who also works for *Country Life*.

'There have been so many milestones in my career, but an outstanding experience for me was receiving my OAM [Medal of the Order of Australia] for services to rural journalism, in 1988. Amazing to think that was more than twenty years ago and I'm still here going strong. I'm very fortunate to have been doing something I love during my working life, and that's writing about rural projects. Meeting the people I write about has been my regular bonus. Of my many and varied experiences over 50 years with *QCL*, I list the "Three Bs"—Brahmans, buffel grass and brigalow lands development—as the most significant for Queensland rural production.'

Malcolm's not sure when he'll retire—'but when I finally hang up my notepad and camera, I want to write novels'. Let's hope we'll be reading the words of Malcolm McCosker for a long time yet.

RON CANLIN

Opal miner, sculptor

Thirteen metres below the scorching hot earth's stony surface, a group of people 'Ooh!' and 'Ahh!' in amazement. The children present mouth irritating Americanisms like 'Awesome!' and 'Hey guys, check this out! Cool!' They are down in an opal mine, but the reason for their astonishment and rapture is a series of fantastic sculptures that line the tunnel they're standing in, and are visible in the shorter drives, smaller tunnels branching off left and right. Lightning Ridge, black opal capital of the world, has provided these tourists with many fascinating sights and attractions, but these sculptures are the icing on the cake.

They are standing in Tutankhamen's tomb, his masked body, rich adornments, and valuables guarded by Egyptian dogs. Up ahead, Bart Simpson peeks out from the next drive to the left, while to the right, African creatures hide amongst tropical jungle. For the tourists, the surprise value when encountering these sights in a working mine has made their long trip to the outback worth the effort.

But wait, there's more . . . for the prolific sculptor cannot stop. Since he began in his mine—mysteriously named the Chambers of the Black Hand—more than ten years ago, Ron Canlin has sculpted literally hundreds of figures and scenes. More are added every year, to what has become one of the most talked-about attractions in rural Australia outside of Uluru and the Kimberley. It began with his sudden desire to down pick and shovel one day, and chisel a word in the soft sandstone at the entrance of his claim—Welcome. An unseen muse was inspiring him, an unseen hand (the black hand, perhaps?) was guiding his first-ever artistic efforts. Then he added a bit of decoration, just a couple of ribbons . . . and before he knew it he was gripped with 'a burning creativity urge' that almost overtook his opal fever.

What would his coalminer father make of all this? Or all his male relatives for that matter, who either were, or still are, Derbyshire miners. Well, the walls of a coalmine don't exactly inspire a man to find his creative side, whereas the soft pastel colours of the sandstone in an opal mine are a very different story. Trust a Pom to come out to the wild west and discover not only the thrill of finding Australia's national gemstone plus, as a bonus, his niche in the world—a place where he feels at home—but to also discover himself, what he really is, and what he is capable of.

Born in 1940 at Kerston, a UK Midlands village, Ron enjoyed a happy rural childhood despite the terrifying and horrible happenings of World War II. 'My earliest memories are of hiding under the stairs during air raids, or running, if there was time, with my mother to the air raid shelter in the park nearby, to spend the night wrapped in grey army blankets. I loved watching the British Lancaster bombers flying over and, like all boys, I ran around with my arms out, pretending to fly. We lived in a row of typical miners' houses, with two bedrooms upstairs, two rooms down [kitchen and sitting room], a coalhouse, toilet and dustbin out the backyard, which was shared with the neighbours. There was also a wooden barrel out there for washing the clothes, and after the clothes were washed we children would all pile in, one after the other, to have a bath.

'In those tight times, my dad would file halfpennies down to the size of a shilling, and pop them in the gas meter—that was common practice. I remember often seeing ice inside the windows in winter, and my poor dad coming home covered in coaldust and having to get clean in a tin tub in front of the gas fire. Despite his hard life in the coalmines, he was a bit of a character who enjoyed a joke. When I was little I asked him, when he was in the bath one night, about all the scratches on his shoulders, which were from the mine. He told me they were from "fighting with a tiger". You can guess what that did to my imagination! Looking back, I can also remember cardboard in my hand-me-down shoes; old Nellie Wainwright delivering milk in her horse and cart, and the taste of warm milk, straight from the cows; the friendly and cheerful German prisoners-of-war putting down pavement slabs . . .

'When the war was over, and the delirious celebrations had died down, food rationing continued, to everyone's disappointment. But mothers were marvellous at knocking up meals and there were always plenty of apples to pinch in summer, so I can say I was never hungry. Despite the frequent rain, we enjoyed an "outdoors" childhood, with lots of mates to join in the old games like "tin-a-lurky", a tin-kicking contest, and "duckstone", where each child had half a brick to throw and try to knock down a tower of bricks. We made up other games and were never bored.

'In that era it was unheard of for a mother to go to work, or own a car—unless she was a movie star—so most children walked or ran everywhere. Many fathers didn't own a car and it was absolutely hugely exciting when Dad bought our first car, an Austin A40. From then on our family enjoyed wonderful outings and holidays at Mablethorpe, a lovely little place near Bournemouth. They were simple beach holidays but great fun.

'I was never fond of school, primary or secondary, and had no thoughts about a particular career. Dad had actively discouraged me from working in the mines, so I simply took the first job I applied for, in a plastics factory, making experimental polystyrene snow for plays and movies. You couldn't get anything much more obscure than that! But at fifteen my first pay packet, containing 2 pounds, 16 shillings and a penny, was pretty exciting. To give a price parallel, a pint of beer was a farthing, or about half a cent. I kept 5 shillings for pocket money, paid Mum 10 shillings board, and banked the rest. As soon as I turned seventeen I bought my first motorbike, a Triumph Tiger 88, for 5 pounds. The filament in the headlight globe made a shadow on the road like a head looking up at me, and my mate Barrie, who had a BSA, used to say, "Look, there's Ming the Merciless, he's gonna get you, yer gonna die on that bike."

Fortunately I didn't, but of course back then there was hardly any traffic where we were riding.

'In the mid 50s, the new "teddy boy" look came in [Australians called them bodgies], and Barrie I went for it, big time. I sported greased hair flicked up in the front, ducktails at the back, with a comb in the back pocket of my pegged [skinny] daks, to ensure a lock was never out of place. My leather jacket featured cartoon layabout Andy Capp on the back. Like all teddy boys, I positively swaggered in my suede, ripple-soled "brothel-creepers". I was still dressing in this appalling outfit when I was to meet the lovely, demure girl who would become my wife, hence, the road to romance started with a very rocky path . . .

'One of my mates, Fred, dragged me reluctantly along on a blind date. To my astonishment Glennis turned out to be an attractive and rather posh nurse from Nottingham. She was less than impressed with my teddy boy get-up—that was obvious—so I tried to make up for that by laying on my nonexistent charm! As the night went on, I was sneaking looks at her figure and thinking what all young fellers think about when they look at attractive girls. Still in my teens, I was not the least bit interested in entering into a "serious, respectful relationship" so, being full of raging testosterone 'n' all, "tried it on" on that first date. Glennis was so upset she burst into tears, making me feel really lousy. I said to Fred later that night, "I don't think she liked me." I knew that she was a "nice girl" and I'd acted badly. Full of remorse, I wrote her a nice letter.

'That won her over, thank goodness. She agreed to go out with me again, so to surprise her I ditched the bad boy look. I arrived to pick her up wearing normal clothes and a crewcut. Like all crewcut boys, I actually ironed the top of my head flat with a red-hot iron! I knew girls love to go dancing, so I set out to impress her with my groovy jiving. It worked! The dance floor's the place to win a bird over, alright. Her opinion of me had changed and in no time we graduated to doing the "Creep" [a slow dance], arms wrapped around each other, with me sucking her neck.

'We fell in love and she agreed to marry me, which was wonderful, but first I had to ask her dad's permission. That was one of the hardest things I've ever had to do, partly because he was a Scot and I could hardly understand a bloody word he said, and he and his wife could hardly understand me. I had to say, no fewer than *three times*, that I wanted to marry his daughter. Finally he got it, and replied with: "An' whae d'ye wanna marry our dochterr for, eh? How can ye marry anyone wi' thart dead-end job ye got?" That was slightly demoralising, so I set about looking for something better.

'I heard I could earn 8 pounds a week at Burran's wire factory—piecework rates—bending wire. That was fantastic money! Monotonous as hell, you can well imagine, feeding wire into a machine all day, but I actually got promoted to doing special jobs, manually shaping wire into various products which no machine could do. My promotion meant another three quid a week and, oh boy, my bankbook was getting fatter by the day. My savings were topped up even further by sales of scrap iron I retrieved with a mate from an old slurry pit.

'Glennis and I were married in 1962. I remember her Uncle Fred promised us a load of coal for a wedding present but we never got it—the old bugger. I also can never forget the first meal Glennis cooked for me after our wedding—squares of luncheon meat in Oxo gravy. Very romantic, that was. By then, I had an ex-army BSA messenger bike, bright orange, with a pillion on a rigid frame for Glennis's "comfort"! She never complained, though.

'While we saved for a house of our own, we rented a big room in a big house owned by a very big lady, Mrs Warrington. Her mum, who was *even bigger*, gave me one of the most difficult and embarrassing jobs of my entire life. After pulling the plug out of her bath one day, she found herself stuck fast in the tub, and had to yell for me to rescue her. I had no choice—she was becoming very upset and I was the only one home at the time. When I went in, not knowing where to look, there she was, wedged, in 2 inches of water. Hauling her out was not easy. Try to imagine how hard it was . . . the suction, the flailing of her enormous limbs . . . dragging a draughthorse out of a trough would possibly have been easier, and certainly less embarrassing. I was mentally scarred for quite a few years. In fact, although that story always makes people laugh when I tell it, I personally find it still ghastly to look back on. Maybe I should try to overcome the trauma of that horrific scene by doing a sculpture of it one day? . . . No, maybe not . . .'

(Like many Poms, Ron has a great sense of humour, which shows in quite a few of his sculptures.)

By the time he became a family man with the arrival of baby Debbie, Ron had joined the Marines, based at Poole, Dorset, for the security of employment, the perks such as housing, and the possibility he would like it enough to have a solid career. He was promoted swiftly to sergeant, then invited to join the Special Boat Services (the equivalent of our Special Air Service), learning many gung-ho skills such as parachuting and clearance diving. After eleven years with the service, he resigned to go for the really big dollars offered to divers in the dangerous environment of the North Sea rigs, by a troubleshooting firm called Oceaneering International. It was challenging work to say the least.

The job involved going down to the ocean floor, at depths of up to 600 feet, in a bell with a workmate, on a wire from the rig. From there they would carry out various tasks, such as lifting equipment into the bottom section of the bell, which is sealed by water pressure, or fixing broken or faulty parts. The bell would hold a pressurised gas mixture of helium and oxygen. The gas must equalise to keep the water out of the bell. One man would stay in the bell, saying to those above, 'Diver leaving bell,' while feeding out cord as he went. The outside diver's task might be, for example, to retrieve a piece of broken equipment. He'd take it to his workmate, who'd work on it in the dry bell. In the bell their voices would sound exactly like Mickey Mouse, the result of the air being 93 per cent helium, 7 per cent oxygen. With their brains starved for oxygen, the divers would have to concentrate twice as hard. Any stuff-up was extremely expensive to the oil company. And, of course, during a breakdown, drilling couldn't proceed and all men employed on the rig were idle. Back then, 40 years ago, when a rig was stopped, it was costing the oil company around half a million pounds per day. So the troubleshooting and repair skills of Ron and his workmates were highly valued by the owners of the rigs.

When they returned to the surface, decompression time in the chamber depended on how long they had been down for and how deep—up to 24 hours or, after saturation diving, 36 hours. The chamber was a round room with a mini bell as an entrance airlock, leading to a further series of airlocks. The diving bell would be brought up and sealed to the chamber, then food, reading matter, etc., was passed in to an airlock for them to retrieve. Ron admits he was anxious at times. Two of his colleagues were killed decompressing too fast.

Ron stuck at that dangerous game for six years. Working two weeks on, two off gave him plenty of time to travel around. Ron and Glennis had bought a nice house in Poole, and enjoyed his favourite hobby of collecting old bottles by spending time searching medieval tip sites.

'England's tax laws were what made us decide to emigrate. I was paying 7000 pounds a year in tax—an exorbitant percentage (almost half) of my salary, that I was risking my neck to earn. We went to the emigration centre and Glennis immediately focused on the posters of Australia, saying: "Look, Ron, this is your sort of country—outdoorsy! That's what you like." I agreed. Young Debbie, who was 18 and very mature and sensible, didn't want to go, so we bought a house for her near my family in Ilkstone. We moved to the Gold Coast first, renting a house in Southport, and bought a shop selling second-hand stuff, Lilliput, which gave us a good income, and I enjoyed running it. I bought our stock at the garage sales, and from the licensed scavengers at the tips. You'd be absolutely amazed what people throw out on the Gold Coast.

'We'd heard a lot about Lightning Ridge—that it was a great place to visit—so we had a holiday there in 1980. We liked the place so much, with its free and easy lifestyle, really friendly people, including a lot of remarkable and interesting characters, we returned to the coast, keen as mustard to up stumps and become "Ridgeites". I was also excited at the thought of getting my own mine. In retrospect, that didn't have anything to do with my father and male relatives all being miners. I was just thrilled at the thought of looking for opals.

'I sold the shop fairly quickly, but kept the house we'd bought by then. To keep up the mortgage payments after we moved to the Ridge, I put an ad in the local paper saying I was prepared to do any work for 8 dollars an hour. I did a lot of crappy jobs, like digging holes in ground hard as rock, for a couple of years in between opal mining. We bought a camp, as the dwellings on the opal fields are called, to live in for 2000 dollars at a mining field right on the edge of town. It was quite comfy until the summer temperatures of 40-plus degrees hit us. Being mad Poms, we stuck with it like the pioneers who came out here from the Old Dart did. We both just loved the Ridge, felt at home and made many friends straight away. "Little Mick" was just one of the locals who welcomed us, helped us in every way. Glennis enjoyed her job on the telephone exchange. It was so old-fashioned and the people were all friendly. Although we were in what's thought of as "the outback", we had a good social life.

'I wanted to start opal mining but wasn't interested in the "big time" way of doing things, with lots of machinery and open-cutting my claim. I wanted to go underground with pick and shovel, just like the old days, and feel that thrill of hitting a seam of opal with my pick, with my face just a couple of feet away from it. After 30 years, I still love mining. When you see good quality opals, they are astonishing in their beauty. Other gems are boring by comparison. The blues and greens remind you of the ocean at its most beautiful, whereas the fire and colour that flash from the reds and yellows is breathtaking. Lightning Ridge opals are the best in the world. The black background brings out the other colours more vividly, and they are tougher than the more fragile opal from other areas. It was so exciting to set off in search of them, on my own little piece of the Ridge.

'My first claim was at a field called "Walsh's" near a famous field called "Pony Fence". I was lucky enough to find a big stone, and not bugger it up with my pick, as sometimes happens. I can't describe the thrill when I prised it gently out of the wall—like delivering your first baby yourself! I took it home and Glennis encouraged me to cut it myself. That was a little nerve-racking but a labour of love, too. When I perfected it, I took it to a valuer. Can you imagine how excited I was? I knew I had a special stone. When he said "Twenty thousand dollars", I was speechless. That was nearly 30 years ago, and I used the money to buy a new vehicle for cash, for the first time in my life. From then on I continued to have luck, but not anywhere near that league. My next claim, at what's called the "Three Mile" field, was named the "Black Hand" because it had a signpost with a black hand pointing to the different opal fields, such as "Lunatic Hill", just nearby.

'When I was working there the shaft entrance was right beside the road, and tourists would pull up and ask if they could come down and have a look. I didn't mind and I met a lot of interesting people from all over the world. They'd naturally want to see the opals I had found, and would want to buy one or more—fresh out of the ground—so that turned into a nice little sideline. I even dug steps down to the main level—60 feet down—on a fairly gentle slant so the less active people could come down for a stickybeak, as well as those fit enough to climb up and down the steep mining ladders.

'About 20 feet up from the opal-bearing level I found there was a soft sandstone reef so I dug out a room there to use as a cutting room, where I could turn stones in the rough, or nobbies, into gemstones. The tourists loved to watch me doing this, and it turned out to be a terrific way to sell stones. I enjoyed the interaction with these visitors so much I carved out the word "Welcome" above the entrance in big letters, then felt a bit creative so added a ribbon either side of it. "Hmmm, not bad," I thought, standing back to admire my work. I enjoyed the feeling of creating something in the stone, so I had a go at shaping a hand, holding the ribbon. "Blimey, that's a pretty good effort," I thought, then suddenly I was gripped by a compulsion to keep carving, so I began fashioning a chain around the entrance, then, in the room itself, an Aboriginal's head. I sort of amazed myself with how good it looked, so then I began doing native animals, roos, koalas, emus, snakes and lizards, and created a real "Aussie room", thinking—rightly so, as it turned out—that the tourists would appreciate it. I continued the Aussie theme for a year then felt confident enough to attempt an Egyptian room.

'First, though, I had to dig the second room out of the sand-stone, which took me a year—countless hours on the jackhammer, shovelling, wheeling the dirt to the bucket and hoist. Up and out it went, one bucketful at a time. Each room, each drive, takes a lot of time and patience, which proves how keen I was to find another "canvas". By the time that second room was finished I was dying to create interesting things to fill it. I couldn't wait to start making mummies. Next came King Tut laid out on his sarcophagus, and all his goodies, then the Egyptian dogs on guard. I loved painting the sculptures, bringing them to life in gorgeous colours. As if that wasn't exciting and satisfying enough, my next project really thrilled me: God touching Adam's hand. I was bursting with ideas by then, so I dug a 15-foot drive leading to where I wanted to dig out another room.

'The artistry—painting the sculptures and decorations in each room—also came naturally to me. When I began, my mind was taken back to my art teacher, Mr Cox, who encouraged me no end when I showed a bit of promise at age ten. He talked me into entering a competition to come up with an idea for a road safety poster, then draw and paint it. I won with my entry that consisted of three big eyes and the caption "Eyes on the Road". I used to carve puppets out of pieces of ply, paint them and sell them to friends. But that aside I never in my wildest dreams imagined I would become a sculptor. I just needed the right time and the right place to discover this natural ability, and my opal mine at Lightning Ridge with its beautiful sandstone was *the place*.

'After creating the Egyptian room, I began on the Last Supper in 2007, and was a third of the way through it when along came a bloke called Trevor Hudson. He took one look, and said I should be charging people to see my work. We immediately worked out an arrangement that suited both of us and I could not wish for a better partner. Trevor began taking the tourists through, and that allowed me to get on with sculpting, almost full-time. I still take a break now and then to dig out a few stones, which end up on sale in the souvenir shop. Trevor and his wife Cheryl did a fantastic job promoting the Chambers of the Black Hand, with advertising, brochures, DVDs—you name it—and now they're so busy they even have a booking office in town and a bus to bring people out here four times a day.'

Trevor recalls Ron's surprise when he told him his work was worth paying to see: 'When I convinced him we should combine our talents, we did our deal on a handshake. That's the sort of bloke Ron is—the most honest, decent bloke I have ever met. He's also the hardest worker I have ever met. Even now at 70 he throws timber props around like matchsticks, and thinks a day on the jackhammer is "fun"! We have built the tourism side up to the point where this is the main attraction of the opal fields now, and more and more people are touring with us every year. A hell of a lot of people are coming to the Ridge mainly to see Ron's sculptures. The way he's going, the Chambers of the Black Hand will soon be known as the Eighth Wonder of the World.'

Ron's business partnership with Trevor has changed his life. 'I still enjoy having a yarn with the people when they come through,' Ron says, 'but all that other stuff that used to take up my time is now taken care of, like talking about opals and mining to my visitors. Trevor gives a fantastic presentation to them about how opals are formed, the history of opal mining, cutting stones, etc. People are fascinated, particularly when he tells them about how hard the miners did it in the old days, and how dangerous it used to be. He shows them the timber props that hold up the roof of what's called a "ballroom", where the original earth and stone pillars have been knocked out gradually while looking for the last gems in that area. As you knock them out, you put up a prop to replace it. When Trevor explains that miners in the old days chose that particular timber—belah pine—because it would give a loud *creak* if the roof was collapsing—which hopefully would warn the miner or miners to run to safety—you can see the horrified but amazed looks on the tourists' faces. Meanwhile I'm somewhere nearby sculpting away, so they realise, as they watch the next work in progress, that I'm not worried about the roof collapsing, and that puts their minds at rest. I am, and have always been, very safety conscious in my mines, which probably stems from my time in the Marines and diving in the North Sea. I would never, for example, ride the bucket up on the hoist. Some blokes used to take that risk. One feller fell all the way down his mine when he was starting his generator with his back to the shaft opening, and the starter rope broke. There used to be quite a lot of accidents, some fatal here, but hardly any—and no fatalities—since a compulsory safety course was introduced about twelve years ago.'

Will he ever stop? 'I don't think I will ever get sick of creating lovely things from stone, and—when I'm in the mood—humorous pieces, like the Simpsons, and Julia Gillard over there sticking the knife into Kevin Rudd. I love to hear the people laughing when they see the pieces I've created specifically for that reason. I put them in unexpected places to give the tour groups a big surprise. It's entertainment—the wow factor. I've bought the claim next to mine, which is 80 per cent good stone for carving, so that should see me out, I reckon. Lightning Ridge is my home forever. I have a wonderful life here. The facilities in the town are night and day compared to what it was like before tourism started to really catch on in the early 70s. Our bowling club and our supermarket are as good as anything you'd see in Sydney. The Ridge has always been multicultural, but now tourists flock here from all over the world, and many come back to stay, like I did. It's the cruisy, no-stress lifestyle, and for some the chance to make their fortune. My good fortune was coming here in the first place. When I visit my family in the UK, I can't wait to get back "home".

'Sadly, Glennis died of cancer three years ago. She was a lovely lady, a wonderful wife and friend, and very popular. I have been lucky enough to recently find another lovely lady to share my life. Isabel and I are great friends and she has just consented to be my fiancée. She has lived in the Ridge for more than 30 years and we share the same interests. She's a metal sculptor. Her late husband Julius was famous for his magnificent opal mosaics.'

Ron's final message just about sums up all there is to say about this remarkable and inspiring man: 'I would say to anyone reading this who has reached a "golden age" and not had a go at what they would really want—in their heart—to do: Just do it. Have a go. That's the Aussie way.'

SHEILA ROSS

British intelligence agent, World War II

While this book was being written there was, and probably still is, a lot of controversy worldwide, including in Australia, about the problem of illegal immigrants 'jumping the queue'. So it's even more astounding that someone like Sheila Ross—who made a great contribution to the British Empire's war effort and was trusted to perform top-secret intelligence work—and her husband Graham, an ex–Royal Scots Guard, were forced to jump through hoops backwards and sideways, for a long time, before being allowed to migrate to Australia.

But that's just one amazing story Sheila recounted to me about her extraordinary life. One of the last representatives of a bygone era, having lived through times extremely different to the present-day world, Sheila also experienced lifestyles, adventures, suffering and danger few people could even imagine—especially when you're looking at this attractive, immaculate and genteel 86-year-old woman. As they say, appearances can be deceiving . . . She's as tough as they come.

Sheila was born in Malaya and enjoyed an idyllic childhood with her two brothers and two sisters on a jungle plantation. Her father was a tea planter, and had married the daughter of another tea planter from Ceylon (as Sri Lanka was known then), which like Malaya was part of the British Empire. The happy family, with their servants and many trips back to England, weren't to know that they were living in what was almost the end of that era.

'My father was a wonderful person, so was my mother. They were both extremely proud of their Scottish roots and regarded themselves as "Scots with no residential qualifications". We experienced the best of both worlds—the freedom to run about and play barefoot in the jungle with the native servants' children at home, then go back to visit the United Kingdom every couple of years and live in completely opposite surroundings with privileged people. Not that my parents didn't live by all the social graces and possible comforts in Malaya, but we were allowed, as children, to go "completely native" out on the plantation with the other children. Our playmates included orangutans, wild and domesticated.

'Our nannies and other staff were all Muslim, so we were brought up to respect their religion. We were the only European children in Malacca [on the southern Malay Peninsula]. At age ten, I was sent off to St Cuthbert's school near Bournemouth, England. In those days you just had to accept that as an inescapable part of life.

While away at school, when I was twelve, my dear mother died—incredibly sad.

'At school my main purpose was ringleader of a group which specialised in night-time infiltration of sweets cupboards. This entailed climbing up and out of skylights, and flitting silently across rooftops, to raid what we felt was rightfully ours. Eventually we were caught. The letter to my father inferred the school might be better off without my bad influence on others. I was instructed to send the letter to my father, which of course I didn't, but he eventually found out. I travelled home for the holidays, dreading what was going to happen and where I'd be sent next year. But there's such a thing as divine intervention . . .

'The Second World War broke out on 3 September 1939—my brother George's wedding day. I can still see the beautifully decorated tables out on the lawn, the house bedecked with flowers, my sister and I in our lovely bridesmaids' dresses, when a sonorous voice from London announced Britain was at war with Germany. I was fourteen, enjoying the long summer holidays in Malaya. My father said, "No going back to England for you now." Schoolchildren were being evacuated out of London and I remember thinking while walking up the aisle behind my sister-in-law that "Hitler has saved me from going to school". However, a school was found prepared to take such a naughty girl, up in the Cameron Highlands [in Scotland]. I got through it, not wanting to cause my father any more worry.

'After school, my sister Diana and I both found jobs in the Medical Auxiliary Service, working in the blood bank of the new army hospital in Malacca during the day, and in the troops canteen at night. When it closed, we were both off to dance in the "fleapits". There weren't many young men around, but in 1941 the Australians arrived; great big chunks of manhood most of them. We were dazzled, especially Diana, who eloped with one of the officers. What a hoot!

'Then came the fatal night of 7 December, when the Japanese invaded Malaya, and dropped their first bombs on Singapore, Hong Kong and Pearl Harbor. Volunteers were mobilised, iron rations carefully stored. Combat troops, including Rex, Diana's new husband, moved south and east. Rumours were rife, stories of fifth columnists and infiltrated Japs on every tongue . . . many were true. Stiff upper lips were the order of the day, but we were all stunned by the sinking of the *Prince of Wales* and *Repulse* only two days after the declaration of war. It's impossible for people to imagine living through that fear and uncertainty if they haven't experienced it.'

By mid February 1942, most of the Malayan Peninsula had been overrun by the Japanese and Sheila and her family were forced to leave their beloved homeland, escaping south on a hairy journey to Singapore. Their focus was on the war effort, and on arrival her father, who was a member of the legislative assembly, spent a lot of time closeted with the governor and armed service chiefs. Her elder sister Betty was snapped up by the British Hospital, while Diana and Sheila joined the Royal Signals. Their brother George literally swam in—'looking like a drowned rat after a night in the ocean'—one of just two survivors of his ship being attacked and sunk on his way back from India. He immediately began driving lorries with the volunteers. Except for her brother Bill, who was in Hong Kong, and her sister-in-law, who had remained in India, Sheila's whole family was concentrated on Singapore Island. Sheila says they didn't believe the British would allow Singapore to fall. 'That was unthinkable.'

Despite her very slow typing, which exasperated the sergeant of the signals unit, and the danger of bombing attacks, Sheila managed to enjoy her first experiences of war. 'When you're sixteen, the only girl amongst a crowd of men, with an identity disc, an armband and World War I tin hat, squatting in the trench with earth falling about you, shrapnel flying overhead, there's no time for fright, just exhilaration. I felt like I was one of the boys.' She made friends with a farmer's son from Ecclefechan, Wales, 'a large raw-boned laughing lad', and whenever the bombing and shelling forced them to dive in the trenches the youngsters clowned about and made a game of it, pushing and shoving each other and giggling behind the sergeant major's back. But one day when the bombing stopped, Sheila couldn't move to get up out of the trench. Her friend lay across her, dead. Sheila says, 'That was the end of any semblance of fun or light-heartedness.'

Then, one morning on their way to work, Sheila and Di were stopped by military officers with the shocking news that the Japanese were on the island. They were told to go home and wait for orders. 'Eventually a truck arrived to take us to a ship that was evacuating the signals unit to Java. To soothe our nerves while waiting, Di had put her record of "Stardust" on the player, on repeat. I can never hear that beautiful song without the heart-breaking vision of my dear father waving goodbye as we sped off. He could have come with us, but would not desert Malaya—our home.

'Our trip to the docks was a nightmare in monsoon rains, and when we arrived it was like Dante's Inferno. The oil islands nearby had been set alight; the roar of the flames deafening, but not quite loud enough to drown out the deeper roar of the bombers, concentrating on the docks. "Take cover where you can! I'll try to find out when you can board," a young second lieutenant was yelling to us, trying to make himself heard above the combined noise of the bombers, fires, ships' hooters, shrieks of the wounded, and steady tramp of boots as men ascended the gangplanks in never-ending lines. Di and I became separated in all the confusion. Imagine the effect all that was going on had on a sixteen-year-old girl?'

Fortunately, Sheila managed to find her sister and together they spent several tense days on the dock, with nothing to eat, waiting. Sheila says she tried not to think about the things she had to leave behind, including her passport and a change of clothes—'We weren't allowed to grab anything.' Finally they were told to board a cargo ship, built to carry six passengers but laden with several thousand men. 'The decks were literally packed with soldiers, shoulder to shoulder, with not enough room for everyone to sit.' While they waited for darkness to fall, as it was deemed safer to travel at night, dive bombers strafed the deck with machine-gun fire. Sheila recalls the English soldiers around her joking about the food they'd soon be eating back in Old Blighty and singing chants like 'Why are we waiting, why o why o why-o . . .' to ease the tension and fill in the time.

'Suddenly the dive bombers came in for an even closer attack. Some men tried to pull their legs or heads in under the meagre cover.

A spatter of bullets ripped up our deck and across the stomach of the previously joking soldier next to me, perforating him like a postage stamp. Great gouts of blood jetted up, then he just seemed to burst open and his entrails oozed out. I had seen quite a few dead men by then but nothing as awful as that and, to my embarrassment, I was sick.'

Another memory of that long and terrible afternoon that has stayed with Sheila was watching the Australian troops disembarking. 'They were big strong noble-looking fellows—all thinking they were going to save Singapore and Malaya—and they didn't realise that they were virtually walking off straight into the prison camps. A dreadful waste. A dreadful disaster. Many of those young Aussie men I saw getting off the ships would not have survived—part of the complete tragedy of the 8th Division.'

Finally, in the bizarre light of the oil fires, the little cargo ship set sail. It was Friday 13 and Sheila says she and Di weren't sure if it was their lucky, or unlucky, day but 'at least we were still alive'.

'After a mostly sleepless night, it was a great relief when we woke at first light to see just empty sea. So far so good. Most of the men on board were Royal Air Force [RAF] who, like us, were heading for Java to continue the war. There was a smattering of infantry and gunners, British and Australian. The other women on board were mostly nurses and included, to our glorious surprise, our sister Betty. Their patients, mostly men in plaster, were all stowed in the hold. An RAF sergeant walked along with two airmen, doling out half a mug of water to each person. "Another half a mug this afternoon, no food till we get to Java."

'Then we heard a dreaded buzzing. Tiny specks materialised out of the sun. There was a moment of hideous panic as men crowded together, in a futile search for cover. Most of them were sitting ducks in the open. There was nowhere to go. We were forced to just watch the planes come in low, guns blazing. Our little tub rocked and bucked as bombs found their target. Betty was thrown down a gangway, seriously injuring her back. Everywhere men slithered and fell and cursed. The airmen manning the Vickers guns rat-tatted impotently as they came in again and again. When a man fell at a gun, his place was immediately taken. Then at last they hit one of the Japs and a huge cheer went up. The remaining planes flew off, leaving havoc behind them. Worse of all, an incendiary bomb had landed in the hold among the injured passengers. The calls of the immobilised men, trapped in their heavy plaster casts, were too pitiful to describe; the screams of those being burnt alive too terrible.

'Later, when the captain stopped to bury the dead, the power and emotion in the soldiers' faces and voices singing "Abide With Me" is something none of us could forget. That night, the captain allowed Betty and me to sleep on his bridge, there being nowhere else to lie down. Another unforgettable moment was the sight of him gently placing his dressing gown over us. A gallant man, he intended to return to Singapore in the hope of rescuing more people, but he went down with his ship in the Mozambique Channel shortly afterwards.

'Battered and torn, listing badly, the lifeboats blasted from their davits, our little ship crept into Tanjong Priok, the port of Batavia (now Jakarta). Two Dutch naval officers came on board, and there was an ominous silence after they announced they had news for us. Then the dreaded words came: Singapore, the bastion between the Dutch East Indies and the Japanese, had fallen. Everyone left behind killed or captured. That, of course, included my father and brother. What a tremendous blow, in more ways than one. It was the greatest bungle of World War II.

'Everyone on board was not only shocked but deflated, having planned on fighting to save Singapore. After hours of miserable waiting, some watery soup—the first food we'd had for a long time—was brought on board, but no one felt hungry anymore. We ate it to keep our strength up. Early next morning the soldiers and airmen were marched off the ship, to God knows where.'

Sheila and the rest of the passengers were now refugees. They were eventually transferred to a Dutch ship, bound for Colombo, and hidden in the hold. 'You don't know what darkness is until you've been confined, as we were, right at the very bottom of the vessel, below the waterline, and battened down. The terror as those hatches were fastened shut was the worst fear I've felt in my entire life. Three hundred of us, huddled down on mouldy straw, too far down to hear the bombers but we could feel the thudding and shuddering of the ship during attacks. Batavia was experiencing its first air raid. All that night, the next day and the next night we were kept down there, trying to mentally prepare ourselves for the worst, how we would handle the unspeakable fate of being burnt to death or drowning in the sunken ship. At last the lights came on, blinding us, but I can remember the tremendous relief very clearly—and to this day, I cannot sleep with curtains or windows closed.'

Sheila recalls the 'huge and hearty cheering' when they reached Colombo, despite the passengers being by then weak from hunger, exhaustion and stress. 'When finally we were taken ashore, the Red Cross gave us a few essentials. Oh, the luxury of a toothbrush!' Despite all she had already endured and her young age, Sheila couldn't wait to 'get back into the war' and continue the fight for her homeland and the British Empire. From Colombo her arduous journey took her to Bombay, Freetown, Trinidad, Halifax and finally Liverpool. On route, she fell in love with a bomber pilot in Cape Town, and decided to join the RAF. But after they arrived on English shores, and a farewell kiss in a park, he went home to his wife.

'Suffering from a broken heart, I went to have my medical, putting my age up a year to seventeen and a half. I had no documents whatsoever, of course, and had a hard time even proving I was alive, as I had been listed as "missing, presumed dead". I remember virtually living at Waterloo Station for five days, sleeping on a bench and eating leftover sandwiches, not a penny to my name. I couldn't wait to get to the RAF training depot if for no other reason than to get a proper meal.

'Training was rigorous and tough, but friendships were formed amid a vast variety of girls—from daughters of aristocrats to the toughest girls from Glasgow. My first posting at a busy coastal fighter station entailed pulling people—alive and dead—out of rubble after air raids. I was so proud of being able to wear my Malaya flashes [the emblem identifying a soldier's unit], which also meant extra blankets as I was from the tropics—a big privilege. One man in the village saw my uniform and said, "Good to know the Empire is with us," while another cranky old sod chased me with a stick, saying, "I know you foreign devils—you're just over here to eat all our food!" My Cornish landlord told me, his accent thick as treacle, "We done found May-lay on a map. 'E be a furriner, like us; we did come up from Carnwall 40 year ago!" Back then, many English people never left their counties or shires.

'Twenty of us were chosen to go to Leighton Buzzard to train as aircraft plotters. Our sergeant instructor told us we had to learn fast, due to staff lost in raids, and there was a lot to learn, including radio-telephone procedure, radar, navigation, air speeds, wind velocity and dead reckoning. Then there were ops room procedures and defence to learn in case of an invasion. We learnt how to throw grenades and operate Sten guns. On the walls were Molotov cocktails to be hurled to destroy everything, but we were never told what to do with ourselves!

'Plots came in relentlessly, nine a minute at times, and I wondered if I would ever make the grade at first. You were supposed to be relieved for five minutes an hour, but often sat there for hours, hunched over huge maps, exhausted, leg and back muscles aching. When you finally went to bed, the huts would resound with girls telling plots in their sleep.

'Once, when I took over my shift at the plotting table, I saw an aircraft was circling over the Cherbourg Peninsula [in north-western France]. My gut feeling told me it was one of ours, in trouble, then a radio-telephone operator picked up his "Mayday". We followed him for a while, then lost him, imagining Germans had intercepted.

A cheer went up as we picked him up again, at last heading in the right direction, but losing height. Then we found out he'd been shot down. We were familiar with that terrible sequence of events, and all tried to settle back into work. Later, a bomber heading home from France reported seeing a dinghy. For nine days the survivor drifted off the French coast, well within range of shore batteries, before he was finally rescued. When we heard the news, the ops room went wild. If only all those stories had such a happy ending . . .

'Coming off nightwatch one day, I returned to the tiny cottage I was staying in, which was on the cliff edge. To take advantage of the rare winter sunshine, I spread a groundsheet out on the grass to sleep outside. A yell from a gunsite a hundred yards away woke me with a start. Then I could hear their "ack-ack" gun, and the sinister, terrifying sound of a lone raider coming in to strafe the cliffs, guns blazing, swooping low, his target the Air Sea Rescue launches below me. I pulled the groundsheet over me, and lay there terrified, till he wheeled around over the top of me and headed back. "Oy, wotyer fink yor in disguise as a rock or sumfin?" a Cockney gunner called out. "You don't arf look silly, wif yer feet stickin' out 'n' all." I got up and shook the dust off myself, then saw the proximity of the line of bullet holes next to where I'd been lying. I could see then that he was relieved I was still alive. "We're brewin' up—come over 'n' 'av' a cuppa wif us." When I got closer to their gunsite, I saw one of his mates lying dead, a handkerchief over his face. "All 'is problems is over. Poor sod copped it." None of the others—all Cockneys—mentioned him. It was easy to see why the spirit of London in the Blitz never failed.

'Always in the back of my mind, I worried about my father, picturing him as he'd waved me goodbye. A pilot friend from Poland introduced me to his priest, whom he thought might be able to help find out if my father was alive. The priest asked me to write a letter to my father and said he would do his best to get it to him. He kept his word. My father received it a year later, and his fellow inmates in Changi told me later on that it transformed him from a worried old man to a bright-eyed optimist, knowing that his daughters were safe. When the Red Cross told me it had been delivered to him, I rushed to tell the priest, but was too late—he'd been killed in an air raid just the night before. My Polish pilot friend was also killed during a raid—I'd plotted him out.'

The strong friendships formed during the horror of wartime had an 'undercurrent of desperation', Sheila says. 'We knew that some of us would not live to see the end of the war. Whenever a group of us met up at the pub for a few drinks or a party, it was always noisy and gay, but no one ever asked about someone who wasn't there. It was highly likely they'd "bought it". Our base was a real "United Nations" and the publican was sometimes heard to call out: "Drinks all round on me. An Englishman just walked in."'

Sheila experienced many amazing things during the war, but none more so than the night a cat saved her life. Sheila had become very close friends with another plotter, Phillipa, and while she was on sick leave, recovering from malaria, she stayed with Phillipa's mother. They were on the rooftop of her home with some other visitors when air raid sirens went off and bombing began. As they looked out at the fires in the city, Phillipa's mother's cat jumped at his owner, grabbing her slacks in his teeth and pulling frantically, snarling at the others who tried to stop him. 'He was telling us to go downstairs, begging us to follow him, so we did. A few moments after we left, the roof where we'd been standing was bathed in flying shards of glass as a landmine landed very close by.'

One of the proudest days of Sheila's life was when she passed her plotting exams with 100 per cent accuracy, to become a leading aircraftswoman. She didn't consider herself to have a mathematical brain, and the exams were notoriously difficult, so she had to work extremely hard to pass, let alone with a perfect score.

'The operation I was associated with, keeping track of hundreds of aircraft and ships, and plotting the paths of our aircraft going out and returning, was so important and requiring dedicated precise people, I was proud to be part of it. There was no room for fools or people who weren't totally focused.

'After that I was called in and told I had been selected to appear before the Air Ministry in London to see if I was suitable for intelligence work. I was sent off to officer training college, in a requisitioned lakeside hotel, after which I would be going to intelligence school. We learnt a lot, and the exams were hard. Drill was even harder. A humorous incident occurred when the drill sergeant, roaring at us out in the freezing snow as usual, was suddenly attacked by a little old lady wielding an umbrella, which she whacked across his kidneys while shouting, "How dare you speak to them like that. They are ladies! Shame on you!"

'At RAF Intelligence School, I learnt more than I had ever learnt before, or since. It was a fascinating new world, with brilliant lectures from outstanding personalities in the field of airforce, army and naval intelligence. At the same time, courses were being held for aircrews, on escape and evasion, if they were shot down. I was trained in Japanese intelligence. I read translations of many Japanese war diaries, which was pretty shattering. The inner sanctum of intelligence was "Top Secret Ultra", manned not by serving officers but officers who were mostly civilians, with no experience of fighting. Very different from my superiors in plotting. At one stage I had my hopes raised I was to be posted to General Mountbatten's HQ at Kandy, my mother's birthplace in Ceylon, but then I was let down— I was being sent to the army.

'My new unit was hidden in the English countryside, and what a relief to be back working amongst people who had all had actual experience in active service. Our work was mainly dealing with escaped or escaping prisoners of war and those who helped them, and we achieved a lot towards saving people—very rewarding. There was a tremendous team spirit amongst the mixture of navy, airforce and army personnel, some of whom had been escapees themselves. One was a wing commander, a splendid personality, who'd lost an eye in a battle at Azerbaijan. He absolutely loved his glass eye because it allowed him to continue smoking without having to remove the ciggie from his mouth. The smoke could curl up into the eye and not annoy him. Consequently there was a perpetual nicotine stain right across the eye, and ash everywhere. Frequently his beautiful wife would phone us, saying, "He has a VIP visitor today. Please dust him off before they arrive." Not that his visitors stayed long as his dogs occupied every comfortable chair.

'As we were within reach of London, I continued, against advice from friends, to see my Cape Town bomber pilot, the youngest commodore in the RAF. I well knew, through my work, of what he had achieved—his raids, his decorations. I also knew that he loved me, but was staying in his unhappy marriage because he was ambitious and the powers-that-be frowned on divorce. I finally found the strength to tell him we mustn't see each other again. We didn't, but he sent me birthday and Christmas cards from all over the world for many years afterwards. When he put me on the train, the last time I saw him, he told me, "You are the only woman I have ever truly loved." The thought hit me, during that tearful journey back to my base, that it was the first time in my life I had been called a woman. Although I was still in my teens, I had grown up.'

Sheila was only twenty years old when World War II ended—and she had already seen so much death and destruction in her life. She recalls: 'Amid the joyous celebrations in Picadilly Circus, I collapsed on the steps of Swan and Edgar's and cried my heart out, thinking of my family, who were POWs. Working all that time in the Japanese section of intelligence, I knew too much—knew of the plans to dispose of prisoners should invasion be imminent; to burn them or bury them alive. Such a cruel enemy, the Japanese. I knew the war must inevitably be concentrated on that area now.

'Soon, released prisoners were streaming back from Europe, and I took part in interrogating them about their ordeal, their attempted escapes, sabotage, collaboration, etc. Most of the escapes entailed amazing tales of determination, courage and survival. There would be many war trials ahead for those who had treated the POWs so cruelly, and for those who had betrayed escapees.

'Then, the bomb dropped on Hiroshima. Horrific though it might have seemed to some people, if it had not happened none of my family would have lived, nor many innocent civilians throughout Asia. I said a prayer of thanks and awaited news. I was torn between taking a posting in Italy, or going to Port Said to join the ships bringing POWs home. We were to interview them from there to London, thus saving delays in reuniting them with their families. Thanks to my commanding officer, the kind brigadier, I was able to do both. He arranged for me to go on the ship bringing my father from Changi. It was the first ship, the *Monowai*, carrying the worst cases plus elderly. As it arrived in Liverpool, flags flying, the Royal Marines playing the national anthem, the living skeletons on the decks tried to drag themselves upright to take the salute—so gallant, so pathetic.

'I went on board to search for my father, sending word out. Eventually a little old man shuffled across the foyer towards me. My father had been a tall, big man who weighed 19 stone. Now he weighed seven. This pathetic creature, skin hanging in folds like an ancient elephant, frowned. "Sheila? But . . . you were a child . . . just a child." We stared at each other in shock.'

Sheila spent the next two years posted in various parts of Italy, which was occupied by Allied forces. She thoroughly enjoyed most of her time there, apart from the few areas where the Allied forces were resented—the sort of places, she says, where girls who consorted with Allied personnel had their heads shaved and were paraded publicly in shame, just as they had been when consorting with Germans when under their occupation. 'A major problem in Italy was the stealing of everything, from vehicles and petrol, to boots and coats. You had to guard everything all the time.'

She was pleased to be posted back to the UK in February 1947. 'It was wonderful to see Phillipa and her family again, but the UK was a sea of depressed drab grey queues—people forced to queue for everything.' However, Sheila soon discovered that the only intelligence work on offer was in Russia, and she 'worked out in half an hour' that she didn't want to learn Russian so took a job in photo interpretation instead. But she found the work, which would have been interesting and vital during the war years, was boring and repetitive.

'Then fate led me to meet my husband-to-be, Graham Ross, a handsome proud kilted officer of the Queens Own Cameron Highlanders. By some miracle he was posted, after our 1947 London wedding, to Singapore and I was able to get a posting there also. I sailed to join him, through the Suez, Aden, Bombay, in a ship transporting some of the last British troops to India and Colombo. On my last "visit" to Colombo as a penniless refugee, the Red Cross had given me a toothbrush; this time I danced in the opulent ballroom of the Galle Face Hotel with my fellow travellers—such a contrast. And, this time, I was going home, not escaping the Japanese.

'We arrived at Singapore on Chinese New Year and were ordered to anchor off until after the holiday. It was fate; I had left Singapore on Friday 13, 1942, now I was returning on Friday 13, 1948. Six years earlier, I had looked out on that wharf—a catastrophic scene then—with fear; now I was looking down at the smiling faces of my new husband and my wonderful family. Home at last.'

Graham's work, first with the Colonial Service and then the Malaya Police Force, had them 'at home' until 1956. For the next ten years after that he took over remote postings in Borneo. They then lived in Spain for 38 years—where Sheila began a new career, as a writer. (Her first book was the best-selling *A Log Across the Road*, a novel about the Malayan Communist insurgency in the 1950s.) After their only child Christine married a Spanish professional diver and moved to Australia, they visited many times and loved it.

'Christine was running a restaurant at Caloundra, a beautiful place. Graham and I didn't need much convincing to apply to migrate here, but amazingly the Australian government officials gave us a hell of a time with our application. Despite our background, we had to fill out hundreds of forms, jump through hoops, produce bank statements, etc. etc. Our only way in was with a four-year visa, with no government perks such as Medicare. We had to stay fourteen months without leaving the country, and my brother, already an Aussie citizen, had to vouch for us. It was a ridiculous exercise, compared with the people who are welcomed here and given everything immediately. Despite the government's double standards, we were very proud and happy to be finally accepted as Australian citizens.'

Sheila is still living near Caloundra and while her days are a lot more peaceful, she continues to face life with the same courage as that sixteen-year-old girl who stepped up to take a place in World War II. 'Sadly, our daughter died at 34. Graham died recently, after

61 years of marriage. I am devastated at losing him but have my writing to keep me going.' Having already written nine books, she is currently working on a quartet of books based on the early Scottish settlers of South China and Malaya. 'My life has never been dull, and I have been lucky enough to have had a wonderful husband and daughter, and to serve in interesting places. Except for the tragic loss of Christine, then Graham, my life has been, on the whole, happy.'

When Sheila marches every Anzac Day, she thinks of the many who didn't make it home, and those who have gone since the end of the war. Like the other people in this book, it is an absolute privilege for me to have met this gracious and gallant lady.

PETER VENABLES

Keeping the past alive

Have you ever wanted to step back in time? Do you wish you were around in the days when everything was done with horses—in a slower era, when life moved at a steady pace? People had time to think things out clearly, with an uncluttered mind. There was always time to stop for a yarn—a *big, long* chat—surrounded by the wholesome smell of leather and horse sweat, and the comforting, peaceful sound of mouthfuls of grass being tugged and chomped while the horses patiently waited for you.

There would have to be few people on earth who would fail to be moved by the majestic, beautiful and heart-warming sight of a team of giant, baldy-faced Clydesdales pulling a wagon or plough across a paddock. If you're travelling between Tenterfield and Texas, and you see a bloke with a flowing grey beard, pipe in mouth, driving such a team, pull up, give him a wave, and I'll bet you ten to one on, he'll mosey over for a chinwag. His name is Peter Venables and he loves a chat and a joke or two almost as much as he loves his magnificent horses. Peter is living his dream—of breeding, training and working with 'Clydies', every day of his life—and he's happy to share it, too.

Although he looks like he has stepped out of a nineteenth-century painting, Peter was born in 1936, at Parkes (home of 'The Dish'). His mother would have been a busy lady, with four boys and three girls to care for, as well as teaching music—a career she carried on until retiring aged 86.

Peter's first introduction to horses was his father's carthorse, which he drove to haul carcasses from the slaughter yards to his butcher shop. He loved to help harness, groom and feed the horse, and by the time Peter was five his parents felt he deserved his own pony. Not long after, Peter went off the rails doing something quite crazy, as all normal boys do from time to time. He pinched a fancy horse and sulky to 'take it for a spin'—and 'going too bloody fast', tipped it over, smashing the seats. He drove home sitting on the axle, wondering how the hell he was going to get out of this fine mess. But instead of giving him a thrashing his father explained what Peter had done wrong, that he must never take anything that didn't belong to him or put himself in danger. Peter was very lucky. His father was an exceedingly patient man! He always took the time to teach his children well, and in Peter's case he passed on a wealth of knowledge about horses, harness and butchering that has stood him in good stead all his life.

At six, riding a new pony, Peter went on a droving trip with his uncle, who couldn't hire a man to help him as they were all away fighting in World War II. So young Peter was it—the offsider. But this was no ordinary, average-sized mob of around 3000—the number two blokes would normally handle. This was a *ginormous* mob of 23 000 head, which the American military in Australia had amassed, and had organised to be delivered to Parkes for slaughter. Peter's uncle was chosen for the job of taking them to Daroobalgie meatworks—a three-day trip—as he was a specialty drover who took mobs on shorter trips to the paddocks belonging to the meatworks. He had a large number of excellent working dogs, which enabled him to handle big mobs, usually with one experienced man. For this important and challenging trip—his biggest ever—he had to put his trust in a six-year-old boy to help him keep them together and deliver every head. His reputation depended on their success.

Peter can still vividly recall the excitement of being part of what was a huge adventure for him, as well as his determination to do a good job for his uncle. He remembers feeling proud as punch as people waved to him from the occasional vehicle that went past, and the romance of sitting round the campfire, eating from camp ovens, drinking a quartpot of billy tea and sleeping out under the stars. He was aware of the responsibility placed on his young shoulders, not to lose any sheep. Their journey followed a fenced stock route, which made the mammoth undertaking possible, but in every mob there are rogues that will try to escape through dicky fences, or hide in scrub or gullies, and those rogues, if they manage to get away, might be followed by other sheep. As well as keeping the tail—the slow sheep and stragglers—moving along, he soon learnt how to trot around and push in the wing—the sheep on the sides—when they were straying too far wide. And when they stopped for the night, he had to help his uncle split the mob into smaller mobs to put them into mesh breaks before sundown. Then it was a case of look after your horses and dogs at the end of the day before you look after yourself. On the first night, Peter was asleep on the ground before he could have his dinner. When their mission was accomplished, they went home from the meatworks in a horse-drawn wagon and the littlest drover slept all the way.

Later that same year, Peter began earning regular pocket money—a shilling a day—leading draughthorses at the wheat silos at harvest time. The wheat had been harvested by eight horses pulling an 8-foot wide stripper. His other task at the silos was to put an endless chain around the bags of wheat that took them up to the wheat lumpers building the stack. Some farmers would give him a penny or threepence to help unload their truck, which would bump up his bank account. That first summer he saved 10 shillings, but spent 5 shillings and threepence of it buying his mother the latest kitchen gadget for Christmas—a bean slicer you put on the table, then wound the handle. It was a miracle of technology, and she was absolutely thrilled.

The next summer Peter was looking forward to earning even more, seeing he was seven years old and much bigger, but some smart bugger had the audacity to invent an elevator, to take the bags of wheat up to the top of the stacks, which eliminated one of his money-making odd jobs. However, the war was on, labour was hard to find, so he soon got another job. A local farmer needed help stooking his crop and asked Peter whether he thought he could drive his three horses pulling the binder. After a short lesson, he was easily driving them round the paddock, then turning them and stopping them at the stacking point.

When the Japanese midget submarines came into Sydney Harbour, it was thought to be the precursor of an invasion. Royal Australian Air Force pilots were being trained at a base at Parkes, which was feared would make the town a target. On being notified of the subs being discovered, the commanding officer at Parkes air base rang sirens and bells in the town to alert people, then put every plane up in the air. Peter remembers the racket being frightening in the middle of the night. The entire town was worried they might be bombed. Many years later when he heard all the planes flying back from the World War II veterans' reunion in Townsville, the drone of the bombers vividly brought back the contagious fear of that night.

From the age of eight, Peter expanded his entrepreneurial skills. He was feeding and exercising four racehorses—riding one, leading one—before school, for a pound a week. He earned another 11 shillings a week delivering papers after school and on Sundays, plus he had always sold rabbit skins for ninepence a pound. At ten, he added six more shillings to his income by cutting chaff for half a day a week at a dairy farm—he was actually paid 10 shillings but four went straight back into the farmer's pocket for chaff for Peter's pony. He was doing well for a school kid.

For Peter, like many of his era, school was something to be endured—he'd rather be working outside earning money. One memory that stands out was learning all about the weather from a nun at his primary school who was very interested in the topic and passed on her enthusiasm. She was ahead of her time with her theory she often spoke about: that if the government would dig a channel from Port Augusta to Lake Eyre, it would keep the lake full permanently and attract rain, thus transforming the 'Dead' Red Centre of Australia. From Grade 4, the ultra-strict Marist Brothers took over from the nuns and he suffered their wrath until inter-mediate high school. Peter liked wood and metalwork and maths, but couldn't wait to leave. A particularly cruel brother caught him wagging school and tried to haul him off his pony. Peter flogged him with his switchy stick and galloped off, never to return. (The bad-tempered brother was later sent off to the New Guinea Highlands as a missionary, and Peter and his mates, who had experienced his cruelty, hoped he would be eaten by cannibals.) The head brother wrote to his parents, saying they would be wasting their money sending him back to school. It was normal then for fourteen-year-olds to leave school and get a job. Peter wasn't worried about missing out on getting his intermediate certificate, as he already knew from experience he would find plenty of work. Fortunately for his personal happiness, his parents agreed.

Peter started riding in amateur picnic races and had a lot of success. He could never forget the thrill of his first win at Orange. He was invited to turn professional and became an apprentice. He did well but had a lucky escape when his horse fell at Cowra, on a track that was cut up from too many races. Peter ended up falling over the fence, which saved him from the pounding hooves behind him. He'd been offered a 20 pound bonus if he won. Another vivid memory from that day was seeing a jockey searched thoroughly by suspicious stewards, who found a battery hidden in a pocket under his bib. The battery would have been fastened to his finger with an elastic band before the start of the race and used to put his mount 'into turbo' by zapping him on the neck with it.

A growth spurt at sixteen years of age meant Peter just couldn't keep his weight down. He had been 6 stone with his saddle but found it impossible to stay at that weight. When he'd started racing, he'd been advised by his trainer to eat nothing on race day in case he was in a fall and had to have an operation. Peter has always held a theory that female jockeys can, in some cases, be stronger riders than males, as their bones are lighter and they don't have to starve themselves. Asian jockeys are becoming more popular in Australia for the same reason. Despite the disappointment of not being able to continue a career as a jockey, he found he could earn a living riding trackwork.

Because trackwork was finished around 8 a.m., and Peter wasn't one to sit around reading comics, he took a second job at Les Solomon's blacksmith shop, in Doncaster Avenue, Kensington, next to Randwick. He had gone there one morning just to watch Les work and enjoy a yarn, when famous trainer Harry Darwin came in with his lead pony missing a hind shoe. The well-respected farrier was very busy, so Peter said, 'I can put that on for you, Les.' Les was surprised but, as it wasn't a valuable thoroughbred, chucked him an apron. When he saw the neat job young Peter did, he offered him a job on the spot, working from 8 a.m. till 3 p.m., when it was time to head back to the track to exercise and feed more horses. Peter learnt how to make shoes using the forge and anvil, plus many invaluable tricks of the trade, while earning a handy 8 pounds a week extra cash. The Australian Jockey Club subsidised wages in a bid to get more blacksmiths—probably, along with shearing, up there with one of the most exacting and physical jobs in the world.

(About this time in our conversation about his early life, Peter was very interested to hear about a sign I saw above a blacksmith's shop in an historical village at Kimba, South Australia. The sign read: 'Apart from prostitution, blacksmithing is probably the oldest profession in the world. Its intricacies and basics have never changed. A blacksmith from seven hundred years ago could walk into this shop, pick up any of the tools, and start working.' He agreed with me that those words certainly provided food for thought. I was also reminded of a thirteenth-century painting of a king holding a gala dinner for all his tradesmen; his blacksmith is on the king's right side—the most valued guest.)

Young Peter looked to the patron saint of blacksmiths, St Clement, for guidance and inspiration, when faced with a challenging problem. A horse without full mobility and a clean gait is not worth much. A clever blacksmith can get a previously useless or inferior horse striding out beautifully with even paces, through ingenious techniques to correct problems, such as putting weights on certain points of the shoe. I can honestly say that Peter is the only blacksmith I have seen who can yap away without pausing while shoeing a horse, and he is the fastest man I have ever seen shoe a horse, but always doing a perfect job. He makes the very hard task look very easy.

Despite his talent, and Les Solomon's attempts to entice him to stay, Peter was a country boy at heart and eventually could no longer stand the hustle and bustle of Sydney. He headed to the far west, to a station called Mt Monara, between Ivanhoe and Wilcannia, to learn how to be a shearing shed rouseabout. This was a job requiring a lot of energy, moving smartly up and down the shearing board all day, swinging a broom, picking up and throwing fleeces. A quick learner, he made a good impression, especially as the other rouseabout hadn't turned up and he was on his own for the first five days, handling a thousand fleeces a day. After a few months, he contracted dermatitis from the yolk in the wool, and his skin was peeling off—big trouble. A doctor made up a potion that smelt like sheep dip, but Peter soon found he couldn't continue to work with wool.

He returned to Parkes and was immediately offered a day's work snigging logs with his horse Trimmer, in the forest near Bogan Gate, west of Parkes. Peter and Trimmer did such a fantastic job they were both invited to stay on permanently. He learnt a lot about timber and, more importantly, how to avoid injuries while working with timber, during the six months he stayed there.

His hands were healed so he risked having a go at shearing, as a real 'goer' can earn big money. Despite being told that a shearer is 'a rousie with his brains knocked out' and that you have to be 'strong in the back and weak in the head', he gave it his best shot. Once 'set' to the rhythm, he managed to shear a best tally of 186, an effort up there with the best—the guns—in the days of narrow combs. He found that when you stopped for a while to try another job, it was difficult because your body was 'set' to shearing.

He took a break to give his father and uncle a hand for three weeks in their Coolah butcher shop. It was a good business; he liked the work and the interaction with the public (especially flirting with the female customers), and stayed for four years. His other uncle, Frank O'Hallorhan, was a saddler, with shops in Parkes and Yeoval, and he taught Peter the ancient craft, enabling him to always make extra money on the side by making and repairing saddlery and harness.

In 1960, aged 24, he went to the ACT to shoe horses full-time—all types of horses, earning very good money. Peter had a natural gift and received his ticket (number 68) from the Master Farriers Association, which allowed him to work on any racecourse in Australia. He holds the unofficial world record for taking the shoes off and plating up 78 racehorses at Queanbeyan one day on his own, when the second farrier didn't turn up. Anyone who has ever shod a horse will understand how amazing that effort was, and if a representative of the Guinesss Book had been there that day, Peter would be in it. 'I was so buggered, that when I had one can of beer at the end of the day, I was silly as a duck and a steward had to drive me home.'

During the ten years of toil since he'd shot through from school, he'd observed this: rouseabouting and shearing are both hard work, but at least you work to set hours; butchering is also hard yakka, but you have fun with the customers; being a farrier brings in the most money, but it's hardest on the body.

'I never had to look for work. Work always found me. In my early twenties I rushed into getting married, like a lot of young blokes do when their mates are all getting married, and I lived to regret that.

Suffice to say when I finally "bushed" her, I was, as far as I know, the first man in Australia to be given custody of girls. I raised my two daughters myself, and I've been told many times I did a good job. I stayed in the ACT for ten years as a farrier, to give them a stable, secure home life.'

While working as a farrier, Peter was kicked in the back at Goulburn races by a horse that was normally very quiet, but horses—especially thoroughbreds—are essentially a nervous animal and their immediate reaction to getting a fright is to either bolt or lash out. The horse hit its head on a low beam and kicked back with such strength it sent Peter's body through the paling fence dividing the back-to-back stalls. Famous trainers George Morrissey and George Vella, who were also friends of his, tried to help him but he was badly hurt—three-quarters of his vertebrae fused.

Despite being in almost constant pain, he was soon back shoeing at the tracks. 'People would say to me, "How the bloody hell do you still shoe horses?" and I'd reply, "It aches like a bastard but I can take it." The income from being a farrier allowed me to give my daughters everything they needed. The three of us had a good life, but it was to get even better.

'I was able to buy a few acres at Bendick Murrell [named after first settlers Ben and Dick Murrell], where I could run sheep, and the girls loved it there. Not long after we settled in, they invited friends from their former school in Canberra up for the weekend. There was an old cemetery on our place, with a kurrajong tree growing out of one of the graves. Local legend had it that a headless horseman was buried there and that his ghost appeared on midnight of the full moon. I egged the girls on to dare their friends to go to the tree after dinner, to see if the ghost would appear—he might come up out of the grave early, I suggested. Then I hid in the long grass near the tree, and as they walked to the grave I couldn't resist grabbing the nearest ankle. Well, you should have heard the squealing and screaming! They made such a racket, the people in the pub down the road all rushed outside to see what was going on. That episode livened up little Bendick Murrell alright!

'When the girls were both married and settled down, I moved north to a warmer climate in the mid-80s on the advice of my doctor, to alleviate the pain in my back. I was told the Bundaberg region had the best climate in Australia—never hot, never cold—so away I went for a look around and discovered a beautiful, quiet area an hour north of Bundy, called Baffle Creek. A big cattle station, Euleilah, was being cut up into 40-acre blocks and I had first pick, so my timing was very good. I built a nice compact brick house, and a huge shed out the back to house my collection of horse-drawn vehicles and harness, and set up my blacksmith shop.'

'I'd always dreamt of owning Clydesdales, and finally in 1990 I achieved that dream by purchasing a pair of fine young well-matched mares, Emma and Ruby. I was happy as a sandboy, harnessing them up, and ploughing up the best area on my block, to grow feed for them. I'd also hitch them to the wagon and give rides to all the neighbours and their kids. Then I started being asked to take them to school fetes and local shows and horse sports days. I raised a lot of money for various local charities with Emma and Ruby. I'd begun collecting other horse-drawn machinery, like a chaff cutter, corn cracker, reaper and binder etc., restored them, and gave demonstrations at these public events, which everyone loved—it took the oldies back in time, and educated the young people about how our pioneers got things done. Their comments and praise inspired me to hold a Heritage Day on my place, for the general public. By then I had several Clydies, and a front paddock full of old horse-drawn farm machinery, as well as the big shed full of saddlery, harness and horse-drawn vehicles. The day was an enormous success, attracting people from a big radius. To show them something really spectacular, I harnessed up all six horses, and did a bit of ploughing with them. The next year I harnessed up nine to plough a few runs. The people were just mesmerised, feeling like they were back in the bush in the pioneering days. Some of the oldies had tears in their eyes, thanking me.

'Then a bus company in Bundy asked if they could bring people out to my place to see all this, and hear me talking about the horses, and how things worked. Well, that gave me a bit of income above what I'd been earning shoeing the locals' horses and repairing their saddlery, plus I enjoyed meeting the people off the bus and yarning with them. The busloads of Japs thought the whole shebang was fantastic. Even the ones who spoke no English at all would shake my hand and yabber away enthusiastically. I could tell they were happy with what they'd seen. And everyone was very impressed with the homemade fruit cake I'd serve up with their billy tea. I've always been a handy cake cook—nice and moist, plenty of fruit, just like Grandma used to make. Of course, I did all the cooking while bringing up my children. The only trouble I ever had with the public was when my pet pig bit a lady on the toe when she sat in a chair to have her smoko. It didn't bite her hard, but she got a hell of a fright and put on a bit of a turn . . .'

As well as a thriving tourist venture, Peter had acquired a magnificent Clydesdale stallion—a Melbourne Royal Show champion—to breed his own foals. He was also competing, and winning, at horse shows with his pair of perfectly matched bay ponies in lighter vehicles like the sulky and the landau, an elaborate open carriage. They were even asked to do weddings so, to really look the part, Peter decked himself out in 'an olden-day outfit, complete with bowler hat'.

'I was finally really enjoying myself,' he says, 'doing what I'd always wanted to do, and earning a bit of money from my hobby. This was my reward, I felt, for working hard all my life.'

Ironically, it was Peter's love for his horses that forced a change— and he had to leave Baffle Creek. 'The problem I had on that coastal country was the continual attacks on my horses by insects, mainly sandflies. They really suffered, no matter what potions I put on them. Ruby and Emma were rubbing their manes all the time, while the ponies rubbed their tails, which made it very difficult to get them looking their best, so I decided to sell up and move away from the coast. The other reason for selling was the need for more room for my expanding herd. Too many horses and not enough acres—that was the situation I'd got into, so I needed to look for a bigger place, suitable for horses, that was reasonably priced.

'I found 800 acres near Yetman, between Tenterfield and Texas—plenty of room, but the catch was I would, once again, be buying just bare land and have to build everything from scratch. It's been bloody hard work—after all, I was nearly 70 when I came here, a bit late to start slaving again—but I saddled up and got stuck into it. The effort was mainly for my horses, which deserve the best I can give them. Their comfort came first—stables, yards, feed and hay sheds and small paddocks—before I could start on the house. Fortunately, while building this property up from bare paddocks, I have had the help of Kath, whom I married in 2002. We share our love of horses and country life. Not many women would be happy camping in a shed while the horses' comfortable accommodation got built first, but she loves them as much as I do.

'Kath and I are both happy with our life here. Texas is a nice little town, with friendly people, no crime, and we're only an hour from Goondiwindi, which is a terrific town with plenty of shops—everything you want. Occasionally I go down south to visit my daughters and grandchildren—and now, two great grandchildren as well—but I love the Sunshine State.

'My herd has increased to eighteen Clydesdales at present, including a new young stallion. They all work and occasionally I can be persuaded to sell one, but only to the right home. I'm still collecting and restoring old farm machinery and the beauty of this place is I have plenty of room to keep collecting. Unlike a lot of women, Kath is happy for me to indulge in what some people might think is a bit of an "untidy" hobby. A lot of the things I buy are a real mess when I get them—sometimes people actually give them to me, thinking they are beyond repair. But I can rebuild anything. Kath also helps me run heritage days here for charities, mainly the rescue chopper. I even hitch up nine or ten Clydies now, which provides a fantastic spectacle for the people who come out. I love the challenge presented by driving a big row of horses—all with different temperaments. Keeps me on my toes, attempting what a lot of people would find impossible.

'I keep myself busy and that keeps me young—when you've got a property and horses, there's always plenty to do. As I get older, I find the best medication for all the aches and pains is a few rums—then a few more rums—it mightn't cure anything, but it helps me have a good night's sleep and also keeps me young. My recipe for happiness is this: a hobby you love, plenty of activity, a few relaxing rums at night and a lovely good-natured wife who likes the same things you do.'

LESLEY WEBBER

Someone who made their dream come true

We all have our dreams—some of them so ambitious or fanciful, it is highly unlikely you will live that dream out in reality. You just spend your life wishing for it to come true. Then, as you get older, you realise you've missed your chance, and your dream slowly died. You simply didn't try hard enough, want it badly enough.

Some people have the determination and guts to *make* their dream come true. Lesley Webber is one of that small percentage, and her triumph will provide inspiration to all girls and young women who read this book. Hers is a story of breaking into what had been once regarded as a man's field, against many odds, then excelling in that field and being held in enormous respect by her male counterparts.

She might not be an 'old' old-timer—she parachuted into

the baby shop at Brisbane general hospital not long after the end of World War II—but she has worked in a tough, extremely challenging industry for a long time. In helicopter-mustering circles, she would definitely be regarded as an old-timer. Helicopter mustering is *not* for people losing their reflexes, not for the faint-hearted, but especially not suited to slack or lazy people. In a job that claims many fatalities, Lesley has survived partly through skill, partly though a totally meticulous attitude to safety. A pilot must have respect for the machine they fly—that is, respect for its capabilities and limitations, and respect for the need for fastidious maintenance—to survive.

In the helicopter-mustering industry, you can also add well-above-average mental and physical stamina as vital requirements. Lesley had exhibited these attributes for years, as a lane-race champion and marathon champion in the sport of waterskiing. In the Grafton Bridge to Bridge, for example, she skied for more than 100 kilometres at speeds of up to 140 kilometres per hour, slowing down only to go round bouys or when boats went past, to be just pipped at the post by the world champion. But that race was a cakewalk compared to her ocean marathon races in which she enjoyed considerable success for years in the 1980s, flying along at high speed—up to 160 kilometres per hour—sometimes through choppy seas, on a piece of wood 6 inches wide. 'If anyone fell off, they were likely to have a broken neck, so you just don't fall off! I was superfit then, but at the end of a marathon ocean race I would be shattered, and almost have to be carried out of the water.'

Lesley has always maintained her fitness, but mustering presented her with a new type of exhaustion. 'You're not just sitting on your bum floating along above the cattle, chasing them. You are striving to out-think them, control them, steady them, continually. You don't want the rogues to break away and lead others off, and you don't want the mob to run their fat off. You have to understand cattle and understand, completely, your machine. Hours of intense concentration . . . at the end of the day you're buggered. Then, while the horse musterers are enjoying a beer, you're carrying out maintenance and checking everything.'

Her affinity with engines was probably inherited from her father Snow Sefton, a Ford dealer, pioneer of motor racing in Queensland, and Australia Grand Prix winner, who developed racetracks using World War II airstrips around the south-east of the state and was the star of the Saturday night speedway in Brisbane. During the war, Snow had been a flight engineer who tested the planes he worked on, often disappearing, a big grin on his face, over the horizon from Rabaul, in Papua New Guinea, or Townsville for a couple of days for a blow-out somewhere. His daredevil, larrikin nature was passed on to Lesley, who has had more fun and adventures than you could poke a stick at.

It was at a party full of polo players at Kooralbyn Resort in the mid 1980s where she got her first chance to fly. She was nearly 40, divorced; her children, who she had raised on her own, were all out in the wide world. Working as a polo groom for friend John Wightman, Lesley had been fascinated that weekend at the Kooralbyn polo carnival with the ultralights continually flying overhead, around the resort. On being introduced at the party to the resort's flying instructors Peter Read and Alan Clarke, she wisecracked, 'So you're the mad bastards who've been buzzing around all day in those mosquitoes!' They convinced her she should go for a flight, so the next day she coughed up the fee to try a new experience. The plane had dual controls, and as soon as she took them, at Peter's invitation, she was hooked, and signed up for lessons. A natural pilot, in no time she'd completed her licence with Peter. 'The first time you fly solo is usually scary for most people but I couldn't wait to get Peter out of the plane!'

Soon she was having the time of her life, flying around the countryside with the Ultralight Club. 'We often had fly-ins to outback places to raise money for the Royal Flying Doctor Service. There'd be a ball or dinner dance on wherever we were headed, also to raise funds, so we'd find somewhere to iron our ballgowns, go to the bunfight and present the cheque.'

Six months after gaining her licence, Lesley teamed up with instructor Alan Clarke to set a world record for the longest unassisted flight in an ultralight. In his Drifter named 'Lollypop', they flew from Brisbane to Darwin, travelling via the Gulf country, attracting wide media coverage along the way. It had been Alan's idea initially, but Lesley *made* it happen by organising the entire trip. A laminated double-page spread in the *Australasian Post* magazine is one of her prized mementoes of an amazing trip and exciting achievement. In the cramped cockpit, their tuckerbox and spare fuel hose were at her feet. There was barely space for a change of clothes, plus a tent—to camp beside the aircraft. Sleeping bags were stored in the wings. It was a great test of personal stamina, but the tremendous publicity they generated helped promote the safety of ultralights.

'Accidents make the news and create a bad impression, but it's not the ultralights that are dangerous, it's the pilots. They try to fly one like you fly a regular plane and they get caught out, or they are simply showing off . . . Oops! Crash! When they are flown correctly, they are safe. I was taking part in a fly-in to Cunnamulla with friends once and saw, to my horror, my friend's wooden propeller fly off. She immediately followed all the procedures we are taught over and over and over again, and she landed that aircraft on a road, with the engine switched off, proving ultralights are safe in sensible, capable hands. We were all taught forced landings and emergencies, until the procedures are second nature. Ultralights are not easy to fly. Pilots of big jets should all get their initial training in ultralights because it's real seat-of-the-pants flying.'

After setting the world record with Alan in Lollypop, she set her sights on the next challenge—getting a helicopter licence. Although the odds seemed almost insurmountable at the time, she decided to do whatever she had to do to become a helicopter pilot before she turned 40, the next big birthday looming up. To acquire the considerable funds necessary she worked at three jobs, as she'd done years before to put her sons through boarding school. First hurdle cleared, onto the next. Despite having had very little secondary schooling, she still managed to grasp the vast amount of complicated technical and navigation information required to pass the exams; a formidable challenge indeed, but Lesley rose to meet and conquer it with remarkable dedication and tenacity. Typically, she took on a double load by studying for her fixed-wing licence at the same time. On the Sunshine Coast she studied and sat for the necessary subjects, but wanted to get her actual helicopter flying licence with the man reputed to be Australia's best helicopter instructor, Howard James, based at Kununurra, in the East Kimberley.

While taking lessons with Howard, she worked at Slingair (now Heliworks)—known locally as the 'Chopper Farm'—near Kununurra, gardening, cleaning the pool and doing odd jobs for the engineers. She achieved her goal, obtaining her licence and mustering endorsement. After telling her she'd passed, Howard called her back for one final instruction. For the umpteenth time, he chanted the golden rule: 'Don't fly downwind with no f . . kin' airspeed.' Lesley attributes the fact she's still alive to Howard's thoroughness.

'The most dangerous thing is low-level flying, checking fences, photographing, etc. If the passenger says, "Slow down," you have to fly away and reposition your machine with nose into the wind. When your passenger is heavy, the extra effort required to fly correctly drains you. Helicopters aren't designed for big people. A pilot dreads seeing big heavy people heading to their small aircraft. So the pilot must always have command decision about "slowing down" at low-level flying, and never let a passenger's demands affect that. The other hard-and-fast rule for safety that was drummed into me was that the pilot must always have the command decision regarding last light—that is, putting the machine down before last light, or taking off with plenty of time to put down at the destination before last light. People will try to override you, but you must not allow them to, no matter who they are. The investigation reports into fatal crashes reinforce those rules, sadly, all too frequently. Even if your passenger is the prime minister, you alone call the shots on those two situations.'

It is extremely hard to get a job in aviation, particularly a specialised field like helicopter mustering, but almost as soon as she got her licence Lesley was offered a job as a stationhand and second pilot on Go Go, near Fitzroy Crossing. Normally, she'd have been competing for work against seasoned Vietnam War veteran pilots, but what she had up on them was stock sense, due to experience with cattle, plus her willingness—unlike most of them—to also help out on the ground with drafting and other manual chores once the cattle were yarded. This willingness to work very hard, go that extra mile, landed her the job—with one of the Kimberley's most demanding employers, Harry Harris.

Not long after she arrived the other pilot resigned, and Lesley became number one. Her dream had come true, but for the next two years she slaved. A second pilot wasn't employed to relieve her, but Lesley was used to hard yakka and took on the lot. There was that female thing, too—she wouldn't ever mention she was buggered, because it might be perceived as 'female weakness'. The tuberculosis (TB) eradication campaign was on and all 35 000 head had to be mustered and tested. Flying long hours, day after day, week after week, month after month, without a break, she was skin and bone and sleep-deprived . . . but she was flying.

The job became a fraction easier once Harry had taught her the run of the enormous paddocks, for she no longer had his extra weight in the chopper, which made manoeuvring more difficult. A photo from those days shows Lesley hovering Harry's Robinson 22 above a big wild red bull which didn't want to be yarded. The bull is rearing up in fury at the machine above him, wanting to kill it. Lesley never let his kind beat her, but also strived to control the travelling speed of each mob so that every little calf would make it to the yard with their mother. On the ground later on, helping push the cattle up towards the drafting race, there'd often be an extra adrenalin rush or two, courtesy of the scrubbers and rogues . . . as if she needed it!

'Big willy-willys can spin you around—you're caught in a vortex ringstate and can suddenly fall 50 feet. At the time it's frightening, but that's part of a musterer's life, and with the huge numbers of cattle I had to bring in for testing, I got a lot of hours up quickly and experience is everything. I had to fly my arse off—hard and fast, crazy flying—day after day, for two years. There should've been at least one other pilot helping me. There was mostly no time to stop for lunch or smoko so I carried food with me—nuts, bananas, sandwiches, eaten on the job. Answering the call of nature had to wait till I was refuelling. While mustering, no matter how exhausted you are mentally and physically, you can't lose concentration. Every second, you are looking, looking, looking for cattle. During that TB eradication muster, you couldn't leave a beast behind—in paddocks of 80000 to 100000 acres. But even in a normal mustering situation, throughout the exercise of getting them together, getting them to the yards, you're constantly thinking ahead of the mob—it's probably the most full-on job there is.'

Then there was the frequent extra physical effort, such as rolling 44 gallon drums of avgas around when refuelling. It was most definitely not a job for a lazy bastard, or someone worried about chipping a fingernail.

After two years of this exhausting but satisfying work, her skills honed to the nth degree, Lesley asked for a raise—not a huge amount above the unimpressive salary she'd accepted as a novice. Harry, like a typical cocky, said no, and lived to regret it. She left, and he found it extremely hard to find another pilot with her ability, stamina and willing attitude. In fact, he never did—eventually two men and two machines were required to do what Lesley had done on her own.

Harry kept phoning her to return, but she had moved on. However, they remained friends. Despite Harry being a very hard boss, Lesley respected him for the lone stand he took against the authorities during the TB eradication scheme, refusing to kill any more of his breeders. Until then it had been a slaughter, quite often of the innocents. He had just got heartily sick of seeing good stock with nothing wrong with them destroyed, and took the powers-that-be in charge of the scheme to court, engaging a QC to assist in his fight for survival. He won, and from then on only cattle that were definitely infected, or lone scrubbers that took a massive effort to yard, were shot. Harry's victory came too late to save other cattle-men's herds from decimation, as Go Go was the last property to be involved in the scheme.

Having established a widespread reputation for excellence in the tight-knit aviation circles, Lesley immediately found another job and a new adventure. She went across to Darwin, to fly a four-seater Kawasaki KH4, known as a 'Kwaka' and made famous by the television series M*A*S*H. The bubble on the version she flew had been elongated by the Japanese to become the KH4. It was a difficult machine to fly, but she piloted it on a refreshing variety of jobs, from search and rescue work with the police, to landing all over Darwin for radio station Hot 100's promotions and towing their huge banner over the town. Another job she enjoyed was dropping incendiaries all over Kakadu to burn off. In between, she was mustering those crazy critters known as tourists and flying them to interesting and beautiful places like Kakadu, Katherine Gorge, Darwin Harbour and the Territory's best fishing spots.

Meanwhile, Lesley breezed through her commercial licence upgrade, having more hours up than most instructors, thanks to her time on Go Go, where she'd clocked 2500 hours.

Flying tourists around gave her many memorable moments. Men would often walk up to her and say, 'Where's the pilot, love?' Once in the air, the next question from them would inevitably be a cautious 'Ah, how long have you had your licence, love?'—to which she would delight in replying with a huge happy smile, 'Just got it last week! Isn't it fantastic!' If they were heading back from a long flight out to the bush, she would have a bit more fun with them by pretending to be lost. 'Ah, any of you fellers got any idea where Darwin is?' The looks on their faces would always give her a big laugh.

Lesley could fill a book with amazing stories of her time flying round the Territory and Kimberley, but the most extraordinary, hard-to-beat one would probably have to be 'the bull camel episode'. She had flown a group of businessmen from Perth on a hunting trip, landing in a spectacular canyon to camp the night. One of them, an American, declared, after he'd had a few drinks, that he'd like to return to the place where he'd shot a big bull camel that day and skin it, because he'd decided it would look great, stuffed, in his house. What his wife would think of that as a decor object can only be imagined! He asked Lesley if she'd fly him back. She explained that as the light was running out and there were tricky crosswinds in the canyon, she would not risk flying a passenger back there. He asked her what she'd charge him to fly there herself, skin it and bring it back. 'A lot!' she replied, laughing at the mad Yank.

But he wasn't joking: 'How about six hundred?' he asked, which was how much he happened to have in his wallet.

To Lesley back then, that was a lot of money. She agreed, and ran to the chopper, whizzed back to the dead camel, skinned it with great difficulty, chucked it in, and took off with its eye staring at her—admiringly, no doubt—from the passenger side. She made it through the crosswinds and landed safely back at camp just before last light. To say the businessmen were impressed is probably a monster understatement. The great postscript to that story is the Yank didn't forget to send her the 600 dollars.

Her former ultralight companion, Alan Clarke, had also moved on to helicopters and was about to start a new business, Heliventures, operating out of Kununurra in the East Kimberley. Lesley's reputation in helicopter circles, particularly up in that area, led him to ask her if she would fly for him. He had a Robinson 22 and a much larger Jetranger. To fly it, she needed a turbine endorsement, which was very expensive, but she got it, even though a pilot's pay in the bush is nothing to get excited about.

'Most employers out there take advantage of your keenness to fly, both from the love of it, and your desire to get hours up. The same thing used to happen with any job that involved riding horses, and that probably hasn't changed either. Luckily I can live on the smell of an oily rag when I have to, and can always get a second job behind a bar when I need extra money.'

To help Alan get his business up and running, Lesley agreed to work for peanuts until things picked up. While she had empty pockets frequently during that time, Lesley still experienced the most magical adventures, flying wealthy people around the fascinating Kimberley on sightseeing trips, fishing and hunting safaris, and ferrying television crews (including *Getaway*'s Ernie Dingo and the Bush Tucker Man) and photographers to the most remote places in Australia. 'I'd land people right beside a gorgeous isolated waterhole to fish for barra, where white people had probably never set foot; take major celebrities to swim under glorious waterfalls, or to see Aboriginal art in caves and rugged red canyons—completely deserted. They'd have these wonderful places all to themselves. I got on well with all the rich and famous.

'To experience all that was worth not having money to buy nice clothes or anything much for several years. On the job, I always wore a smart, professional pilot's uniform. Apart from looking neat, that professional appearance gives confidence to people who are nervous about flying—especially with a female.

'Alan set up a base camp on one of the thousands of islands off the north-west coast, with a great fishing boat he'd built himself moored there. I would either leave guests there to camp in comfort and privacy, looking after themselves, or stay and look after them, cooking seafood for them straight out of the ocean.

'Alan and I were fishing and snorkelling with guests once on a reef out from our island camp. Back on board, we noticed a bow wave heading towards us, from where we'd been snorkelling earlier in the day. As it came closer, we could see it was actually an enormous croc. It swam around the boat, looking straight at us with its truly evil eye. The boat was 6 metres long and it was longer than that. We watched that angry prehistoric creature circling us for quite a while, then discretion became the better part of valour and we vamoosed, being responsible for our guests. I think that encounter was even scarier than the one I'd had at Go Go. I was about to dive in the pool there one morning and suddenly saw there was a croc in the pool. It was the wet season, when they travel all over the place. We had fun getting the bugger out, I can tell you!'

While she was based at Kununurra, Lesley was honoured at a ceremony in the Civic Centre during WA Week, as a 'WA Week Woman of the Year'. That impressive plaque joined her huge collection of trophies and medals from her waterskiing days.

Unfortunately, after three years of struggle, just when the business was getting on its feet, Alan contracted the debilitating Ross River fever and had to call it quits. After he closed down Heliventures, Lesley was offered a great position at the opposite end of the country, geographically and in every other way. She was appointed senior pilot for a chopper operation flying out of Dreamworld on the Gold Coast. As well as joyflights over the Gold Coast, she flew many types of aircraft for the next five years, on many different jobs, all over Queensland: everything from television and movie crews, multi-zillionaires sussing real estate, to mapping out new powerlines. 'One job that sticks out in my mind is picking up six jockeys from Eagle Farm, where they'd ridden in earlier races, to fly them to Southport and Toowoomba racecourses. When requesting permission for take-off, I gave the "persons on board" as seven. Out ran these gorgeous little blokes, and when I was granted clearance for take-off, the bloke in the tower said, "Have a nice flight, Snow White". What a laugh we all had at that!

'I often had to pick up the Channel 10 helicopter and deliver it back to Mt Cootha. Flying over busy cities like Sydney and Brisbane presented new challenges, but my ultralight training, all those years ago, came back to me: "Look, look, look, look—never stop looking." My years of experience flying in and out of Kununurra—one of the busiest uncontrolled airports in Australia, with no tower—also stood me in good stead in busy flight zones.'

Lesley's favourite task of all was fighting bushfires. She became hooked on that formidable exercise during her first encounter in the Blue Mountains. Based at Blackheath and Lithgow with a Jetranger and a Hughes 500, she relished the dangerous challenge of missing the powerlines in heat that was, in her words, 'hot as a bastard'. Later on, fires in the Snowy Mountains also gave her a lot to think about, after the mostly glamour jobs on the Gold Coast.

'After flying round the Kimberley for so long, over and alongside those majestic red rugged ranges that I loved, I found the scenery around south-east Queensland bland by comparison. It took a year before the green, gold and blue beauty of the Gold Coast won me over. It's an incredibly wonderful, inspiring experience to fly right past places like Mt Warning and Mt Tibrogargan—places I had driven past much of my life but, like the Kimberley ranges, really need to be seen just metres away, from a chopper, to fully appreciate them.'

After four years, Lesley was yearning for outback adventures again, so next came a stint flying huge pigs out of the Daly River area in the Territory to the pig chillers at their base camp. One of the best shots in Australia, Steve Warburton, flew with her, picking them off at an astonishing rate, while her son Lee was on the swampy ground below, retrieving them and hooking them under the hovering chopper. A daredevil himself, young Lee carried a revolver as protection against boars that suddenly jumped up to attack him and, of course, the ever-present crocs. Like mother, like son . . . take anything on!

Then it was off to Strathmore Station, 2 million acres in the Gulf of Carpentaria, to muster for new owner Scott Harris, son of Harry, her first 'flying' boss from Go Go. During one dry season, when Harry was visiting Strathmore, she was flying over a big bushfire on a neighbouring property, directing Scott, who was down below madly grading firebreaks. You could only see the fire jumping a break from the air. Harry was with her and she'd put him down whenever they saw small outbreaks, to put them out with his trusty old damp hessian bag. At one stage, he jumped back in the helicopter, the bag in his lap, when suddenly it started burning him between his legs. Harry's head literally hit the roof. 'Land, love! Land!' Harry bellowed, which she managed to do safely, and while he attended frantically to his burning bits, Lesley was laughing so much she was rolling around on the ground. Just the sort of incident to brighten up your day on a remote station, and make a good yarn to spin for years to come.

She mustered for Scott for three years—till he got his own licence—then decided she had had enough. Without any regrets, Lesley said farewell to flying a year ago, and has gone on to enjoy herself in many other adventures from her Kingaroy base.

As she gets older (in years only!), she certainly hasn't slowed down—powerful motorbikes are her choice of transport. But with a rum in hand at sunset, reminiscing about what she has seen and experienced—beyond ordinary people's ken—she can thank not her lucky stars but herself, for making her almost-impossible dream come true.

ACKNOWLEDGEMENTS

A huge, heartfelt thankyou to all my wonderful 'subjects', who gave me their time and their stories. It was a privilege to meet you.

And thank you Helen Cameron, former co-editor of *The South Burnett Times*, for allowing me to use some quotes and photos from your wonderful book on Lady Bjelke-Petersen.

Thanks also to Stuart Neal, Ann Lennox and Angela Handley of Allen & Unwin, for their expert advice and assistance.

GLOSSARY

Aussie lingo

balloted out   to miss out on being drawn for a start in a rodeo

bangtail   where half a horse's (or steer's/cow's) tail switch is cut off to denote status

Bell 47   a three-seater plane

big show   a large station

breaks   temporary stockyards

BSA   a common motorbike of the 1950s and 60s, from the Birmingham Small Arms factory, pronounced 'beezer'

bulldogging   jumping from a horse and wrestling a steer or small bull to the ground

butterfly knife   a double-bladed knife

chillers	large cold rooms in rural towns that take kangaroos and pigs from shooters; they are then sent to specialist butcheries
cleanskins	unbranded or wild cattle
cotton chippers	casual labourers who 'chip' weeds between rows of cotton
dead wool	wool from a dead sheep
drafting	sending stock into different yards
drafting race	where cattle are sorted, or 'drafted', and sent into different yards
Dragon Rapide	a British short-haul passenger airliner of the 1930s
fettlers	railway labourers
fifth columnist	a traitor or spy
flashes	the emblem identifying a soldier's unit on his uniform
fleapits	dance halls or nightclubs
gidgee limb	gidgee trees are found in the outback and have very tough timber
Hughes 500	a five-seater turbine-powered helicopter
inside country	as opposed to outback; the coastal strip or the mid-west

GLOSSARY

Jetranger a five-seater turbine-powered helicopter

K wagon a wagon for livestock

Kawasaki KH4 a four-seater piston helicopter

lamb-markers men who castrate male lambs, usually contractors

lumpers men who 'lump' or carry bags of wheat

medium wool wool that is not fine or strong

No. 8 wire very thick wire

party line a phone line linking several properties to the exchange

pick-up rider a strong, very capable rider who lifts riders off bucking broncos at rodeos

plating up putting very light horseshoes (plates) on before a race

Quickcat a brand of catamaran

repat a repatriation clinic for returned servicemen

riding one and leading one a bush term that means having a girlfriend as well as a wife

Robinson 22 a two-seater piston-engine helicopter made by the Robinson Company

rouseabout person in shearing sheds who picks up the fleeces and throws them onto the wool table for the classer

saturation diving where the body is saturated with helium to stop it surfacing quickly

shunter a man who shunted engines back onto wagons; a highly dangerous procedure which is now automated

Silver Spur a type of Akubra hat

smoko morning or afternoon tea-break (from the days when everyone smoked during a break)

snigging pulling logs behind horses or tractors

stencil the tin stencil bearing the wool classer's registered number, to be put onto each bale of wool

ten bob ten shillings in pre-decimal currency

ultralight a small aeroplane made with ultra-light materials and small motors, making them cheap to run

vortex ringstate flying term: a hazardous condition encountered in helicopter flight, which can cause a catastrophic loss of altitude

wing cattle at the side of a herd which tend to wander

yolk colouration and grease which contaminates inferior wool